Communications in Computer and Information Science 594

Commenced Publication in 2007
Founding and Former Series Editors:
Alfredo Cuzzocrea, Dominik Ślęzak, and Xiaokang Yang

More information about this series at http://www.springer.com/series/7899

Vitaliy Yakovyna · Heinrich C. Mayr
Mykola Nikitchenko · Grygoriy Zholtkevych
Aleksander Spivakovsky · Sotiris Batsakis (Eds.)

Information and Communication Technologies in Education, Research, and Industrial Applications

11th International Conference, ICTERI 2015
Lviv, Ukraine, May 14–16, 2015
Revised Selected Papers

Springer

Editors
Vitaliy Yakovyna
Lviv Polytechnic National University
Lviv
Ukraine

Heinrich C. Mayr
Institute of Applied Informatics
Alpen-Adria-Universität Klagenfurt
Klagenfurt
Austria

Mykola Nikitchenko
Taras Shevchenko National University of Kyiv
Kyiv
Ukraine

Grygoriy Zholtkevych
V.N. Karazin Kharkiv National University
Kharkiv
Ukraine

Aleksander Spivakovsky
Kherson State University
Kherson
Ukraine

Sotiris Batsakis
University of Huddersfield
Huddersfield
UK

ISSN 1865-0929 ISSN 1865-0937 (electronic)
Communications in Computer and Information Science
ISBN 978-3-319-30245-4 ISBN 978-3-319-30246-1 (eBook)
DOI 10.1007/978-3-319-30246-1

Library of Congress Control Number: 2016931283

Printed on acid-free paper

This Springer imprint is published by SpringerNature
The registered company is Springer International Publishing AG Switzerland

Preface

This volume contains a number of selected and extended contributions to ICTERI 2015, the 11th International Conference on Information and Communication Technologies (ICT) in Education, Research, and Industrial Applications: Integration, Harmonization, and Knowledge Transfer.

The conference was held in Lviv, Ukraine, during May 14–16, 2015. It was a real pleasure for all ICTERI players, that in contrast to 2014, the 11th edition could bring scholars and experts physically together again for exchanging and discussing new ideas and findings, and for networking across political borders. This was all the more pleasing as, despite all the current challenges, the Ukrainian ICT community proved its vigor and global integration.

ICTERI as a conference series is concerned with interrelated topics of ICT development, deployment, and use; topics that are vibrant for both the academic and industrial communities, namely: education, research, industrial applications, and cooperation in ICT-related aspects. ICTERI 2015 continued the tradition of hosting co-located events, this year by offering four workshops.

As in previous years, the ICTERI 2015 proceedings have been published as a CEUR-WS volume (http://ceur-ws.org/Vol-1356/), containing 45 papers selected from a total of 119 submissions from 12 countries. Thus the acceptance rate for ICTERI 2015 was 38 %. Of these papers, the best 19 were identified and selected by the program and workshop chairs to be submitted in substantially extended and revised versions for a proceedings volume. All authors resubmitted. Again, these papers were reviewed by at least two experts regarding scientific and technical quality, anticipated reader interest, and coverage of the conference scope. Finally, the proceedings committee selected the nine most mature and interesting papers for publication after further revision. The acceptance rate thus is 7.5 % regarding the overall number of ICTERI 2015 submissions and 47 % of the proceedings submissions.

The selected papers are grouped into two parts in this volume: (I) ICT in Education and Industrial Applications, and (II) Formal Frameworks.

In the first paper of Part I, Aleksandr Spivakovsky, Maksim Vinnik, and Yulia Tarasich present an approach of developing dissertation committees and ICT infrastructure for graduate schools. As a continuation of their research, the authors are actively working on the creation of an open course on the use of ICT for undergraduates and postgraduate students.

Mykola Tkachuk, Konstiantyn Nagornyi, and Rustam Gamzayev discuss a framework for effectiveness estimation of post-object-oriented technologies in software maintenance. They define complex estimation measures based on fuzzy logic, and embed these into a CASE tool, which has been successfully tested on real-life software applications.

Oleksandr Gordieiev, Vyacheslav Kharchenko, and Mario Fusani give a survey of software quality models and related metrics, and analyze their evolution with respect to covering aspects of "greenness" and reliability. Using the elsewhere published "cumulative matching characteristics metric" they also calculate a forecast on quality model evolution for the year 2020.

Bohdan Volochiy, Bohdan Mandziy, and Leonid Ozirkovskyy in their paper deal with safety models of complex technical systems for critical applications. They propose to extend and improve the state space method such that a model also reflects independencies between accidental situations in contrast to the traditional methods FTA and FMEA/FMECA.

Part II presents formal and algorithmic frameworks for advancing ICT foundations.

Andrei Alexandru and Gabriel Ciobanu describe an extension of the theory of invariant sets to a theory of invariant algebraic structures that allows one to work with (infinite) structures in terms of finitely supported objects. The advantage of such "finitely supported mathematics" is shown by means of some applications in experimental sciences.

Bogdan Aman and Gabriel Ciobanu first introduce a polynomial solution of the SAT problem (satisfiability problem) by using polarizationless P systems with active membranes, without division, but with a pre-computed alphabet. Secondly, they present how to efficiently simulate polynomial space Turing machines by using a logarithmic space P system with active membranes and encoding the positions on the Turing machine tape by use of a binary representation.

Nadezhda Baklanova, Wilmer Ricciotti, Jan-Georg Smaus, and Martin Strecker discuss a new kind of small-step semantics for imperative programming languages, based on the zipper data structure. They show that this semantics has decisive advantages for abstracting programming language semantics to automata.

Grygoriy Zholtkevych formalizes the implementation of black boxes by Moore machines for synchronous black boxes and by pre-machines for asynchronous black boxes, i.e., black boxes with an asynchronous interdependence between input and output. Using this approach, event processing in distributed systems can be modelled and analyzed.

Finally, Elena Zaitseva, Vitaly Levashenko, Jozef Kostolny, and Miroslav Kvassay address the problem of reliability analysis of multi-state systems, and propose an approach to the analysis of the boundary states of such systems based on direct partial logic derivatives.

This volume would not have materialized without the support of many people. First, we are very grateful to all the authors for their continuous commitment and intensive work. Second, we would like to thank the Program Committee members and additional reviewers for providing timely and thorough assessments, and also for being very cooperative in doing additional review work at short notice. Furthermore, we would like to thank all the people who contributed to the organization of ICTERI 2015. Without their efforts there would have been no substance for this volume.

November 2015

Vitaliy Yakovyna
Heinrich C. Mayr
Mykola Nikitchenko
Grygoriy Zholtkevych
Aleksander Spivakovsky
Sotiris Batsakis

Organization

General Chairs

Yuriy Bobalo	Lviv Polytechnic National University, Ukraine
Aleksander Spivakovsky	Kherson State University, Ukraine

Steering Committee

Vadim Ermolayev	Zaporizhzhya National University, Ukraine
Heinrich C. Mayr	Alpen-Adria-Universität Klagenfurt, Austria
Mykola Nikitchenko	Taras Shevchenko National University of Kyiv, Ukraine
Aleksander Spivakovsky	Kherson State University, Ukraine
Mikhail Zavileysky	DataArt, Russian Federation
Grygoriy Zholtkevych	V.N. Karazin Kharkiv National University, Ukraine

Program Chairs

Sotiris Batsakis	University of Huddersfield, UK
Heinrich C. Mayr	Alpen-Adria-Universität Klagenfurt, Austria
Vitaliy Yakovyna	Lviv Polytechnic National University, Ukraine

Workshop Chairs

Mykola Nikitchenko	Taras Shevchenko National University of Kyiv, Ukraine
Grygoriy Zholtkevych	V.N. Karazin Kharkiv National University, Ukraine

Tutorial Chair

Vadim Ermolayev	Zaporizhzhya National University, Ukraine

IT Talks Chairs

Aleksander Spivakovsky	Kherson State University, Ukraine
Mikhail Zavileysky	DataArt, Russian Federation

Local Organization Chair

Dmytro Fedasyuk	Lviv Polytechnic National University, Ukraine

Publicity Chair

Nataliya Kushnir	Kherson State University, Ukraine

Web Chair

Eugene Alferov	Kherson State University, Ukraine

Program Committee

Eugene Alferov	Kherson State University, Ukraine
Sotiris Batsakis	University of Huddersfield, UK
Anatoliy Doroshenko	National University of Technology Kyiv Polytechnic Institute, Ukraine
Vadim Ermolayev	Zaporizhzhya National University, Ukraine
David Esteban	TECHFORCE, Spain
Hans-Georg Fill	University of Vienna, Austria
Brian Hainey	Glasgow Caledonian University, UK
Jason Jung	Yeungnam University, South Korea
Samia Kamal	Oxford Brookes University, UK
Vitaliy Kobets	Kherson State University, Ukraine
Hennadiy Kravtsov	Kherson State University, Ukraine
Sergey Kryukov	Southern Federal University, Russian Federation
Vladimir Kukharenko	National Technical University Kharkiv Polytechnic Institute, Ukraine
Heinrich C. Mayr	Alpen-Adria-Universität Klagenfurt, Austria
Mykola Nikitchenko	Taras Shevchenko National University of Kyiv, Ukraine
Tope Omitola	University of Southampton, UK
Dimitris Plexousakis	Institute of Computer Science, FORTH, Greece
Klaus-Dieter Schewe	Software Competence Center Hagenberg, Austria
Wolfgang Schreiner	Research Institute for Symbolic Computation of Johannes Kepler University Linz, Austria
Vladimir A. Shekhovtsov	Institute of Applied Informatics, Alpen-Adria-Universität Klagenfurt, Austria
Maria Shishkina	Institute of Tools of Education, Ukraine
Maxim Vinnik	Kherson State University, Ukraine
Paul Warren	Knowledge Media Institute, Open University, UK
Vitaliy Yakovyna	Lviv Polytechnic National University, Ukraine
Grygoriy Zholtkevych	V.N. Karazin Kharkiv National University, Ukraine

Additional Reviewers

Michael Walch	University of Vienna, Austria
Volodymyr Skobelev	Kyiv National Economic University, Ukraine

ICTERI 2015 Sponsors

Oleksandr Spivakovsky's Educational Foundation (OSEF)	http://spivakovsky.fund/
DataArt	www.dataart.com
Lviv Polytechnic National University	http://lp.edu.ua/
Logicify	http://logicify.com/

Contents

ICT in Education and Industrial Applications

Web Indicators of ICT Use in the Work of Ukrainian Dissertation Committees and Graduate Schools as Element of Open Science

Aleksandr Spivakovsky, Maksym Vinnyk(✉), and Yulia Tarasich

Kherson State University, 27, 40 rokiv Zhovtnya St., Kherson 73000, Ukraine
{Spivakovsky,Vinnik,YuTarasich}@kspu.edu

Abstract. Today an enormous amount of problems in building a system of efficient education and science is on the discussion agenda in Ukraine. A decrease in the number of scientists in the country has been observed in the last 15 years. At the same time, the amount of postgraduate students and people aiming at obtaining their doctorate is increasing. Notably, similar indicators are also observed in the majority of post-soviet countries. One complicating factor is that the system of scientific personnel training in Ukraine is very restrictive and closed. The proportion of research results published using a free access scheme to the overall bulk of publications is still very small, in particular if compared to the level of ICT development. Therefore, a major part of the publications still remains inaccessible from the outside. In this study we investigate the openness and accessibility of the preparation of the academic staff in Ukraine. To partly overcome some of the problems, we propose an our vision on ICT development of DC & GS infrastructure. In this article we analyzed the performance of DC and GS through their web indicators.

Keywords: Web · Information and communication technology · Education and learning process · ICT infrastructure · Open science

"If it's not on the Web, it doesn't exist at all"
Sarah Stevens-Rayburn & Ellen N. Bouton, 1997.

1 Introduction

The main catalyst for socio-economic development of a state potential is the ability to create, collect, and effectively manage knowledge that is comes out from the best scholarly research practices. The countries which have made it to their development strategy and implemented the effective interaction with the business enjoy TOP ratings in the World rankings. In the age of information technologies, it takes one not years, but rather days to bear the bell of scientific research and excel the competitors. The companies which are the first in the market are more likely to benefit from a positive effect caused by the introduction of new knowledge. Globalization is adjusting the cooperation

V. Yakovyna et al. (Eds.): ICTERI 2015, CCIS 594, pp. 3–19, 2016.
DOI: 10.1007/978-3-319-30246-1_1

between science and industry. More and more funds are invested in scientific research and development to capture the leadership in the market. A modern country's development is stimulated by the transition from aresource-based economy to hi-tech. There is an opportunity to create "intellectual dollars" without any resource, but people. The results of intellectual work become a hard currency. For example, Japan, though it had no natural resources, managed to become the leader in world's economy. The monetary value of the biggest hi-tech (IT) companies is at a scale of the budgets of some developed countries (Apple– $ 711 billion, Microsoft – $ 349 billion, Google – $ 365 billion).

The Open Science (OS) movement gains popularity in the world of clerisy, aiming to make research results and source data accessible to public at all levels. However, there is a conflict between the desire of scientists to have access to shared resources and make profit by using these resources [1]. In recent years, many governments try to impose the policy of openness regarding scientific knowledge, especially, if it is funded with public money. One way is the enforcement of providing open access to the results of all research projects performed at public expense. An indicative example is the US, which grant annually about $ 60 billion for research. In 2008, the US Congress imposed the obligation to grant free access in a year after the first publication to all the research papers based on the studies conducted by the National Institute for Health (which receives circa the half of the total public funding for science). Similar measures are now considered by many other countries.

Today, a lot of research in Ukraine is devoted to the problems of higher education and, in particular, the use of ICT for training students, creating information and communication environments in the universities, etc. However, in the scholarly literature insufficient attention is paid to the development of information and communication models of interaction with ICT in academic staff training. Moreover, today we are talking about the need for openness and accessibility of scientific activity, whereas a substantial part of the scholarly output never reaches its reader within and even more outside the professional academic community. This problem is particularly acute in the post-soviet countries. Regionalism of entire areas in science, convention, low connection with contemporary scientific trends, low level of foreign language knowledge by scientists, lack of self-developing scientific community, low competition with other countries, lack of motivation, poor funding, brain drain, and a number of other factors result in the continuing archaism of scientific brainpower training in Ukraine.

Scientometrics is rapidly developing nowadays. Using information technology allows creating new services for the development of scientific and research activity. Many global companies invest billions of dollars in services to support research activity, thereby creating a serious market not for the research results but for the research process support. Herewith the trend shifts toward commercial projects. The examples of such companies are Apple, Microsoft, Google, Elsevier, Thomson Reuters, not to mention many others. The most outstanding services with rapidly growing impact are Google Scholar, Scopus, Orcid, Academia.edu, Research Gate, Mendeley, arXiv.org, cs2n, Epernicus, Myexperiment, Network.nature, Science-community. These services contribute to satisfying the needs of the scientific community. In fact, these positively influence scientific and technical progress and create a new paradigm of scientific research. A big number of the recently created scientometric services allow assessing the relevance of the research results by a scientist, the number of his publications, citations, storage, etc. Having these measurements at hand opens up new opportunities and prospects. Our time ischaracterized by the high rates of the accumulation of new knowledge, in particular in the form of research results. Provided that the integration of research activities is currently (and naturally) low, a huge amount of scientific and research information falls out of search visibility and accessibility. Information technology is the only way to arrange and create effective search tools for acquiring the necessary knowledge. The objective of our research is to investigate the transparency of specialized scientific bodies and offer the vision of their supporting ICT infrastructure. Accordingly, the rest of the paper is structured as follows.

Present article includes such sections, as description of the methodological and experimental parts (2–4), discussion of basic components of Dissertation Committees (DC) and Graduate Schools (GS) ICT infrastructure and main ways and methods of their realization (5).

2 Related Work

David [2] mentions that the goal of Open Science is to do scientific research in a way that facts and their distribution is made available at all the levels of the concerned public. The same article states that the movement arose in the XVII century. Due to the fact that the public demand for access to scientific knowledge has become so large that there was a need for a group of scientists to share their resources with each other, so that they could conduct research collectively [2].

The term E-Science (or eScience) was proposed by John Taylor, the Director-General of the United Kingdom Office of Science and Technology in 1999 and was used to describe a large funding initiative, starting from November 2000. E-Science has been interpreted more broadly since as “the application of computer technology to the implementation of modern scientific research, including training, experimentation, accumulation, dissemination of results and long-term storage and access to all materials obtained through the scientific process. These may include modeling and analysis of facts, electronic/digitized laboratory notebooks, raw materials and built-in data sets, handwritten production and design options, preprints and print and/or electronic publications” [3].

Koichiro Matsuura, the President of UNESCO, wrote in his preface to [4]: “Societies that are based on the knowledge will need to share them to keep their human nature”.

In 2014, the IEEE eScience community proposed a condensed definition [5]: “eScience encourages innovation in collaborative, computationally or facts intensive research in all the disciplines throughout the research life cycle”.

Michael Nielsen, a physicist and propagandist of Open Science, colorfully describes in [6] the way the new instruments need to look like to facilitate the dissemination of the culture of cooperation and openness among scientists. One of such tools exists now. This is arXiv – a site that allows physicists to publish preprints of their works before the official publication of the article. This promotes to get in faster feedback and to disseminate the new discoveries. Nielsen also acts for publishing not only conclusions, but all the original data – this is the thing physicistshave been dreaming of for a long time. Journals could help them do that if they wanted to [6].

The most basic obligation of a scientific journal is to perform peer review, arXiv founder Ginsparg says. He laments that a large proportion of open-access scientific publishers "clearly are not doing that." Ensuring that journals honor their obligation is a challenge that the scientific community must rise to. "Journals without quality control are destructive, especially for developing world countries where governments and universities are filling up with people with bogus scientific credentials," Ginsparg says [7].

The peer review system for scientific papers on one hand offers an opportunity to obtain a (preliminary) critical assessment of a manuscript, but on the other hand it slows down the publication of research results. In this system, a review process is rarely accomplished in less than a month. The reviewers often request authors to revise some parts of the material or conduct additional studies. As a result, the time before the publication stretches for about six months or more. However, Michael Eisen, the co-founder of the Public Library of Science (PLoS), mentioned that according to his experience the "most serious incompletes are detected only after the article is published." The same applies to other scientific works, including dissertations for a degree [8].

It is a big problem in modern conditions of development of information technology is a plagiarism. Although information technology can be used in recognition of plagiarism, it is one of the major problems of scientific research. So, the American researcher Bela Gripp in her dissertation says that "… even today's best performing systems cannot reliably identify more heavily disguised forms of plagiarism, including paraphrases, translated plagiarism, or idea plagiarism. This weakness of current systems results in a large percentage of disguised scientific plagiarism going undetected. While the easily recognizable copy & paste-type plagiarism typically occurs among students and has no serious consequences for society, disguised plagiarism in the sciences, such as plagiarized medical studies in which results are copied without the corresponding experiments having been performed, can jeopardize patient safety" [9].

The cases are known in history when after many years after the defense a person was divested a degree and even was fired after the examination of his work regarding qualitative or even plagiarism.

Tugo Pagano and Maria Alessandra Rossi suggest [10] that politics aimed at overcoming the disadvantages of excessive privatization of knowledge can play an important role in stimulating the economy. Efforts should be focused to maintain and enhance the role of open science. The institutions of open science have allowed the flourishing of industrial development from the beginning, and should have a much more important role in the architecture of the future post-crisis global economy. This can be achieved through the institute of World Research Organization (WRO) which can master some of the benefits of open science to overcome the well-known free rider problem associated with contributions to the last.

In 2004, the research group Laboratorio de Internet from Spain, which studies educational and scientific activities on the Internet, started the Webometrics (www.webometrics.info) project with the aim to rate University web sites. The subject of their analysis is the university domain. Webometrics researchers emphasizethat the presence of a university website allows to simplify the publication of scientific works by faculty and research staff, compared to the publication in print, and also provides the information the fields of their professional activities. Online publications are much cheaper than paper publications and have broader potential audience. Publishing online facilitates to broadening the access to academic resources for scientific, commercial, political, and cultural organizations both from within a country and abroad. The rating scale is based on the four criteria that take into account the entire Web data within the university domain: Visibility, Presence, Openness, and Excellence. Each criterion has a weight corresponding to its importance [11].

The report by UNESCO on information technology in education [4] shows that in Ukraine there is a "rapid advancement of ICT into the sphere of education, which needs continuous improvement in the efficiency of use of the new ICT in the educational process, timely updates of educational content, and an increase in the quality of ICT training". However, there are some problems which are primarily associated with the low psychological, methodological, and pedagogical readiness of teachers to the rapid changes in information technology.

The issue of the openness of an education system and science often comes up in relation to international research funding instruments, such as Tempus, Erasmus, and others, and related projects. Every year, they attract the attention of many Ukrainian and foreign universities, research organizations and structures.

In 2006–2008 our Kherson State University (KSU) participated in the following European projects: Tempus TACIS CP No 20069-1998 "Information Infrastructure of Higher Education Institutions"; Tempus TACIS MP JEP 23010-2002 "UniT-Net: Information Technologies in the University Management Network"; US Department of State Freedom Grant S-ECAAS-03-GR-214(DD) "Nothern New York and Southern Ukraine: New Partnership of University for Business and Economics Development", which resulted in the development and implementation of scientific and management processes of analytical information systems and services. More detailed information can be found in the articles by G. Gardner [12], V. Ermolayev [13], A. Spivakovsky [14].

The results on the interrelation of ICT and educational process and the influence of ICT on professional and information competencies of the future university graduates have been presented in our previous publications [15, 16]. The authors have also conducted the investigation of the technical component of the feedback services implementation in KSU [17] and their impact on the preparedness of the students to use ICT for educational and non-educational purposes, and forming the ICT infrastructure in a higher educational institution [18, 19].

3 Experimental Settings

Today, Ukraine possesses a historically established system of scientific training. The foundations of this system were laid in the Soviet Union. This system is very similar to the system of post-soviet countries.

According to the State Statistics Service, 2011 [19], Ukraine had 14 895 "doctors of science" and 84 979 "candidates of science" (the analog of a PhD) covering arts, legal studies, and sciences. Among them 4 417 doctors and 16 176 candidates of science work in sciences. In addition, as reported by the "Voice of Ukraine" newspaper, the National Academy of Sciences of Ukraine employs today 2 564 doctors and 7 956 candidates of science [20].

In the last 19 years the number of researchers in Ukraine, decreased by more than 100 thousand people, while the number of graduate students increased by almost 2 times. The trend similar to the decrease in the research staff members can be observed in the numbers of domestic research and development organizations.

In Ukraine there are 988 Dissertation Committees [21]. DC are the expert councils in different scientific domains which form the National organizational infrastructure, accepting candidate and doctoral dissertations for examination, doing the expertise, hosting the defenses of dissertations, and further awarding advanced academic degrees. The aim of this infrastructure is to foster the development of the innovative elite of Ukraine which is considered as a driving force for scientific and technological progress. Preparatory work before the work of Dissertation Committee is carried out in the Graduate Schools. In Ukraine, there are about 300 universities, in which Graduate Schools operate, where about 34 thousand graduate students conduct the researches.

Given the importance of the DC infrastructure, the foci of this study are to:

- Assess the openness and accessibility of the preparation of academic staff in Ukraine within the system using the DC.
- Specify the requirements for the construction of the ICT infrastructure in this area.

We will analyze web indicators the performance of DC and GS based on the following principles:

1. The availability of information;
2. Openness;
3. Weight;
4. Scientific;
5. Social significance.

The research into the current state of the system of interaction with ICT of the DC, the Higher Attestation Commission of Ukraine, and graduate students is impossible without the analysis, comparison and synthesis, abstract approach to the definition of the basic patterns of the use of information technologies, and logical approach to the description of possible implementations of innovative teaching methods. Hence, the study of this issue requires the use a carefully designed combination of exploratory, empirical, and statistical methods. Therefore, several methods are used:

- Exploratory – the analysis, synthesis, comparison, generalization and systematization of relevant information acquired from psychological and educational literature legal documents, standards and information resources. These sources are consulted and further generalized to define the essence of the information competency of university students and assess the theoretical and methodological bases of information competency formation. Pedagogical modeling is employed to build the model of informatics competency;
- Empirical – questionnaires, surveys, testing, and self-esteem; pedagogical experiments are used to test the hypotheses of the study;
- Statistical – the methods of mathematical statistics are employed to determine the reliability of the results on the basis of quantitative and qualitative analysis of the empirical data.

The analysis of the public (available on the Internet) information on the availability of data on DC and GS, and collecting the opinions of graduate students using a questionnaire on the use of information technology in their dissertation projects are the main research methods.

Considering that the DCs function as university bodies, such sites as Top 100 universities in the World, Top 10 European universities, Top 50 universities in Russia, Top 25 universities in Poland, Top 10 universities in the USA, Top 15 universities in UK, Top 20 universities in Asia [22], DC of Ukraine were the object of information analysis. Overall, 300 university sites were analyzed in the reported research.

The study of the current status the use of ICT to support the activities of DC/GS the following assessment aspects:

1. The availability of a web site for a DC/GS and its analysis;
2. The degree of openness of the information provided for a DC/GS: information about the members, dissertation abstracts, theses, etc.;
3. Information security;
4. The existence of DC/GS pages in social networks;
5. The availability of a feedback service.

Let us consider in more detail each of the assessment aspects.

1. While exploring the web sites of universities regarding the availability of information about the activities of the respective DC and GS, we have selected to use the following four criteria:
   - A university web site provides the information on the DC and GS and a link to its own website;
   - A DC and GS does not have a separate web site, but it has a page on the university web site;
   - A University website provides a brief information about the DC and GS;
   - There is no information about the DC and GS neither on the university website nor in social networks.
2. The openness to the information about a DC and GS for public:
   - Any Internet user can see the information;
   - A user can view the data only after registration on the web site;
   - Only the staff and students of the university can see the information.
3. Feedback facilities:
   - Providing a contact phone number;
   - Providing a contact e-mail address(es);
   - Providing the list of contact persons;
   - Providing the Skype ID for contacts;
   - Providing the schedule of DC and GS works.
4. The availability of information (pages) in social networks:
   - Due to a substantial impact of social networks on the communication among people today, it has been decided to account for the relevant indicators in our study an analysis of the availability of information about DC and GS: the availability of accounts or groups in social networks such as Vkontakte, Facebook, Google +, Twitter;

- To analyze the availability of video records of defense meetings the analysis of the YouTube content relevant to a DC and GS has been also undertaken.

5. The technical characteristics of DC and GS web sites.

With this common name we have combined the following criteria of examination of the sites:

- Number of pages on the website - research on the number of pages of the DC and GS or part of the website of the University with information about DC and GS, as one of the indicators influencing the position of the site in the search results;
- Dynamic - in this case we are not talking about the dynamic of the site per se, but about the frequency of updating information on the activities of the DC and GS. Thus we examine the frequency of updating information in the categories - weekly, monthly and annually;
- Authentication System - a study of the main elements and authentication mechanism;
- Usability - the assessment of convenience of use and ease of operation of the system, namely how well, clearly and correctly interface and website structure are implemented. Whether the site user can quickly find the information he needs. In order to evaluate the site based on this criterion, we conducted a brief analysis of the layout of the site; availability is checked on the website of dynamic elements, the availability of search and so on;
- Platform - by means of specialized web services was implemented the management system review site. Thus we have divided the sites into two categories - implemented using CMS and handwritten;
- CEO - the study of site positions in the results of search engines for specific user requests;
- Validity - the number of errors found by the validator;
- Multimedia content - a study on the website of the libraries of audio and video recordings protections scientific papers, photographs, etc.

The questionnaire which has been used to survey the use of ICT by graduate students in their preparation to defense consisted of 3 components:

- Quantitative indicators of the use of ICT by graduate students in the process of working with their DC;
- The availability of training courses for the use of ICT in the preparation to defense;
- The readiness of the subjects to authorize the open storage of their research results (articles, theses, dissertations) and review materials such as audio, video, etc.

4 Experimental Results

The result of the analysis of the websites of the universities of Ukraine regarding the information on DC and GS, personal web pages and sites of DC members is pictured in Table 1.

Table 1. The availability of information on the websites of the Universities on the DC and GS

	DC	GS
Have own web sites	9 %	2 %
Part of the University's website with detailed information DC and GS	47 %	3 %
Part of the University's website with short information DC and GS	37 %	84 %
No information about DC and GS	7 %	14 %
Information about the courses on IT in science		1 %
Information scientific leaders at the GS website		2 %

Only 9 % of the reviewed DC have their own web sites. 84 % of DC related information can be found on University web sites, taking into account that full information concerning the DC activities has been found only for 47 % of the reviewed DC. 7 % of the reviewed DC have no presence on the Internet. As for GS sites, we see, only 2 % of its have their own sites. Full information concerning the activities of the GS is placed only on the 3 % of the studied by GS, and 14 % of GSfrom the total number is not placed on the Internet for almost any information about themselves. These results pinpoint the major problems in the transformation of the contemporary Ukrainian scientific community into the Open Science community.

Only 4 DC web sites exploit a user authentication functionality distinguishing user roles. So, it can be stated that only 1 % of the reviewed DC have created some ICT based prototypes for the interaction between the applicants and the Ministry of Education.

About 30 % of the reviewed DC (and 2 % of GS) update the information on their web sites every week, whereas 51 % (94 %) of the information on these sites is updated several times per year (Fig. 1 shows an example). Consequently, the question arises on the reliability and relevance of this information.

As per the information on the reviewed web sites, the DC have no means to track scientometric indicators of the members of the DC, the candidates for a degree, and persons that had defended their theses in a particular DC, not to mention the presence of analysts defended dissertations and access to them, which makes the qualitative assessment of their activities impossible. 32 websites have usability problems in terms of the ease of use of their interfaces and poorly implemented site (keyword-based) search functionality. The latter is implemented on only 27 of the reviewed resources. Only 17 of the examined web sites provide the information on or references to resources like a "library".

Regarding the minimally present contact information of a DC (a phone number, address, contact person name, document templates), it is provided only on 4 of the reviewed web sites. Moreover, the contact phone number is mentioned only on 2 of them. Thus, in order to find the information a DC of relevance to a PhD project, one should get their list and addresses in the Ministry of Education and Science of Ukraine (where one also needs to go) and search for a relevant DC at the specified address.

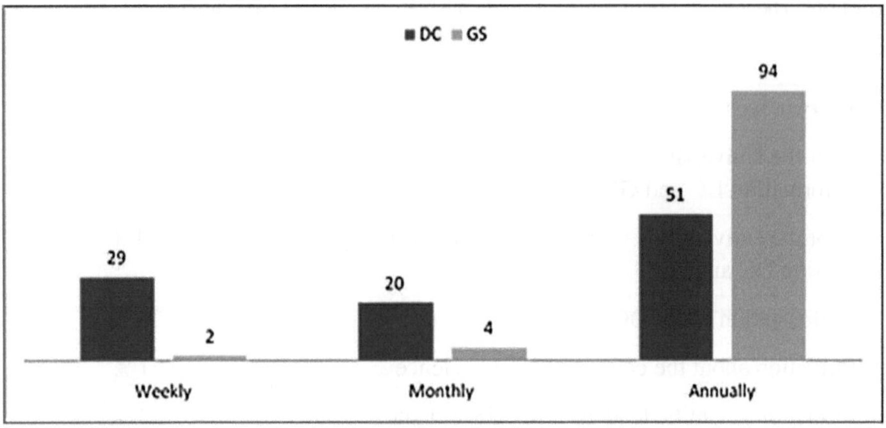

Fig. 1. Frequency of updates.

This is only the first problem in the application process. The required documents have also to be submitted to a DC by coming in person, since there is not a single web site that allows you to exchange the information and documents with a DC in the process of registration, filing and review of the thesis and so on.

The results of the review of the availability of information about Ukrainian DC and GS in social networks are shown in Fig. 2.

As can be seen in Fig. 2, 14 DC have a personal group or page in Vkontakte, 11 – in Facebook, 7 – in Twitter and 4 – in Google + . As for GS we see that only 5 of it have a personal group or page in Vkontakte, 3 in Facebook, 1 - in Twitter and 1 in Google +.

It is also important that YouTube is used, though to a small degree. So, a certain degree of openness of our science may be noted, in particular the openness of the preparation of the scientific staff.

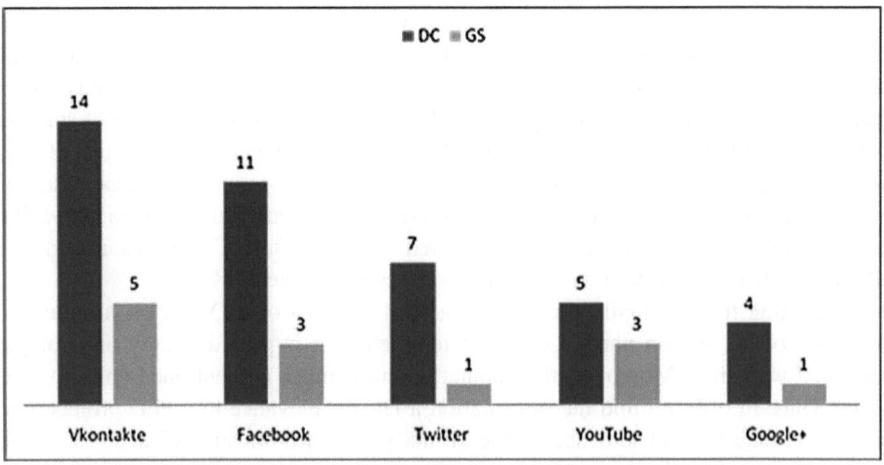

Fig. 2. The use of social networks in the work of DC and GS

The analysis of quantitative indicators of the use of ICT by graduate students for working with a DC is shown in Table 2.

Table 2. Quantitative indicators of the use of ICT by graduate students for working with a DC.

		Do not use	Rarely use	Always use
Usage of the Internet to search for information about DC	Working with DC website	80 %	15 %	5 %
	Search of information about the members of DC in SDB	93 %	5 %	2 %
	own profiles in SDB	95 %	4 %	1 %
	Work with El. repositories (dissertation and author's abstract)	40 %	50 %	10 %
Usage of El. Mail		30 %	40 %	30 %
Usage of Skype		84 %	10 %	6 %

The study reveals that only 2–3 % of the respondents know what is a scientific database (SDB) or a citation index, 7 % use these systems from time to time to find the necessary information, and only 4 % have their own profiles in such scientometric systems and databases like Scopus, Google Scholar, Mendeley, RSCI or others. It is important that the majority of the respondents are not interested in creating their own profiles in such scientometric systems. The main reason for that is the lack of recognition of their utility. Moreover, some of the profiles were created directly by the organizations where scientists work, or automatically by the systems that store their scientific articles. Thus the majority of respondents did not know whether they have a profile in any of the systems, whether these exist or not.

80 % of respondents do not think much about how their scientific publications are stored –in a paper or electronic form, and they believe that it is not of great importance. Thus, the majority of publications are going out of press in a paper form and are not further digitized – so remain unavailable to the scientific world.

93 % of respondents answered negatively about attending any course (or lectures) to get prepared for the use of ICT in their dissertation project (SDB, repositories, etc.).

Analyzing the readiness to the open storage of research results (articles, theses, dissertations) and materials of dissertation defense such as audio or video, we observes the following:

1. The majority of the respondents (80 %) support the publication of electronic copies of their scientific papers on the Internet, but at the same time consider it unnecessary and inconvenient. Further, all the respondents point out that the Ministry of Education and Science of Ukraine (MESU) has the publication requirements (regarding

the number of papers and form of publication, paper or electronic) to qualify for a degree which do not motivate providing open access. MESU requires that a qualified candidate has 5 publications at the MESU approved venues, one of which can only be published in an electronic edition and another one in an international or indexed international SDB. Thus, none of the applicants target to publish the electronic copies of their papers on the Internet. In some cases, this problem is solved by posting electronic copies on a digest web site or putting these into an electronic repository of a scientific institution of the applicant. Otherwise the articles remain inaccessible to the outside world;

2. The Problem with open access to the protected dissertations and abstracts is identical to the previous. In addition, the human factor needs to be taken in consideration. Providing free access to abstracts or theses means making these open for further examination after publication, hence the increase of the author's responsibility for its contents and quality. Therefore, open storage of scientific work of this type stimulates quality improvement. We see it in the results of the evaluation of the respondents ' answers to this question. Notably, 80 % of the respondents agree that the understanding that their work could be read by any other scientist clearly affects the quality of publications.

As an example, let us compare the quantities of the full versions of theses and abstracts stored in the repositories in Ukraine to numbers in the repositories in Germany, Great Britain, and Spain (top 30 repositories of each country rated by Webometrics, http://www.webometrics.info, were examined) – see Table 3. Ukraine has 46 repositories (Table 3) in total while having more than 300 universities.

Table 3. Numbers of dissertations and abstracts in open access repositories.

	Ukraine	Germany	UK	Spain
Numbers of repositories	46	117	146	64
Dissertation	1858	71656	16724	3586
Abstract	3532	22882	23617	18582

Only 15 % of the respondents agree that online video protection is useful, 30 % – to deposit their audio and video files providing open access, while the remaining 45 % believe that audio and video recording is unnecessary or even harmful as it bothers and disturbs focusing on the defense talk. To the question "if they would like and are ready to use specialized systems to work with a DC and MESU" 90 % of the respondents gave a positive answer. The most significant motive to this answer is potential reduction of time and financial expenses for data processing (sending and receiving documents, access to the proper information and so on).

5 Our Vision on ICT Development of DC & GS Infrastructure

As experimentally proven above, the effective implementation of the elements of OS must assume the existence of an appropriate ICT infrastructure as a scientific and educational system as a whole and its component parts (schools, universities, DC, and others) in particular.

The main elements of the ICT infrastructure of OS are researchers (academic staff), data and processes.

Speaking of ICT infrastructure DC we can determine its components as follows:

- Researcher – the applicants, the members of a DC/GS, the employees of MESU, and other users of the system have access to relevant information and participate in information processing, communication, and computing processes;
- Data – information about the work of DC, their employees, applicants, archives of theses, scientific publications, etc. as a tool to open exchange, recombination, and reuse are the important components of the infrastructure;
- Process – the procedures, services, tools, and methodologies that are used to collect, perform the transformation, analysis, visualization and storage of data, build models and simulations. The management of these processes is done both on the side of users (researchers) and of the specialized services and systems.

All the user roles have both generic and specific abilities in using the system. All roles can retrieve publicly available information while working with documentation is allowed only to certain roles.

One of element of the activity openness of DC and postgraduate study, we see in the creation of their accounts in scientometrics and bibliometrics systems, databases, scientific social networks. Today 345 scientific institutions of Ukraine have the profile in Googlescholar. We created the profile of DC K 67.051.02 and on the May 2015 it is the only one in Ukraine (data of the project "Ukrainian Bibliometrika Science").

Using these resources, we can combine the results and indicators of scientific activities of applicants, post-doctoral students and members of the DC, and thus show their scientific orientation, number and topics of publications of DC members, their citation, the geography and dynamics. Thus, it will clear for each graduate student in what kind of field the GS/DC operates, and how valued the scientific activities of its members in the scientific world are, it will be the opportunity to compare and analyze GS and DC in real time.

The next important element is to develop a service that enables to conduct analytical processing of scientometric indicators and promote the adoption of administrative decisions in the scientific and educational activities by IT resources.

An example of such a resource is a service developed by us called Publication (http://publication.kspu.edu). Functional features of the service are:

- Collect information of scientometric indicators of scientists, organizations, research groups.
- Ordering and ranking the results. For example, the construction of ratings of departments, faculties, universities, research groups and scientists.

- Facilitation of user access to information about scientific publications.

The service creates the conditions for effective work of postgraduate students and collaboration of scientists. In addition, today, thanks to the work of the service, we will create some motivational environment conducive to increase quantitative and qualitative indicators of scientific activity.

As mentioned above, one of the major factors, influencing on scholar's rank, as well as its openness and visibility is posting the results of his scientific work in electronic repositories. Most often, there are books, some articles, theses. Much less often, there are dissertation and abstracts. And this is one of the main factors, which shows open, academically activity of DC and graduate schools. Currently, we have a working repository, which stores the results of the scientific work of the university and other research organizations operating on its base (http://ekhsuir.kspu.edu/).

The next element of the considered infrastructure should be the sites of a DC and postgraduate schools, as well as their pages on the sites of the university on the basis of which they operate.

Appropriate Web-resources we divide into 2 categories:

- Information site;
- Web-service.

Web-service we call the type of Web-resource, which supports not only the availability of information on the activities of DC/GS, and communications options for users to automate the "paper" processes of their work, namely:

- Possibility of supplying and receiving applications for entry into postgraduate school, registration in the special council;
- Ability to supply and reviewing of abstracts and dissertations (for DC);
- The ability to supply reports on the work of graduate students;
- Ability to create new accounts of all users of the service;
- Possibility of electronic document;
- Feedbacks.

Today there is a first version of the site DC K 67.051.02 (http://www.kspu.edu/About/ScientificCouncil/Specvchenarada.aspx) corresponding to most of the described requirements. Currently, we are working to transfer from "Information sites" to Web-Service corresponding to the fundamental principles of OS.

The site DC states:

- Basic information about the activities of a DC and its members (with links to their personal Web-page).
- information about past and future presentation;
- information about applicants and their scientific advisers;
- list of defended dissertations;
- links of DC profile in scientometric system GoogleScholar, and a page with the scientometric indices according to Scopus;
- created examples and documentation requirements which are necessary for filing and defence in DC;

- links of collection of scientific papers published by the University, and other "useful" links.

The feedback in this case is carried out by means of electronic mail. The new version of the site DC feedback will be implemented through the implementation of special modules and forms, such as Online-chat, presence of user's personal accounts with the ability to send and view messages, etc.

An important element of the OS, we see the use of video and audio services such as YouTube, Dailymotion.com, Yandex.Video, RuTube.ru and others. Their use provides the following features:

- Online broadcast the defense of theses;
- Storing audio and video dissertations defense;
- Storing video and audio lectures for teaching in postgraduate school, etc.

You should also pay attention to where and how the research results are published. From 1400 relevant scientific editions in Ukraine there is less than the third part has a website, while the main principle of the OS is the availability of research results to the outside world. Guided by these principles, we are working on the development and publication of a collection of scientific papers "Information Technologies in Education" (http://ite.kspu.edu/en), our scholars and scientists around the world are published. Today the collection has its own website there are the electronic versions of all the articles and the associated metadata, and pages with the ranking list of authors and publications.

Another element that we would like to note is the creation of online-resources for training postgraduate students. Studies show that in our country, very little attention is paid to this problem; there are no online-courses or disciplines in postgraduate school, which considered the potential of ICT as basic mean and the environment for scientific research.

Today, we are actively working on the creation of an open course on the use of ICT for undergraduates and postgraduate students.

6 Concluding Remarks and Future Work

Building a system of efficient education and science in Ukraine today is complicated by many serious problems. A system of training of scientific personnel in Ukraine is among the most restrictive and closed ones in the world. A similar trend is observed in the majority of post-soviet countries. The proportion of scientific research results published under a open access is still very small compared to the level of ICT development. The main part of research results still remains inaccessible for external users.

Today we are all talking about scientometrics, but at the same time have not the ability to track scientometric indicators DC, GS, candidates, not to mention the presence of analytics the defended dissertations and access for them, which makes it impossible for a qualitative assessment of their activities.

As the results of the research have shown, extremely weak is applying of ICT in training of scientific personnel. Processing of all documents required for graduate studies or for the protection of dissertations is going manually, requiring a lot of time and resources.

The creation as many services which allow an understanding of the existing sciencemetric systems and databases, presenting them their own researching results, as well as services that contribute to the analysis and ranking of the results that received, reflecting the work of a DC and graduate schools, will allow us to create an environment that will match the essential requirements of the OS.

Working in it, scientists can not only efficiently receive, but also to pass scientific knowledge to each other and the world community. Using of the electronic repositories, publication of research results in collections that have electronic copies and indexed by international databases will increase the coverage of scientific publications that will help to improve their visibility, citation, the development of interdisciplinary research.

As we see from Sect. 5, today we have not only offer to build a system of this level, but also some ready-made solutions to efficiently manage many operations of post-graduate and DC. The next step is the developing of the Web-services for the automation of a DC and GS, the establishment of guidelines and training courses for candidates to use ICT in science, in the course of post-graduate studies and dissertations defense.

References

1. Savchenko, O.Y.: The Learning Abilities as a Key Competence of Secondary Education Competence Approach in a Modern Education: World Experience and Ukrainian Prospects: Library of Educational Policy, pp. 35–46. K.: « K.I.S. » (2004) (In Ukrainian)
2. David, P.A.: Understanding the emergence of 'open science' institutions: functionalist economics in historical context. Ind. Corp. Change **13**, 571–589 (2004)
3. Bohle, S.: What is E-science and How Should it Be Managed? Nature.com, Spektrum der Wissenschaft. http://www.scilogs.com/scientific_and_medical_libraries/what-is-e-science-and-how-should-it-be-managed
4. Towards knowledge societies: UNESCO world report. http://unesdoc.unesco.org/images/0014/001418/141843e.pdf
5. IEEE International Conference on eScience. https://escience-conference.org
6. Science under lock. The second part. http://habrahabr.ru/post/190046
7. Bohannon J.: Who's Afraid of Peer Review? http://www.sciencemag.org/content/342/6154/60.full?sid=39ce10dc-f70e-4ee2-a349-b59053b88bd7
8. PLOS is anti-elitist! PLOS is elitist! The weird world of open access journalism. http://www.michaeleisen.org
9. Gipp, B.: Citation-based Plagiarism Detection. Detecting Disguised and Cross-language Plagiarism using Citation Pattern Analysis, Magdeburg (2013)
10. Pagano, U., Rossi, M.A.: The crash of the knowledge economy Camb. J. Econ. **33**(4), 665–683 (2009)
11. Ranking Web or Webometrics. http://www.webometrics.info
12. Gardner, G.G.: On-line education: developing competitive. Inf. Technol. Educ. **1**, 22–25 (2008)
13. Ermolayev, V.A., Spivakovsky, A.V., Zholtkevych, G.N.: UNIT-NET IEDI: an infrastructure for electronic data interchange. Inf. Technol. Educ. **1**, 26–42 (2008)
14. Spivakovsky, A., Alferova, L., Alferov, E.: University as a corporation which serves educational interests. In: Ermolayev, V., Mayr, H.C., Nikitchenko, M., Spivakovsky, A., Zholtkevych, G. (eds.) ICTERI 2012. CCIS, vol. 347, pp. 60–71. Springer, Heidelberg (2013)

15. Vinnik, M., Lazarenko, Y., Korzh, Y., Tarasich, Y.: Use of computer communication means for future software engineers' preparing. J. Pedagogical Almanac **21**, 100–108 (2014). (In Ukrainian)
16. Kravtsov, H.M., Vinnik, M.O., Tarasich, Y.H.: Research of influence of quality of electronic educational resources on quality of training with use of distance technologies. Inf. Technol. Educ. **16**, 83–94 (2013). (In Ukrainian)
17. Spivakovsky, A., Klymenko, N., Litvinenko, A.: The problem of architecture design in a context of partially known requirements of complex web based application "KSU Feedback". Inf. Technol. Educ. **15**, 83–95 (2013)
18. Spivakovsky, A., Vinnik, M., Tarasich, Y.: To the Problem of ICT Management in Higher Educational Institutions. Inf. Technol. Learn. Tools **39**, 99–116 (2014). (In Ukrainian)
19. Spivakovska, E., Osipova, N., Vinnik, M., Tarasich, Y.: Information competence of university students in ukraine: development status and prospects. In: Ermolayev, V., Mayr, H.C., Nikitchenko, M., Spivakovsky, A., Zholtkevych, G. (eds.) ICTERI 2014. CCIS, vol. 469, pp. 194–216. Springer, Heidelberg (2014)
20. State Statistics Service of Ukraine. http://www.ukrstat.gov.ua
21. Ministry of Education and Science of Ukraine. http://mon.gov.ua
22. World University Rankings. http://www.timeshighereducation.co.uk/world-university-rankings

Models, Methods and Tools for Effectiveness Estimation of Post Object-Oriented Technologies in Software Maintenance

Mykola Tkachuk(✉), Konstiantyn Nagornyi, and Rustam Gamzayev

National Technical University "Kharkiv Polytechnic Institute", Frunze Str., 21, Kharkiv 61002, Ukraine
tka@kpi.kharkov.ua, k.nagornyi@gmail.com, rustam.gamzayev@gmail.com

Abstract. An intelligent framework for effectiveness estimation of post object-oriented technologies (POOT) is proposed, which is based on structuring and analyzing of domain-specific knowledge about such interconnected and complex data resources within a software maintenance process as: (1) structural complexity of legacy software systems; (2) dynamic behavior of user requirements; (3) architecture-centered implementation issues by usage of different POOT. These 3 components are formalized and combined in form of the algorithmic model, and the final estimation values of POOT effectiveness are defined using fuzzy logic method and CASE-tools elaborated, which were tested successfully at the maintenance case-study of real-life software application.

Keywords: Post object-oriented technology · Effectiveness · Crosscutting functionality · Knowledge-based approach · Algorithmic model · Metrics · Fuzzy logic · CASE-tool

1 Introduction: Problem Domain Actuality and Research Aims

Nowadays the most part of real-life software systems are designed and implemented using the object-oriented programming (OOP) paradigm [1]. A well-known and important problem of support and maintenance for such applications is often modifications of many of their subsystems and a need to develop new components for additional business logic, taking into account new user requirements. In order to emphasize this issue we propose to use in this paper tshe notion of "legacy software system" (LSS), similarly to terms in software reengineering domain (see, e.g. in [2]). Permanent changes in LSS lead to design instability which causes a so-called crosscutting concern problem [3, 4]. The OOP actually does not solve this issue, and usage of OOP-tools increases the complexity of an output source code.

During last ten years some post object-oriented technologies (POOT) were elaborated and became intensively used in development process, especially the most known POOT are: aspect-oriented software design (AOSD) [5], feature-oriented software design (FOSD) [6] and context-oriented software development (COSD) [7]. All these

V. Yakovyna et al. (Eds.): ICTERI 2015, CCIS 594, pp. 20–37, 2016.
DOI: 10.1007/978-3-319-30246-1_2

POOTs utilize the basic principals of OOP, but at the same time they have additional features, which allow solving the crosscutting problem electively. From the other hand usage of any of POOT for LSS maintenance and reengineering is concerned with an additional time and other efforts in software development. That is why many researchers emphasize an actual need to elaborate appropriate approaches for complex estimation of POOT effectiveness usage in real-life software projects. It is additionally to mention that within the context of this paper we are talking about the POOTs which are focused on programming techniques exactly, but not about such software management trends as Extreme Programming (XP), Rapid Application Development (RAD), Scrum and some others [8], which are also can be characterized as "post object- oriented" approaches.

Taking into account issues mentioned above, the main objective of the research presented in this paper is to propose an intelligent complex approach to effectiveness estimation of POOTs usage in software maintenance. The rest of this paper is organized in the following way: Sect. 2 analyses some critical issues in OOP and reflects the phenomena of crosscutting functionality in software maintenance. In Sect. 3 existent POOTs are analyzed and results of their comparing are shown with respect to software maintenance problems. In Sect. 4 we present the knowledge-based approach for effectiveness estimation of POOT, which is based on structuring and analyzing of domain-specific knowledge about interconnected and complex data resources within a software maintenance framework. Section 5 presents first implementation issues and results of test-case for the proposed approach. In Sect. 6 the paper concludes with a short summary and with an outlook on next steps to be done in the proposed R&D approach.

2 Crosscutting Functionality Phenomena in Software Maintenance: Related Work

To meet new requirements existing LSS have to be refined with new classes, which must implement their new functionality. Standard OOP toolkit "proposes" to support additional associations between already existent and new program objects, to modify inheritance tree for classes, to implement new or additional design patterns, e.g. the Gang-of-Four (GoF) patterns [9]. Because of permanent modifications of a source code and doing software system re-design, developers face with "bottlenecks" of OOP: increase coupling among classes [10]; increase of depth inheritance tree (DIT) for classes hierarchies [11]; modification of design patterns instances [12, 13]; emerging lack of modularity in functionality realization [14].

A number of studies investigate problems of OOP mentioned above, and their negative influence on LSS maintenance. High dynamic of requirement changes and these critical issues of OOP induce and propagate an additional development problem: this is a crosscutting concern phenomenon. Crosscutting concern (hereby referred as "crosscutting functionality" - CF) is a concern emerged on user requirements level and often crosscuts on software design level, this is a part of a business logic, which can not be localized in the separate module on source code view, but it stays separate on requirement view [15]. In literature exist a lot of researches related to CF's properties, multiple patterns of CF and it's interaction with the source code of non-crosscutting functionality, and it's further propagation in a system source code (see e.g. in [13–16]). There are some widespread examples of software system features which could be considered as CF: exception management, logging, transaction management, data validation [17]. Nevertheless our own experience in software development and LSS maintenance exposes that almost any system feature, emerged by requirements, on source code perspective could be transformed into CF.

CF has two main properties [18]: scattering and tangling. CF's source code *scatters* among classes (components) of non-crosscutting functions, this happens because of mismatch on end user requirement level of abstraction, and final realization of this requirement as a feature on the source code level. CF's source code *tangles* (mixes up) with source code of the other functionality, no matter crosscutting or non-crosscutting. Moreover CF could be divided into several types [19]: homogeneous and heterogeneous. *Homogeneous* CF represents the same piece of source code which crosscuts multiple locations in multiple OOP-classes of a software system. *Heterogeneous* CF represents each time unique piece of source code which crosscuts multiple locations in multiple OOP-classes of a software system (see Fig. 1).

```
  public class Line {
  private Point p1, p2;

   Point getP1(){
  return p1;
  }
   Point getP2() {
  return p2;
  }
   void setP1(Point p1){
   this.p1 = p1;
  Display.update(this);
  }
  }
  public class Oval {
  void setPosition(Point
p2){
    this.p2 = p2;
  Display.update(this);
}
  }
  //Homogeneous CF
```

```
public class
CreditCardProcWithLogging
{
  Logger _logger;
  public void debit(CreditCard
card, Money amount)
  throws InvalidCardException,
NotEnoughAmountException,
CardExpiredException
  {
    _logger.log("Starting
debiting"
   + "Card: " + card
   + " Amount: " + amount);
  // Debiting
    _logger.log("Debiting
finished"
   + "Card: " + card);
  }
  }

// Heterogeneous CF
```

Fig. 1. Crosscutting functionality types

As a result, presence of the CF in software system increases it's complexity for the maintenance process [20]:

- CF complicates traceability of various software design artifacts, e.g. requirement traceability [21];
- CF decreases understandability of a source code and functionality it realizes;

- Source code of LSS becomes redundant;
- Almost impossible to reuse CF solutions, because of lack of modularity.

These common negative CF-features cause specific problems in maintenance of a given LSS, which also are considered in some already existent publications. E.g., according to the research presented in [22] there is a strong positive correlation (with Spearman's rank-order coefficient approx. from 0.650 to 0.744) between the degree of scattering and the number of defects in LSS source code. Authors [23] also report about the correlation between the number of defects in design-pattern classes of LSS and scattering of induced crosscutting concerns. Another study on CF-consequences with respect to the quality of maintenance process deals with modularity problem in source code [24]. From the other hand, exactly because of these problems arose, attempts to improve CF-issues in maintenance exist, e.g. a model-based approach to reuse crosscutting concerns [25], and some others.

A conceptual approach, which allows dealing with CF, is the separation of concerns (SoC) [26]. It envisages a *decomposition* and further non-invasive *composition* of CF source code with the rest code of LSS. Decomposition mechanism allows to split source code into fragments and to organize them into easy-to-handle CF-modules. Composition mechanism supports reassembling of isolated code fragments in easy and useful way. Usage of SoC principles make possible to decrease coupling in LSS, to decrease code redundancy, to reuse isolated CF-modules, to configure system by add/remove functionality if it is needed.

Finally, the existing POOTs provide SoC principles and offer a lot of toolkits to manage CF-problem in an effective way.

3 A Short Survey of Post Object-Oriented Technologies: Main Features and Comparative Analysis Results

As already mentioned above (see in Sect. 1) nowadays there are 3 main well-defined approaches in POOT-domain, namely: aspect-oriented software development (AOSD) [5], feature-oriented software development (FOSD) [6] and context-oriented software development technology (COSD) [7]. In order to reflect their essential features with respect to the problem of CF it is useful to represent an interaction between basic components of OOA and POOT [20].

AOSD was proposed in Research Center Xerox/PARC and now it is implemented in many programming languages such as Java /AspectJ, C ++, .NET, Python, JavaScript and some others [4]. AOSD allows concentrating CF in separate modules called *aspects*, which should be localized in source code infected with CF using such means as points of *intersection* (point-cut) and *injection* (injection). Schematically this interaction is shown in Fig. 2, (a), where the white vertical rectangles C1, C2, C3 represent OOP-classes and gray horizontal rectangles A1, A2, A3 represent aspect-modules.

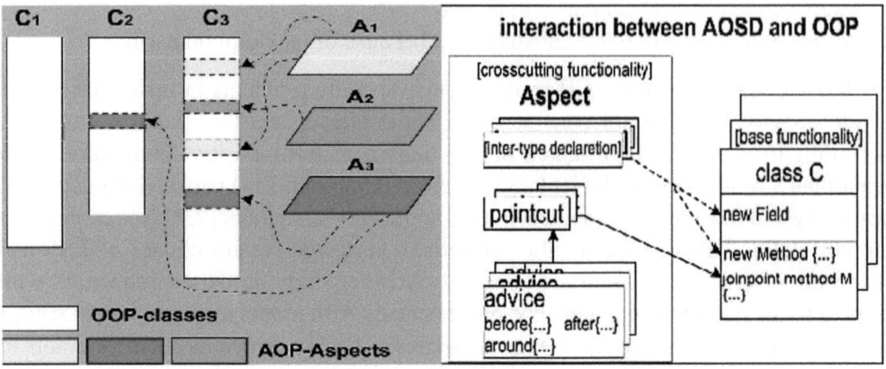

Fig. 2. AOSD: (a) the conceptual scheme; (b) the implementation facets (to compare with [19])

More detailed the structure of aspect is shown in Fig. 2, (b). Any *aspect* consists of interconnected point-cut, of a *notification* (advice), and of an *introduction* (inner declaration). The task of *point-cut* is to define a connection point between *aspects* and basic methods in OOA-classes, in other words, *point-cut* determines those lines of code in the OOA-methods, were *notification* code has be introduced. A *notification* is a peace of code in OOA-language (e.g. in Java), which implements an appropriate CF, therefore notifications can belong to three types: *before* – a notification is performed before an OOA-method is called; *after* – a notification acts after this call; and *around* – a notification is executed instead of an OOA-method calling. Also AOSD allows the introduction into OOA-classes new fields and methods that can be defined in aspects.

In the same way the FOSD and COSD schematically can be represented and analyzed carefully (see in [20] for more details). The result of this comparative analysis is presented in the Table 1.

Table 1. Results of comparative analysis for several POOT

POOT features / Estimation marks	Type of POOT		
	AOSD	FOSD	COSD
Modeling CF features at a higher level of abstraction	+	+	+
Implementation of homogeneous CF	+	±	±
Implementation of heterogeneous CF	±	+	+
Provide CF layers separately from a OOA-class	+	+	+
Context-dependent activation/deactivation of layers	–	–	+
Possibility to use several approaches simultaneously	±	±	–
Availability of CASE-tools to support this POOT	+	+	±

Even a cursory analysis of this comparison shows that for a decision making concerning the appropriateness and effectiveness of using an appropriate POOT to solve CF-problem in given LSS, it is necessary to take into account a number of other additional factors, which will be considered in the proposed approach.

4 Knowledge-Based Approach to Effectiveness's Estimation of Post Object-Oriented Technologies

Taking into account results of performed analysis (see Sect. 2), and basing on some modern trends in the domain of POOT-development (see Sect. 3) we propose to elaborate a knowledge-based approach for comprehensive estimation of POOT-effectiveness to use them in software maintenance. Thus we proceed from one of possible definition of the term "knowledge" within the knowledge management domain [27], namely: *a knowledge is a collection of structured information objects and relationships combined with appropriate semantic rules for their processing in order to get new proven facts about a given problem domain.*

Then our next task is to define and to structure all information sources, and to elaborate appropriate algorithms and tools to process them with respect to the final goal: how to estimate usage effectiveness of different POOTs in software maintenance.

4.1 Metaphor of Multi-dimensional Information Space and Algorithmic Model for POOT Effectiveness Estimation

To elaborate the proposed knowledge-based approach a metaphor of the multi-dimensional modeling space is proposed in [20], and its simplified graphical interpretation is shown in Fig. 3.

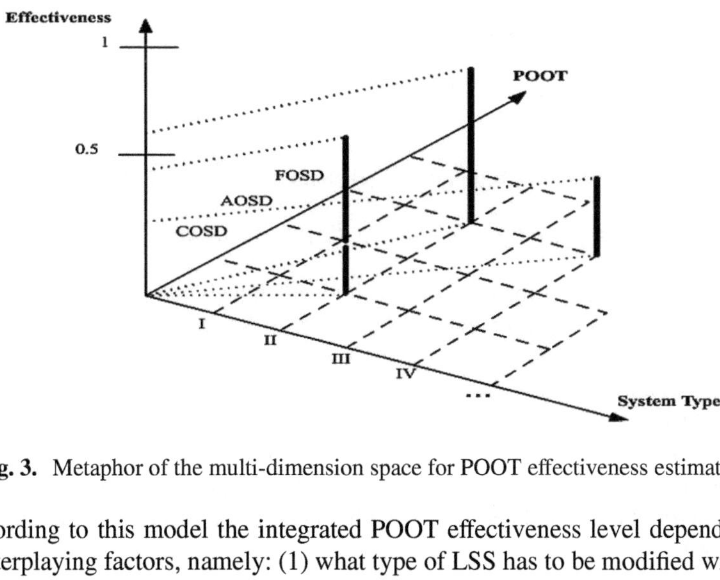

Fig. 3. Metaphor of the multi-dimension space for POOT effectiveness estimation

According to this model the integrated POOT effectiveness level depends of two main interplaying factors, namely: (1) what type of LSS has to be modified with usage of an appropriate POOT; (2) what kind of POOT is actually used to eliminate the CF in this LSS. In order to answer these questions the following list of prioritized tasks can be composed:

(i) to define a type of given LSS with respect to its structure complexity and to behavior of requirements, which this LSS in maintenance process is facing with;
(ii) to calculate average effort values for different POOTs, if they were used to eliminate CF in an appropriate LSS;
(iii) to elaborate metrics for CF assessment before and after LSS modification using a given POOT;
(iv) to propose an approach for final effectiveness estimation of POOT usage taking into account results, provided by activities (i) – (iii).

In order to generalize the proposed knowledge-based framework described as steps (i)–(iv) it is useful to utilize the algorithmic modeling approach (e.g. see in [28]). This one can be given as the following tuple:

$$AM = \langle Infospace, Workflow(Methods), CFMetrics\rangle \tag{1}$$

where the *InfoSpace* is the multi-dimensional informational space (the part of this one is shown in Fig. 3), the *Workflow(Methods)* are algorithms which implement appropriate methods to define all values requested for the final POOT effectiveness estimation, and *CFMetrics* is the collection of specific metrics for the CF-assessment. Basing on the formula (1) it is possible to evaluate several aspects of CF-issues in LSS by usage of complex and heterogeneous data structures, to process them with various algorithms, and to estimate achieved results with appropriate quantitative or qualitative metrics.

Tasks (i) – (iv) are solved sequentially below, using knowledge-based and expert-centered methods and relevant software tools.

4.2 Definition of Legacy Software System Types

To solve task (i) from the list given in Sect. 4.1 the approach for analyzing and assessment of LSS's type which is proposed in [29] can be used, which is based on following terms and definitions.

Def#1. *System Type* (ST) is an integrated characteristic of any LSS given as a tuple:

$$ST = \langle StructuralComplexity, RequirementRank\rangle \tag{2}$$

The first parameter estimates a complexity level of a given LSS, and the second one represents status of its requirements: their static features and dynamic behavior.

To calculate structural complexity (SC) the following collection of metrics was chosen: *Cyclomatic Complexity* (V), *Weighted Method Complexity* (WMC), *Lack of Cohesion Methods* (LCOM), *Coupling Between Objects* (CBO), *Response For Class* (RFC), *Instability* (I), *Abstractness* (A), *Distance from main sequence* (D). The final value of SC can be calculated using formula (2), where appropriate weighted coefficients for each metric were calculated in [29] with a help of the Analytic Hierarchy Process method [30].

$$SC = K_V avgV + K_{WMC} avgWMC + K_{LCOM} avgLCOM + K_{CBO} avgCBO \\ + K_{RFC} avgRFC + K_I avgI + K_A avgA + K_D avgD \tag{3}$$

To evaluate the final value of SC of given LSS in terms of an appropriate linguistic variable (LV): *"Low"*, *"Medium"*, *"High"*, the following scale was elaborated [29]:

$$\begin{aligned} & SC_{Min} \leq Low < \frac{2 \cdot SC_{Min} + SC_{Max}}{3} \\ & \frac{2 \cdot SC_{Min} + SC_{Max}}{3} \leq Medium \leq \frac{SC_{Min} + 2 \cdot SC_{Max}}{3} \\ & \frac{SC_{Min} + 2 \cdot SC_{Max}}{3} < High \leq SC_{Max} \end{aligned} \tag{4}$$

To define the second parameter given in formula (1), two relevant features of any requirement were considered [29], namely: a grade of its *Priority* and a level of its *Complexity*.

Def#2. *Requirement Rank* is a qualitative characteristic of LSS defined as a tuple:

$$RequirementRank = \langle Priority, Complexity \rangle \tag{5}$$

It is to note that in modern requirement management systems (RMS) like IBM Rational Requisite Pro, CalibreRM and some others, the *Priority* and the *Complexity* of requirements are usually characterized by experts in informal way, e.g. using such terms as: *"Low"*, *"Medium"*, *"High"*. The real example of such interface in RMS is presented in Fig. 4, with requirement's attributes "*Priority*" and "*Complexity*" (or "Difficulty" in terms of RMS-technology).

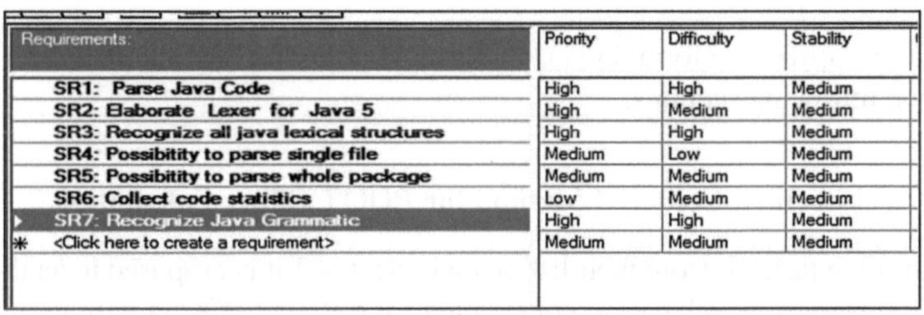

Requirements:	Priority	Difficulty	Stability
SR1: Parse Java Code	High	High	Medium
SR2: Elaborate Lexer for Java 5	High	Medium	Medium
SR3: Recognize all java lexical structures	High	High	Medium
SR4: Possibitity to parse single file	Medium	Low	Medium
SR5: Possibitity to parse whole package	Medium	Medium	Medium
SR6: Collect code statistics	Low	Medium	Medium
SR7: Recognize Java Grammatic	High	High	Medium
<Click here to create a requirement>	Medium	Medium	Medium

Fig. 4. The list of requirements completed in RMS Rational Requisite Pro

Taking into account the definition for linguistic variable (LV) given in [26], the appropriate term-sets for LVs *Priority* and *Complexity* respectively were defined in [29] as follows:

$$X{:}Priority;\ T(Priority) = \{\text{"}neutral\text{"}, \text{"}actual\text{"}, \text{"immidiate"}\} \tag{6}$$

$$X{:}Complexity;\ T(Complexity) = \{\text{"}low\text{"}, \text{"}medium\text{"}, \text{"high"}\} \tag{7}$$

Basing on definitions (2) – (7), the mapping procedure between 2 attribute spaces was elaborated in [29]. These attribute spaces are defined with appropriate LVs, namely:

the space *"Requirements Rank"* with axes *"Priority"* and *"Complexity"*; the space "*System Type*" with axes "*Requirements Rank*" and "*Structural Complexity*". This mapping procedure in details is presented in [29], and the final result of this approach is shown on Fig. 5. It illustrates the main advantages of the proposed approach, namely: (1) we are able to estimate current state of system requirements w.r.t. their static and dynamic features; (2) basing on this estimation, we can define an appropriate type of investigated software system (e.g., some LSS in maintenance process), taking into account its structural complexity and dynamic requirements behavior as well.

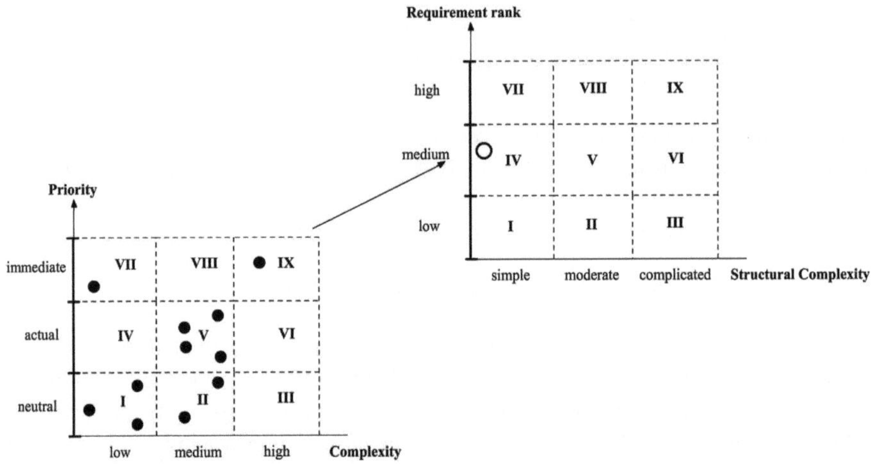

Fig. 5. (a) initial allocation of system requirements in the space "*Requirement Rank*"; (b) mapped system position in the space "*System Type*"

Further, according to formula (1), we have to elaborate next methods and metrics, listed in the following sections.

4.3 An Architecture-Centered Method for POOT Effort Calculation

In order to solve task (ii) from their list given in Sect. 4.1 it is proposed to analyze basic architectural frames, which can be constructed for different POOTs with usage of their OOP-specification. In [20] the following definition is proposed for this purpose.

Def#3. *Enhanced architectural primitive* (EAP) is a minimal-superfluous component-based scheme, which is needed to implement an interaction between basic OOP-elements (class, field, method) and specific functional POOT-elements.

Obviously, to perform the comparative analysis of different EAP in the correct way, preliminary they have to be represented in some uniform notation. As such notation the architecture description language (ADL) family should be used, because: (1) this notation does not depend on any specific programming tools; (2) in this way static and dynamic features of AP both can be described and analyzed.

It is proposed to use Acme-ADL, because it operates with an irredundant set of basic abstracts, for static modeling (see e.g. in [31]), such as: *components*, *ports* and *connectors*, and there are several additional Acme-ADL features for dynamic modeling, like *role* and *interaction.* They have following definitions within the context of this paper.

Def#4. *Component* is a complex of functional items, which implements a certain part of a business-logic in LSS, and which is supposed to have special interfaces (ports) for communication with other entities in an operating environment.

Def#5. *Port* is an interface to provide an interaction between several components.

Def#6. *Connector* is a special architectural item to join ports of different components.

Def#7. *Role* is a special feature of a given connector to identify its communicating ports.

Def#8. *Interaction* is a special feature of a given connector defined which uses its roles.

More detailed the notion of the *port* can be characterized in the following way: (1) there is so-called *single port* – this is an interface of any component to communicate with some another one via exactly one connector; (2) furthermore there is a *case-port* – this is an interface of any component to communicate with another components via more then one connector (e.g., using an appropriate Boolean variable as a flag to switch communication, etc.). Similarly, the notion the *connector* can be classified as follows: (1) a *binary connector* – this is a connector with 2 fixed roles only; (2) a *multiply connector* – this is a connector, which has exactly 1 input role and more than 1 output roles; (3) a *case connector* – this kind of the connector can have a lot of input and output role as well.

Using definitions Def#3 – Def#8 appropriate EAPs for all mentioned above POOTs were elaborated [20]. As one example the EAP for the AOP is shown on Fig. 6, which reflects how specific AOP-features such as *advice* and *inner declaration* (they are shown as rectangular icons in grey color) are interacting with basic OOP – elements, namely: *class, field* and *method* (they are represented as crosswise icons in white color).

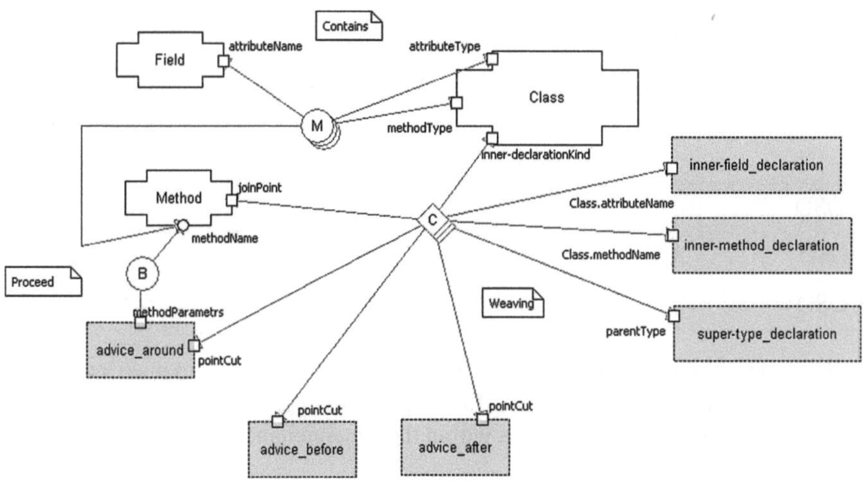

Fig. 6. ADL-specification for the aspect-oriented EAP

To calculate the complexity coefficients (CC) of the elaborated EAP the following formulas are proposed in [20], namely:

$$Component = 0.6 \cdot \#POOT + 0.4 \cdot \#OOP \quad (8)$$

where the *Component* is the CC of an appropriate EAP, *#OOP* is a number of architectural OOP – components, and *#POOT* is a number of POOT-components included in this EAP. These values are multiplied with weight coefficients: *0,6* and *0,4* respectively, and these coefficients can be defined using some expert methods (see in [20] for more details).

$$Connector = 0.2 \cdot \#BinCon + 0.3 \cdot \#MultyCon + 0.5 \cdot \#CaseCon \quad (9)$$

where the *Connector* is the CC of connectors included in an appropriate EAP, which is calculated using a number of binary connectors: *#BinCon*, a number of multi-connectors *#MultyCon* and a number of case-connectors: *#CaseCon*, with respect to the appropriate weight coefficients *0.2, 0.3* and *0.5,* which also are defined by some experts [20];

$$Port = 0.8 \cdot \#SinglePort + 0.7 \cdot \#CasePort \quad (10)$$

where the *Port* is the CC of ports included in an appropriate EAP, which takes into account a number of single ports: *#SinglePort*, and a number of case ports: *#CasePort* with appropriate weigh coefficients.

Using formulas (8) – (10) a summarized value the *Complexity* of an appropriate EAP, measured in so-called architectural units (a.u.) [20] can be calculated as follows:

$$Complexity = Component + Connector + Port \quad (11)$$

The final value of CC for all POOTs, were calculated using the formula (11), and they are represented in Table 2 (see in [20] for more details).

Table 2. Values of an architectural complexity for different POOT

POOT type	CC for components (a.u.)	CC for connectors (a.u.)	CC for ports (a.u.)	Summarized values of CC (a.u.)
AOSD	4,8	1	4,3	10,1
FOSD	3,6	1	3,9	8,5
COSD	2,8	0,7	4,1	7,6

Based on estimation values aggregated in Table 2 it is possible to make conclusions about average implementation efforts for usage of an appropriate POOT, to solve CF-problems in legacy software systems within their maintenance.

4.4 Quantitative Metrics for Crosscutting Functionality Ratio in Legacy Software

There are various ways to characterize a nature of the CF and its impact to software source code. A number of studies are dedicated to a classification, qualitative and quantitative description of CF problems [3, 14–16]. The aim of our research is to assess an impact, which CF makes to a structure of OOP-based software system during its evolution in maintenance; therefore we are focusing on quantitative facet of a crosscutting nature. To reach this goal it is proposed to perform next three steps.

Step 1: Localize source code belonged to a particular CF in a given LSS. Although there are exist several source code analysis tools for CF localization, e.g., tool CIDE [32], this problem remains really complicated for autoimmunization and demands an expert in code structure and business-logic of an appropriate LSS.

Step 2: Calculate a specific crosscutting weight ratio of a particular CF in the system indicated as CF_{ratio} [20]. This coefficient shows a ratio between OOP-classes, "damaged" by a particular CF and all OOP-classes in the system, or its projection, e.g. business-logic realization without subordinate classes of a framework. This coefficient possible to represent as

$$CF_{ratio} = \frac{C_{cf}}{C_{cf} + C} \tag{12}$$

where C_{cf} – a number of classes in LSS, "damaged" with CF, C – a number of classes free of CF. Obviously $CF_{ratio} \in [0;1]$, and if $CF_{ratio} = 0$, it means that a particular functionality is not crosscutting; and if $CF_{ratio} = 1$, it means that all classes are "damaged" with a particular CF.

Step 3: Calculate a residual crosscutting ratio indicated as RCR_{ratio}. This metric, based on DOS (Degree of Scattering) value, proposed in [14], namely "*...DOS value is normalized to be between 0 (completely localized) and 1 (completely delocalized, uniformly distributed)*". Nevertheless this metrics does not allow to asses "damage" degree, done by a particular CF, therefore we propose to refine DOS-metric in a following way

$$RCR_{ratio} = DOS \cdot CF_{ratio} \tag{13}$$

where DOS – Degree of Scattering; CF_{ratio} – the specific crosscutting weight ratio of a particular CF. Similarly to CF_{ratio}, $RCR_{ratio} \in [0;1]$, if $RCR_{ratio} = 0$, it means that CF is localized in a separate module and it is no more crosscutting; if $RCR_{ratio} = 1$, it means that CF affects the whole system and it is uniformly distributed.

Thus proposed quantitative metrics (12) – (13) provide to experts a possibility to assess a distribution nature of a CF, and to estimate a "CF-damage" in a given LSS.

4.5 Fuzzy Logic Approach to Complex Effectiveness Estimation of POOT

Based on assessment of a POOT average implementation efforts (see Sect. 4.3), and assessment for the residual CF ratio (see Sect. 4.4) it is possible to estimate an integrated effectiveness of a POOT usage. Although because of different scale and units of measurement for proposed assessments, it is hard to evaluate them within a single analytical method. Therefore, for further evaluations it is proposed to use one of algorithms of the fuzzy logic [33], namely the Mamdani's algorithm, which consists of 6 steps. According to this algorithm it is necessary to compose fuzzy production rules (FPR). In this paper a verbal description for these rules is omitted, instead of this the widespread symbolic identifiers for short description of FPR are listed in Table 3.

Table 3. The symbolic representation form for the FPR description

Symbolic form	Description
Z	Zero
PS	Positive Small
PM	Positive Middle
PB	Positive Big
PH	Positive Huge

The whole system of elaborated FPR consists of 20 definitions (see in [34] for more details), and the fragment of this FPR-system is listed below:

1. RULE_1: If "β_1 is **PS**" and "β_2 is **Z**", then "β_3 is **Z**";
2. RULE_2: If "β_1 is **PM**" and "β_2 is **Z**", then "β_3 is **Z**";
3. RULE_9: If "β_1 is **PS**" and "β_2 is **PM**", then "β_3 is **PM**";
4. .....

Corresponding to the Mamdani's algorithm, the next step is fuzzifying of variables in FPR, therefore average implementation efforts, residual crosscutting ratio, and effectiveness of POOT usage have to be represented as a LV. The output LV E_{POOT} is the effectiveness of POOT-usage, the LV E_{POOT} is bounded on universe X, and it belongs to the interval [0;1]. The term set for this LV looks like:

$$E_{POOT} \in \{non-effective, low-effective, mid-effective, effective, very-effective\},$$

and it could be represented in a short form as $E_{POOT} \in \{Z, PS, PM, PB, PH\}$. The corresponding identifier for E_{POOT} is β_3 (see FPR above), and it is shown in Fig. 7.

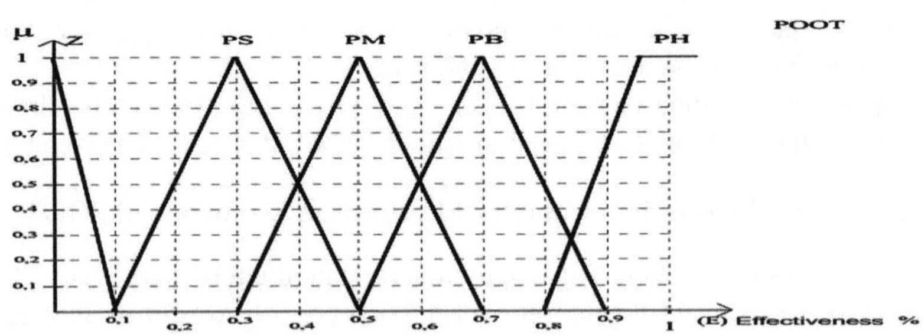

Fig. 7. The graphic form for LV "Effectiveness" E_{POOT}

The input LV C_{POOT} represents average implementation efforts, C_{POOT} is bounded to universe X and belongs to an interval [(EAP)min; (EAP)max], where EAPmin, EAPmax are minimum and maximum values of architectural complexity (measured in a.u.) for an appropriate LSS type respectively. The term set for the C_{POOT} linguistic variable (LV) looks like: $C_{POOT} \in \{low, middle, high, huge\}$ and could be represented in a short form $C_{POOT} \in \{PS, PM, PB, PH\}$. The corresponding identifier for C_{POOT} is β_1 (see FPR above). The graphical interpretation for this LV is similar to the graphic, depicted on Fig. 7.

The input LV P_{POOT} is the residual crosscutting ratio, see formula (13). The LV P_{POOT} is bounded to universe X and belongs to interval [0;1]. The term set for this variable looks like: $P_{POOT} \in \{useless, low, middle, high, huge\}$, and it could be represented in a short form as $P_{POOT} \in \{Z, PS, PM, PB, PH\}$. The corresponding identifier for P_{POOT} is β_2 (see FPR-system above). The visual interpretation is similar to the graphic depicted in Fig. 7.

5 First Implementation Issues, Test-Case and Results Discussion for the Proposed Approach

To prove the proposed approach an appropriate software tool was implemented, its functionality allows to automate the most routine data processing operations of the CF / LSS – estimation methods introduced in the previous Sect. 4. This tool is designated below as a CASE, and its interaction with such additional facilities as RMS and Java source code parser can be considered as the completed information technology (IT) to estimate POOT effectiveness.

5.1 An Informational Technology to Support the Proposed Approach

The proposed IT can be represented as the diagram in IDEF0 [34] notation, and it is depicted in Fig. 8. It consists of 6 functional blocks: 1. "*Requirements Rank assessment*", 2. "*Structural Complexity calculation*", 3. "*System Type definition and LSS modification with POOT*", 4. "*POOT-modification Costs calculation*", 5. "*Residual CF ratio calculation*", 6. "*Estimation of POOT usage effectiveness*". Each block, corresponding to the IDEF0 notation, has 4 kinds of interfaces: *Inputs* –arrows enter into a block from the left, they represent the data to be processed in this block; *Controls* – arrows enter from the top, they define all business logic algorithms and models; *Mechanisms* – arrows enter from below, and they reflect all implementation issues related to this block (including human actors, if needed); *Outputs* – arrows leave the block from the right, and they are the results of data processing in this block.

Block 1 operates with functional requirements, obtained from an RMS-system and the result of block 1 is a value of the *Requirement Rank*, represented as a linguistic variable. Block 2 analyzes Java source code of a given LSS and defines its value of *Structural Complexity*, which is also represented as a linguistic variable. Block 3 operates with both parameters: *Requirement Rank* and *Structural Complexity*, and allows to define a value of *System Type*. After this operation it is possible to perform

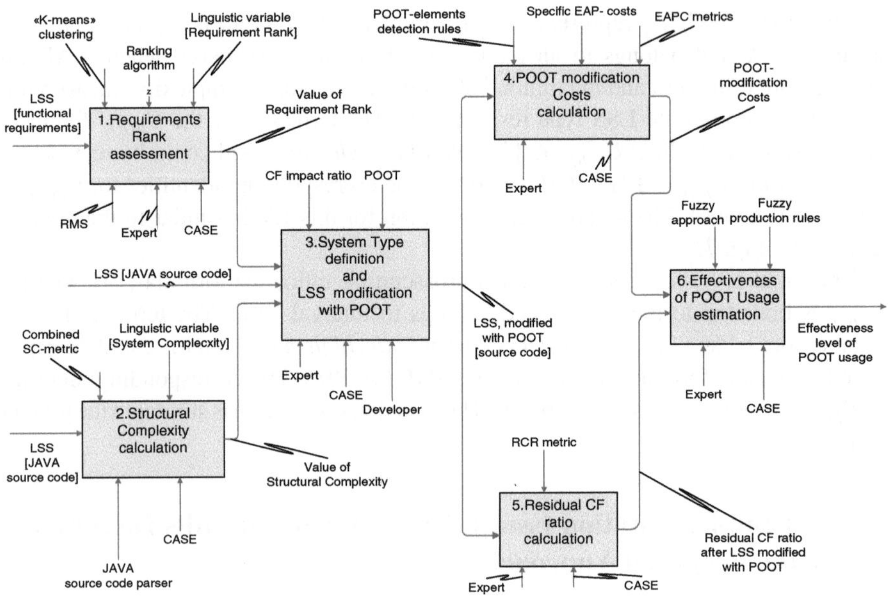

Fig. 8. The information technology scheme of a proposed approach

POOT-modification on LSS source code level, in order to localize and to isolate CF-concerns in separate POOT-modules. Functional blocks 4 and 5 deal with received POOT-modified source code to calculate values of *POOT modification costs* (block 4) and *Residual CF ratio* (block 5). Finally, block 6 realizes a fuzzy logic approach to assess the final value of POOT usage effectiveness. As the human actors the *Expert* (a person, who is interesting in POOT estimation results) and the *Developer* (a person, who is responsible for LSS maintenance) are supposed to participate in the data processing within the proposed IT-scheme (see Fig. 8).

5.2 Test-Case Data Description and Results Discussion

To illustrate the proposed approach the real LSS for personal data management was analyzed [35]. It consists of 115 java-classes, and it contains a homogenous realization of "logging" crosscutting functionality. Accordingly to the LSS – type definition method (see Sect. 4.2) this application belongs to the III-rd system type with rank: {"Low structural complexity"; "High requirement rank"}. The source code of this LSS was sequentially modified using 3 several POOTs: AOSD, FOSD, and COSD respectively. Final results of the POOT effectiveness estimation are shown in Table 4. The first column lists all LSS – modifications to be compared: an initial OOP-version, which has to be restructured with respect to the CF-problem, and its 3 modifications done with usage of a different POOT. In the second column there are summarized efforts needed for these modifications with respect to architectural-centered complexity are calculated (see Sect. 4.3). The data given in the third column of Table 4 show the level of the residual CF ratio which is presented (for initial OOP-version) or which is remained after its

Table 4. Effectiveness values of POOT usage in the target system

OOP / POOT	Architectural complexity (a.u.)	Residual crosscutting ratio (%)	Effectiveness level (%)
OOP	122.51	69.52	6,7
AOSD	79.43	0,15	73,3
FOSD	116.16	29.06	34,4
COSD	115.88	8.78	32,8

re-design with an appropriate POOT. The forth column indicates the final effectiveness estimation values for all LSS-versions.

Results achieved show, that OOP actually is not enough effective to solve crosscutting problem (it is done with 6.7 % only). The most preferable approach to eliminate the CF-issue in the given type of LSS (as mentioned above, this is the III-rd system type according to LSS-classification proposed in Sect. 4.2), is the AOSD which provides effectiveness level over than 70 %.

It is also to mention, although the effectiveness level of COSD and FOSD is lower than AOSD, over 30 % for a homogenous CF, it is still much better result than OOP. Taking into account a qualitative advantage of these two another technologies, namely: a possibility to implement a heterogeneous CF also (see Table 1), it can be reasonable to use one of them for the LSS-maintenance to deal with such kind of CF in more effective way than AOSD.

6 Conclusions and Future Work

In this paper we have presented the intelligent approach to effectiveness estimation of modern post object-oriented technologies (POOT) in the software maintenance, which aims to utilize domain-specific knowledge for this purpose. This knowledge is complex and interconnected data resources organized in a form of the multi-dimensional information space, where the following characteristics can be defined: (1) the structural complexity of a legacy software; (2) the dynamic behavior of user's requirements; (3) architectural-centered implementation efforts of different POOTs.

To process these data quantitative metrics and expert-oriented estimation algorithms were elaborated, which are formalized and combined logically in a form of the proposed algorithmic model. Final complex estimation values of POOT effectiveness assessment are defined using the fuzzy logic method and the appropriate CASE-tool, which were successfully tested on real-life legacy software applications.

In future we are going to extend the collection of metrics for POOT-features assessment, and to apply some of alternative (to fuzzy logic method) approaches to final decision making support. Besides that it is supposed to continue our research with respect to the correlation issues between different kinds of CF and programming defects arose in an LSS source code.

References

1. Sommerville, I.: Software Engineering. Addison Wesley, Boston (2011)
2. Eilam, E.: Reversing: Secrets of Reverse Engineering. Wiley Publishing, Indianapolis (2005)
3. Apel, S. et al.: On the structure of crosscutting concerns: using aspects of collaboration? In: Workshop on Aspect-Oriented Product Line Engineering (2006)
4. Przyby³ek, A.: Post object-oriented paradigms in software development: a comparative analysis. In: Proceedings of the International Multi-conference on Computer Science and Information Technology, pp. 1009–1020 (2007)
5. Official Web-site of Aspect-oriented Software Development community. http://aosd.net
6. Official Web-site of Feature-oriented Software Development community. http://fosd.de
7. Official Web-site of Context-oriented Software Development group. http://www.hpi.uni-potsdam.de/hirschfeld/cop/events
8. Highsmith, J.: Agile Project Management. Addison-Wesley, Reading (2004)
9. Gamma, E., et al.: Design Patterns: Elements of Reusable Object-Oriented Software. Addison-Wesley, Reading (2001)
10. Sheldon, T., Jerath, K., Chung, H.: Metrics for maintainability of class inheritance hierarchies. J. Softw. Maintenance Evol. **14**, 1–14 (2002)
11. Harrison, R., Counsell, S.J.: The role of inheritance in the maintainability of object-oriented systems. In: Proceedings of ESCOM 1998, pp. 449–457 (1998)
12. Aversano, L., Cerulo, L., Di Penta, M.: Relating the evolution of design patterns and crosscutting concerns. In: Proceedings of the Seventh IEEE International Working Conference on Source Code Analysis and Manipulation, pp. 180–192 (2007)
13. Hannemann, J., Kiczales, G.: Design pattern implementation in java and aspectJ. In: Proceedings of OOPSLA 2002, pp. 161–173 (2002)
14. Eaddy, M., et al.: Identifying, assigning, and quantifying crosscutting concerns. In: Workshop on Assessment of Contemporary Modularization Techniques (ACoMT 2007), Minneapolis, USA, pp. 212–217 (2007)
15. Filman, R., Elrad, S., Aksit, M.: Aspect-Oriented Software Development. Addison Wesley Professional, Reading (2004)
16. Figueiredo, E.: Concern-Oriented Heuristic Assessment of Design Stability. Ph.D. thesis, Lancaster University (2009)
17. Official Web-site of MSDN. https://msdn.microsoft.com/en-us/library/ee658105.aspx
18. Clarket, S., et al.: Separating concerns throughout the development lifecycle. In: International Workshop on Aspect-Oriented Programming ECOOP (1999)
19. Apel, S.: The role of features and aspects in software development. Ph.D. thesis, Otto-von-Guericke University Magdeburg (2007)
20. Tkachuk, M., Nagornyi, K.: Towards effectiveness estimation of post object-oriented technologies in software maintenance. J. Prob. Program. **2-3**(special issue), 252–260 (2010)
21. Taromirad M., Paige, M.: Agile requirements traceability using domain-specific modeling languages. In: Extreme Modeling Workshop, pp. 45–50 (2012)
22. Eaddy, M., et al.: Do crosscutting concerns cause defects? IEEE Trans. Softw. Eng. **34**(4), 497–515 (2008)
23. Aversano, L., et al.: Relationship between design patterns defects and crosscutting concern scattering degree. IET Softw. **3**(5), 395–409 (2009)
24. Walker, R., Rawal, S., Sillito, J.: Do crosscutting concerns cause modularity problems? In: Proceedings of the ACM SIGSOFT International Symposium on Foundations of Software Engineering (SIGSOFT/FSE 2012), pp. 1–11 (2012)

25. Gottardi, T., et al.: Model-based reuse for crosscutting frameworks: assessing reuse and maintenance effort. J. Softw. Eng. Res. Dev. **1**, 1–34 (2013)
26. Tarr, P.L., et al.: N degrees of separation: multi-dimensional separation of concerns. In: Proceedings of the International Conference on Software Engineering (ICSE), pp. 107–119. ACM, Los Angeles (1999)
27. Official Web-site of System Thinking World community. http://www.systems-thinking.org/kmgmt/kmgmt.htm
28. Ramesh, K., Karunanidhi, P.: Literature survey on algorithmic and non-algorithmic models for software development effort estimation. Int. J. Eng. Comput. Sci. **2**(3), 623–632 (2013)
29. Tkachuk, M., Martinkus, I.: Model and tools for multi-dimensional approach to requirements behavior analysis. In: Kop, C. (ed.) UNISON 2012. LNBIP, vol. 137, pp. 191–198. Springer, Heidelberg (2013)
30. Saaty, T.L.: Fundamentals of the Analytic Hierarchy Process. RWS Publications, Pittsburgh (2000)
31. Garlan, D., Monroe, R., Wile, D.: ACME: an architecture description interchange language. In: Proceedings of CASCON 1997, Toronto, Canada, pp. 169–183 (1997)
32. Official Web-site of CIDE-project. http://wwwiti.cs.uni-magdeburg.de/iti_db/research/cide/
33. Zadeh, L.A.: Fuzzy Sets. WorldSciBook (1976)
34. Official Web-site of IDEF Family of Methods. http://www.idef.com
35. Nagornyi, K.: Elaboration and usage of method for post object-oriented technologies effectiveness's assessment. J. East-Eur. Adv. Technol. **63**, 21–25 (2013)

Software Quality Standards and Models Evolution: Greenness and Reliability Issues

Oleksandr Gordieiev[1(✉)], Vyacheslav Kharchenko[2], and Mario Fusani[3]

[1] University of Banking of the National Bank of Ukraine, 1 Andriivska Street, Kyiv, Ukraine
alex.gordeyev@gmail.com
[2] National Aerospace University «KhAI», 17 Chkalova Street, Kharkiv, Ukraine
v_s_kharchenko@ukr.net
[3] System and Software Evaluation Center, ISTI-CNR, Via Moruzzi, 1, 56124 Pisa, Italy
mario.fusani@isti.cnr.it

Abstract. New attributes (characteristics, requirements) are proposed as an essential part of a software quality model related to green software. It consists of two main attributes, namely resource (energy) saving and sustainability. Evolution of software quality models is analyzed in context of greenness and reliability. In particular, well known software quality models beginning from on the first McCall's model (1977) to models described in standards ISO/IEC9126 (2001) and ISO/IEC25010 (2010) are analyzed according to green and reliability issues. Comparison of the software quality models is carried out using a special metrics of complexity and technique considering the number of levels and attributes and their semantics. Prediction of complexity for the next software quality model (2020) is fulfilled and variants of green software attributes inclusion in model are proposed. Metrics for assessment of reliability, green related and other quality attributes are analyzed considering the standards ISO/IEC25023 and ISO/IEC9126. Results of comparing metric sets of for these standards are described.

Keywords: Software quality model · Green software · Software reliability · Evolution analysis · Metrics · ISO/IEC9126 · ISO/IEC25010 · ISO/IEC25023 · Structure-semantic analysis · Software metrics

1 Introduction

1.1 Motivation and Work Related Analysis

A set of Software Quality Models (SWQM) has been introduced since the evolution of software engineering [1]. Software quality is the degree to which a software product satisfies stated and implied needs when used under specified conditions [2]. Software Quality Model (SWQM) is usually defined as a set of characteristics and relationships between them which actually provide the basis for specifying the requirements of

V. Yakovyna et al. (Eds.): ICTERI 2015, CCIS 594, pp. 38–55, 2016.
DOI: 10.1007/978-3-319-30246-1_3

quality, evaluating quality and SWQMs comparison [3–9]. There are a lot of models suggested during «software engineering era» [10]. Some of SWQM, described in IEEE, ISO, IEC standards, became well-known and can be called basic. New significant SWQM appear just about once in 10 years. The characteristics and subcharacteristics set and structure (graph-based hierarchy and semantic content) of such SWQMs are changed [11–14]. Generally, these sets are extended and the next SWQM becomes more and more complicated. Changes of SWQMs are caused by evolution of technologies, new challenges in software engineering and so on.

One of the challenges is development of energy-saving (green) information technologies. It has been caused by appearance of a concept «green software» [15]. «Green software» (GSW) is described by the following words: «decrease» (energy or other resources consumption), «don't do much harm and preserve» (energy, resources, environment) and «improve» (make environment more comfortable and safe). More wide aspects and directions of green and safe/reliable computing are discussed in [16, 17].

«Green» or «greenness» characteristics for software are resources saving and sustainability, which were not explicitly defined in well known SWQMs described by standards ISO/IEC9126-1 [18], ISO/IEC25010 [2]. Analysis of [3, 4, 6–8] indicates that SWQMs do not include such characteristics in explicit form.

Taking into consideration the prerequisites for emergence of green characteristics in future SWQMs in direct form we analyze the evolution of the characteristics associated with GSW for existing quality models and try to predict their changing. The analysis will allow the definition tendencies of green characteristics and suggest variants of including some in future SWQMs.

Besides, it is important to analyse the changing of metric set during last ten years considering standards ISO/IEC9126-2 [19] and ISO/IEC25023 [20].

1.2 Goal and Approach

In previous works we:

- described the technique of structure-semantic analysis, which was applied for comparative research of SWQMs [11];
- represented conception for SWQMs analysis [21];
- analysed more competitive characteristics of SQMs, such as greenness, usability and security, and their combinations «usability-security» , «security-greenness» and «usability-greenness» in point of view standard's evolution [22].

A **goal of the paper** is carrying out of additional analysis of known software quality models and their development in context of GSW and software reliability. We aim to investigating SWQMs using metric-based approach to assess "weights" of different software quality attributes, first of all, green and reliability characteristics. Expected results of this analysis are also to assess the changing of the attribute weights during evolution of the models and to predict their changing in future.

Stages of the research are the following:

1. Determination of occurrence rates for different SWQM attributes (characteristics at the first level of hierarchy and subcharacteristics at the second one) in different quality models;
2. Selection and analysis of SWQM characteristics which are implicitly associated with green software;
3. Analysis of SWQMs in context green software and reliability by use of complexity metrics and calculation of corresponding weights for attributes;
4. Research of relationship/dependency between metric values for green software, reliability and the years of emergence for known basic SWQMs;
5. Calculation of complexity metric for using results of SWQMs relationship/dependency comparison, described in [11];
6. Calculation of complexity metric for green and reliability attributes of new SWQMs using function describing of dependency between metric values and years of SWQMs emergence;
7. Analysis of SWQM in use in context of green software and definition of possible variants of inclusion of green attributes in new models;
8. Analysis of metrics for assessment of reliability, green related and other quality attributes considering the standards ISO/IEC25023 and ISO/IEC9126.

2 SWQM Analysis in Context of Green Software and Reliability

2.1 Analyzed Models

Let's select and analyse SWQM characteristics which can be implicitly associated with green software and reliability. The results of analysis are shown in Tables 1 and 2 for green characteristics and reliability characteristics correspondingly. Numeration of the characteristics corresponds with their "places" in hierarchy of SWQMs.

To assess "weights" of green characteristics the technique of SWQM structure-semantic analysis (SSA-technique) can be applied [11]. The technique describes quality models as a facet-hierarchy structure (graph). Nodes correspond to quality attributes and links take into account hierarchy dependencies. To briefly characterize the proposed analysis technique, let us introduce some initial terms:

- conceptual model is a model which a model under study is compared with;
- characteristic under study is a conceptual model characteristic which is compared with model under study characteristics.

2.2 Metrics

SSA-technique is based on comparing a model under study with the conceptual model, i.e. every SW Quality Model is compared with the conceptual model. So, the analysis is equivalent to semantic comparing characteristics and subcharacteristics of a model under study and the conceptual model with regard to their structures. Selecting a reference model is usually performed by an expert who has relevant experience and qualifications.

At the following stage comparison of models among themselves should be performed. The simplest and most obvious metrics are offered. Hierarchy of these metrics is presented in Fig. 1. The metrics are used to compare models with reference model bottom up, i.e. first at the level of subcharacteristics (subcharacteristics matching metric SMM, cumulative subcharacteristics comparison metric CSCM, characteristics matching metric CMM), then at the level of characteristics (cumulative matching

Table 1. SWQM characteristics associated with GSW.

№	SWQMs (years)	GSW characteristics
1.	McCall (1977)	4. Efficiency
		4.1 Execution efficiency
		4.2 Storage efficiency
2.	Boehm (1978)	2.2 Efficiency
		2.2.1 Accountability
		2.2.2 Accessibility
3.	Carlo Ghezzi (1991)	–
4.	FURPS (1992)	4 Performance
		4.1 Velocity
		4.2 Efficiency
		4.3 Availability
		4.4 Time of answer
		4.5 Time of recovery
		4.6 Utilization of resources
		1.2 Capacity
5.	IEEE (1993)	1 Efficiency
		1.1 Temporal efficiency
		1.2 Resource efficiency
6.	Dromey (1995)	2.2 Efficiency
7.	ISO 9126-1 (2001)	4 Efficiency
		4.1 Time behavior
		4.2 Resource utilization
8.	QMOOD (2002)	6 Effectiveness
9.	ISO 25010 (2010)	2 Performance efficiency
		2.1 Time behavior
		2.2 Resource utilization
		2.3 Capacity

Table 2. Reliability characteristics of SWQM.

№	SWQMs (years)	Reliability characteristics
1.	McCall (1977)	2. Reliability
		2.1 Accuracy
		2.2 Error tolerance
		2.3 Consistency
2.	Boehm (1978)	2.1 Reliability
		2.2.1 Self contentedness
		2.2.2 Integrity
		2.2.3 Accuracy
3.	Carlo Ghezzi (1991)	3. Reliability
4.	FURPS (1992)	3. Reliability
		3.1 Frequency and servity of failures
		3.2 Recoverability
		3.3 Time among failures
5	IEEE (1993)	2. Reliability
		2.1 Non deficiency
		2.1 Error tolerance
		1.3 Availability
6.	Dromey (1995)	1.2 Reliability
7.	ISO 9126-1 (2001)	2. Reliability
		2.1 Maturity
		2.2 Fault tolerance
		2.3 Recoverability
8.	QMOOD (2002)	–
9.	ISO 25010 (2010)	5. Reliability
		5.1 Maturity
		5.2 Availability
		5.3 Fault tolerance
		5.4 Recoverability

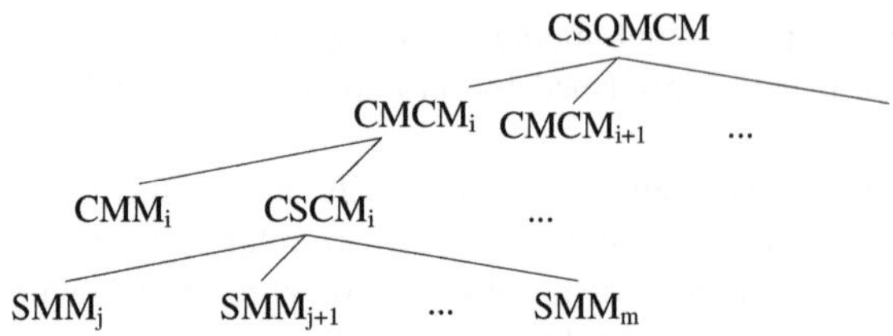

Fig. 1. Metrics hierarchy.

characteristics metric CMCM) and finally at the level of models as a whole (cumulative software quality models comparison metric CSQMCM).

Features of the metrics are the following [11]:

- subcharacteristic matching metric (SMMj). Every subcharacteristic match value is identified as SMMj = 0,5/number of reference (conceptual) model elements subcharacteristics of the characteristic under study. Weights of characteristics are not considered when calculating metrics;
- cumulative subcharacteristics comparison metric (CSCM) is evaluated as a sum of SMM:

$$CSCM_i = \sum\nolimits_{j=1}^{k} SMM_j; \quad (1)$$

- characteristics matching metric (CMM) takes the value of 0.5 in case of matching or 0 if the characteristics are different;
- cumulative matching characteristics metric (CMCM) is calculated as a sum of CMM metric and $\sum\nolimits_{j=1}^{k} CSCM_j$:

$$CMCM_i = CMM_i + \sum\nolimits_{j=1}^{k} CSCM_j; \quad (2)$$

- cumulative software quality models comparison metric (CSQMCM) is calculated according to the formula:

$$CSQMCM = \sum\nolimits_{j=1}^{n} CMCM_j \quad (3)$$

2.3 Results of SWQM in Context of Green Software and Reliability Characteristics

Let us conduct SW QM analysis and first of all, define the reference (conceptual) model. SW Quality Model ISO/IEC 25010 will be considered as uppermost and reference [11] regarding to all other models. It is the newest introduced model and takes into account main modern software peculiarities in point of view quality evaluation. This model is described by international standard of top level.

According with results of analysis CMCM is calculated for set of characteristics presented in Table 1. The results of calculation are shown in Table 3 (Chs – characteristics, SChs – subcharacteristics) for GSW characteristics and Table 4 for reliability characteristics.

The histogram of CMCM values for software quality models is presented on Fig. 2. An abscissa axis corresponds to years of SWQM emergence. Initial point (year) is 1970 (as a first year after 1968 which is multiple of a ten years).

CMCM values will be further represented and analysed only for so-called basic SWQMs [18]. Basic models were selected considering their support by standards, the international reputation and application. The models of McCall and Boehm are similar, hence first one was selected. Hence, the models of Boehm, Ghezzi, FURPS, Dromey, QMOOD were excluded (Fig. 3).

The analytical dependency between SWQM appearance year (X axis) and CMCM value (Y axis) for characteristics associated with GSW may be represented by regressive linear function:

$$y = ax + b \tag{4}$$

Table 3. Results of GSW characteristics comparison and calculation of CMCM.

Conceptual model (ISO 25010)		**McCall model**				**Boehm model**				**Ghezzi model**			
Chs	SChs	Chs	SChs	CMM	SMM	Chs	SChs	CMM	SMM	Chs	SChs	CMM	SMM
2		4		0,5	0	-	2.2	0	0,5	-	-	0	0
	2.1	-	-	0	0	-	-	0	0	-	-	0	0
	2.2	-	-	0	0	-	-	0	0	-	-	0	0
	2.3	-	-	0	0	-	-	0	0	-	-	0	0
				CMCM=0,5				CMCM=0,5				CMCM=0	
Conceptual model (ISO 25010)		**FURPS Model**				**IEEE Model**				**Dromey model**			
Chs	SChs	Chs	SChs	CMM	SMM	Chs	SChs	CMM	SMM	Chs	SChs	CMM	SMM
2		-	4.2	0	0,5	1	-	0,5	0	-	2.2	0	0.5
	2.1	-	-	0	0	-	-	0	0	-	-	0	0
	2.2	-	4.6	0	0,17	-	1.2	0	0,17	-	-	0	0
	2.3	-	1.2	0	0,17	-	-	0	0	-	-	0	0
				CMCM =0,84				CMCM =0,67				CMCM =0,5	
Conceptual model (ISO 25010)		**ISO 9126 model**				**QMOOD model**							
Chs	SChs	Chs	SChs	CMM	SMM	Chs		SChs		CMM		SMM	
2		4	-	0,5	0	2		-		0,5		0	
	2.1	-	4.1	0	0,17	-		-		0		0	
	2.2	-	4.2	0	0,17	-		-				0	
	2.3	-	-	0	0	-		-		0		0	
				CMCM=0,84						CMCM=0,5			

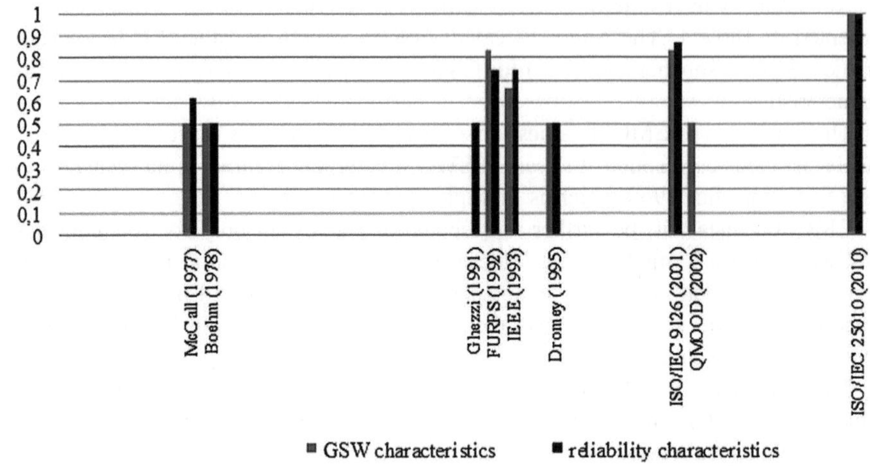

Fig. 2. CMCM values for GSW and reliability characteristics of SWQMs.

Table 4. Results of reliability characteristics comparison and calculation of CMCM.

Conceptual model (ISO 25010)		**McCall model**				**Boehm model**				**Ghezzi model**			
Chs	SChs	Chs	SChs	CMM	SMM	Chs	SChs	CMM	SMM	Chs	SChs	CMM	SMM
5		2.	-	0,5	0	-	2.1	0	0,5	3	-	0,5	0
	5.1	-	-	0	0	-	-	0	0	-	-	0	0
	5.2	-	-	0	0	-	-	0	0	-	-	0	0
	5.3	-	2.2	0	0,125	-	-	0	0	-	-	0	0
	5.4	-	-	0	0	-	-	0	0	-	-	0	0
				CMCM=0,625				CMCM=0,5				CMCM=0,5	
Conceptual model (ISO 25010)		**FURPS Model**				**IEEE Model**				**Dromey model**			
Chs	SChs	Chs	SChs	CMM	SMM	Chs	SChs	CMM	SMM	Chs	SChs	CMM	SMM
5			3.	-	0,5	2		0,5	0		1.2,2.3, 3.4,4.4	0	0,5
	5.1	5.1	-	-	0	-	-	0	0	-	-	0	0
	5.2	5.2	-	4.3	0	-	2.3	0	0,125	-	-	0	0
	5.3	5.3	-	-	0	-	2.2	0	0,125	-	-	0	0
	5.4	5.4	-	3.2	0	-	-	0	0	-	-	0	0
				CMCM =0,75				CMCM =0,75				CMCM =0,5	
Conceptual model (ISO 25010)		**ISO 9126 model**				**QMOOD model**							
Chs	SChs	Chs	SChs	CMM	SMM	Chs		SChs		CMM		SMM	
5		2	-	0,5	0	-		-		0		0	
	5.1	-	2.1	0	0,125	-		-		0		0	
	5.2	-	-	0	0	-		-		0		0	
	5.3	-	2.2	0	0,125	-		-		0		0	
	5.4	-	2.3	0	0,125	-		-		0		0	
				CMCM=0,87						CMCM=0			

where x – variable, a and b- regression coefficients. For 1970 year variable (x) has value 0, for 1980 year x = 10, for 1990 year x = 20, for 2000 year x = 30 and for 2010 year x = 40.

Linear subjection was chosen by graphic data analysis (Fig. 3). Satisfiability of applying linear subjection is confirmed by coefficient of determination (R2) which equals 0,94.

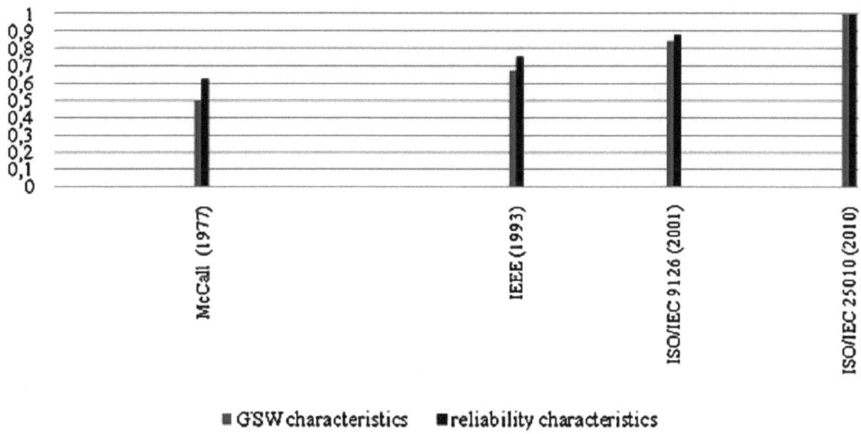

Fig. 3. CMCM values for GSW and reliability characteristics of basic SWQMs.

The values of parameters a and b can be calculated using Least Square Method:

$$a = \frac{n \sum_{i=0}^{n} x_i y_i \sum_{i=1}^{n} x_i \sum_{i=1}^{n} y_i}{n \sum_{i=1}^{n} x^2 \left(\sum_{i=1}^{n} x_i\right)^2}, \tag{5}$$

$$b = \frac{\sum_{i=1}^{n} y_i \; a \sum_{i=1}^{n} x_i}{n} \tag{6}$$

As a result a = 0.0146, b = 0.4108 and function:

$$y = 0.0146x + 0.4108. \tag{7}$$

The obtained function may be called a law of increasing of characteristics associated with GSW for SWQM.

The similar dependency can be obtained for reliability characteristics. In this case a = 0.011, b = 0.5 and function:

$$y = 0.011x + 0.5. \tag{8}$$

Formulas 7 and 8 illustrate a tendency of SWQMs characteristics/ subcharacteristics changes. Analysis of dependencies (Fig. 3) allows concluding that weights of green and reliability characteristics became equal in 2010 (the standard ISO/IEC 25010). Hence, since first SWQMs the characteristics/subcharacteristics related to green attributes have faster dynamics of increasing.

2.4 Development of SWQM in Context of Green Software

We can assume that the next general SWQM will include GSW characteristics in an explicit form. Let's analyse SWQM evolution tendency in context GSW as a whole. CSQMCM for SWQM may be calculated as shown in formula (3). It may be appeared for future model (2020 year). In compliance with [11] and based on the analytical relationship between SWQM appearance year (X axis) and CSQMCM value (Y axis) the following formula may be obtained:

$$y = 0,153x + 1,363. \quad (9)$$

Besides, considering that each new SWQM approved as a standard is received about once per 10 years, and that the last model was introduced by the standard ISO/IEC 25010 appeared in 2010 the prediction of the CSQMCM value can be done. With this in mind:

$$\text{CSQMCM} = 0,153^{*}50 + 1,363 = 9,013. \quad (10)$$

CSQMCM values change is illustrated in Fig. 4 as a histogram for the well known base SWQM as columns of gray and subsequent SWQM 2020 as a column of light gray column.

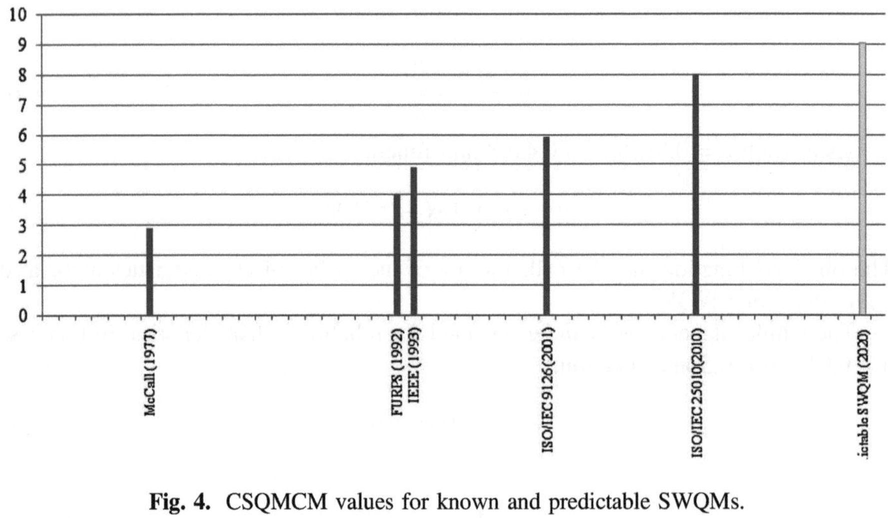

Fig. 4. CSQMCM values for known and predictable SWQMs.

According to the obtained dependence (4) CMCM for green software characteristics is calculated for predictable SWQM 2020 (Fig. 5).

$$y = 0,0146^{*}50 + 0,4108 = 1,1408. \quad (11)$$

And CMCM for reliability characteristics is calculated for predictable SWQM 2020 (Fig. 5).

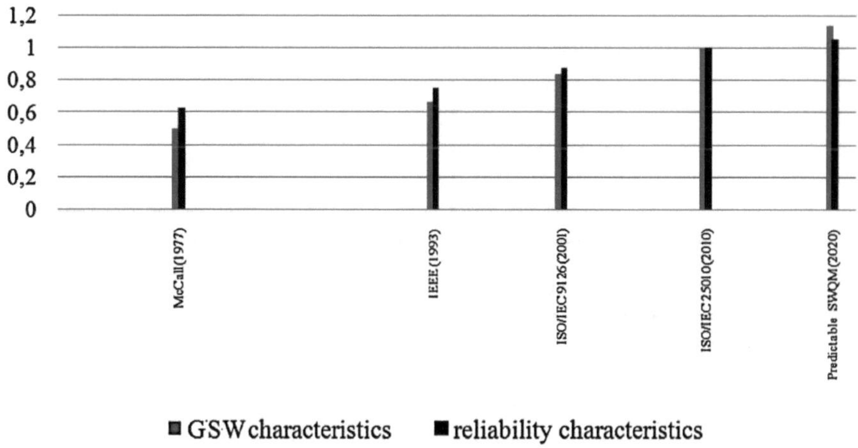

Fig. 5. CMCM values for reliability characteristics and green characteristics for basic SWQMs.

CMCM values of SWQM 2020 for characteristics associated with «green» software exceed the value of the same metric for SWQM ISO/IEC 25010 by 0.1408.

$$y = 0,011^{*}50 + 0,5 = 1,05. \quad (12)$$

CMCM values of SWQM 2020 for reliability characteristics exceed the value of the same metric for SWQM ISO/IEC 25010 by 0.05.

Analysis of dependencies (Fig. 5) allows predicting that green characteristics number will increase faster comparing with other more conservative characteristics.

3 GSW Oriented oN Extending of SWQMs

Taking into account predictable changing of SWQMs let's analyse how content of such models may be added including software quality models in use.

3.1 Variants of GSW Characteristics Inclusion in SWQM

In the following, possible variants are shown of inclusion of GSW characteristics and its components in a SWQM.

1. GSW characteristic can be introduced in SWQM as a separated characteristic with subcharacteristics *resources saving* and *sustainability*. It should be noted that usually *resources saving* excludes *resource utilization* from *performance efficiency* characteristic (Fig. 6).

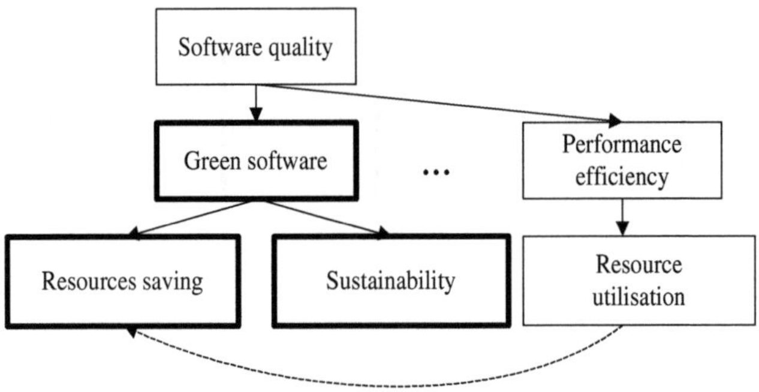

Fig. 6. Green software characteristics in SWQM at the level of characteristics (1).

2. Green software characteristics are not included in SWQM explicitly, but subcharacteristics can go in to SWQM (Fig. 7). *Resources saving* goes in to SWQM as the subcharacteristic in place of *resource utilization*. Subcharacteristic *sustainability* goes in to SWQM as separated characteristic.

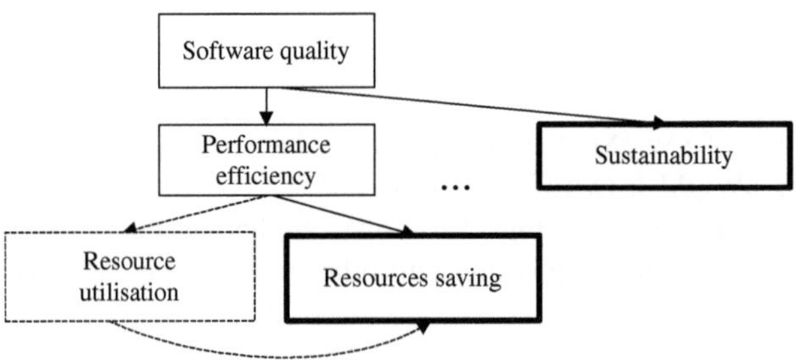

Fig. 7. «Green» software characteristics in SWQM at the level of characteristics and subcharacteristics (2).

3. GSW characteristic cannot be explicitly included in SWQM, but subcharacteristics can be explicitly included (Fig. 8). *Resources saving* is included in SWQM as

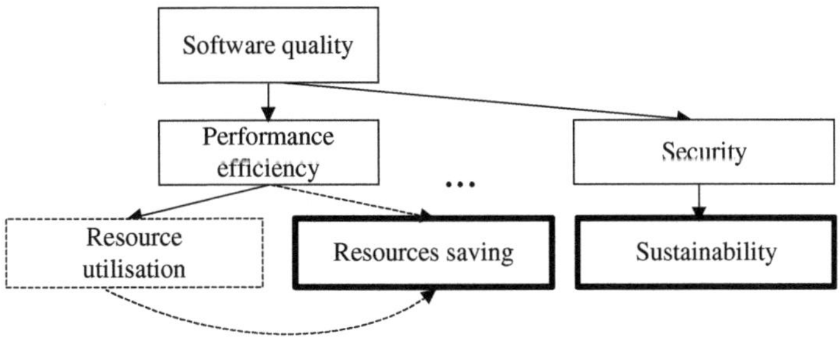

Fig. 8. Green software characteristics in SWQM at the level of subcharacteristics (3).

subcharacteristic in place of *resource utilization. Sustainability* is included in SWQM as subcharacteristic to characteristic *security.*

3.2 SWQM in Use. Analysis in Context of GSW

The standards ISO/IEC9126 and 25010 describe a separate type of model - software quality models in use (SWQM-U). SWQM-U is a capability of the software product to enable specified users to achieve specified goals with effectiveness, productivity, safety and satisfaction in specified contexts of use [18]. The SWQM-Us include characteristics, which can be associated with GSW subcharacteristics, in particular resources saving and sustainability:

- **for SWQM-U, ISO/IEC 9126**: *resources saving – productivity; sustainability – safety. Productivity* is a capability of the software product to enable users to expend appropriate amounts of resources in relation to the effectiveness achieved in a specified context of use. *Safety* is a capability of the software product to achieve acceptable levels of risk of harm to people, business, software, property or the environment in a specified context of use. Risks are usually a result of deficiencies in the functionality (including security), reliability, usability or maintainability;
- **for SWQM-U, ISO/IEC 25010**: *resources saving – efficiency*; *sustainability – freedom from risk, which include 3* subcharacteristics – *economic risk mitigation, health and safety risk mitigation and environmental risk mitigation. Efficiency* is a ratio of expended resources to the accuracy and completeness with which users achieve goals. *Freedom from risk* is a degree to which a product or system mitigates the potential risk to economic status, human life, health, or the environment.

Correlation of SWQM-U characteristics for standards ISO/IEC 9126 and 25010, which are implicitly associated with «green software» and among themselves is shown in Fig. 9.

Thus, GSW related characteristics should be taken into account on development of the next SWQM (SWQM-U) as well.

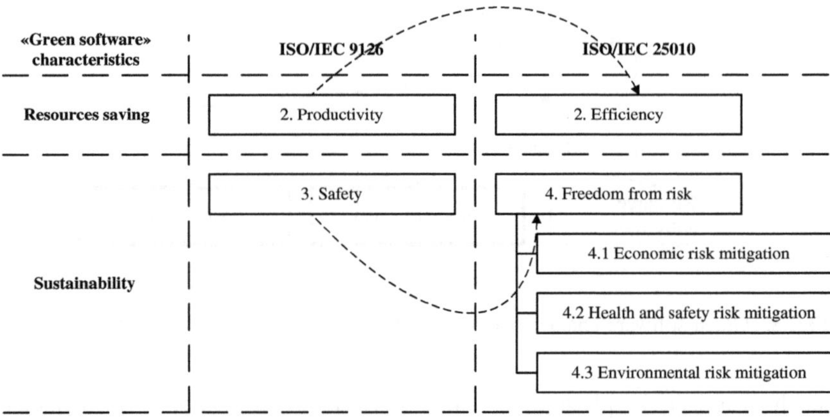

Fig. 9. Correlation of characteristics of SWQM-Us (ISO/IEC 9126 and ISO/IEC 25010) with GSW characteristics.

4 Software Quality Assessment Metrics Analysis

4.1 Standards ISO/IEC 9126-2 and ISO/IEC 25023: Comparing of Metrics

To assess software quality different metrics are applied. As a rule, nomenclature of metrics corresponds to SQMs. Hence, analysis of the changing of metrics set can be done considering evolution of standards by using an approach similar to that mentioned above. Two most known international standards of the last years ISO/IEC 9126:2003 and ISO/IEC 25023:2015 will be analyzed. The standards describe each a set of software quality metrics.

Our procedure of metrics analysis is based on comparison of metrics sets of these standards (Table 5). As far as each set of metrics in standards corresponds to hierarchy of measures software quality assessment, such hierarchy for ISO/IEC 9126-2 [19] has been chosen as an etalon. To implement a quantitative analysis of SWQ metrics evolution (changing of metric sets from standard to standard) the following indicators are suggested:

- general number of metrics for ISO/IEC 25023 (it equals 59);
- number of full compliances of metrics for standards (26);
- number of partial compliances of metrics for standards (5);
- general number of metrics for ISO/IEC9126-2 (83).

The values of these indicators are shown in Table 6.

As a result of the analysis, it was established the following:

- number of the metrics in the standard [20] is less on 24 metrics than in the standard [19];
- more than half of the metrics (considering partial compliance of the metrics) in the standard [20] concur with metrics of the standard [19] (31 metrics out of 59);

Table 5. Results of software quality assessment metrics analysis.

Characteristics measures	Sub-characteristics measures	Metrics	Metrics	Sub-characteristics measures	Characteristics measures
ISO/IEC 25023			ISO/IEC 9126-2		
1 Functional suitability	1.2 Functional correctness	Computational Accuracy	Computational Accuracy	1.2 Accuracy	1Functionality
2 Performance efficiency	2.1 Time behaviour	Response time (*)	Response time	4.1 Time behaviour	4 Efficiency
			Response time (Mean time to response)		
			Response time (Worst case response time ratio)		
		Throughput (*)	Throughput		
			Throughput (Mean amount of throughput)		
			Throughput (Worst case throughput ratio)		
		Turnaround time (*)	Turnaround time		
			Turnaround time (Mean time for turnaround)		
			Turnaround time (Worst case turnaround time ratio)		
	2.2 Resource utilization	I/O devices utilization	I/O devices utilisation	4.2 Resource utilisation	
		Memory utilization	Maximum memory utilisation		
3Compatibility	3.1 Co-existence	Available co-existence	Available co-existence	6.3 Co-existence	-
	3.2 Interoperability	Data exchangeability(*)	Data exchangeability (User's success attempt based)	1.3 Interoperability	
			Data exchangeability (Data format based)		
4 Usability	4.2 Learnability	Completeness of user Documentation and/or help facility	Effectiveness of the user documentation and/or help system	3.2 Learnability	3 Usability
	4.3 Operability	Message clarity	Message understandability in use	3.3 Operability	
		Customizing possibility	Customisability		
		Operational consistency	Operational consistency in use		
	4.5 User interface aesthetics	Appearance customizability of user interface	Interface appearance customisability	3.4 Attractiveness	
5 Reliability	5.1 Maturity	Fault removal	Fault removal	2.1 Maturity	2 Reliability
		Test coverage	Test coverage		
		Mean time between failures	Mean time between failures		
	5.3 Fault tolerance	Failure avoidance	Failure avoidance	2.2 Fault tolerance	
	5.4 Recoverability	Mean recovery time	Mean recovery time	2.3 Recoverability	
6 Security	6.1 Confidentiality	Access controllability	Access controllability	1.4 Security	
	6.2 Integrity	Data corruption prevention	Data corruption prevention	-	-
	6.4 Accountability	Access auditability	Access auditability	-	-
7 Portability	7.1 Adaptability	Hardware environmental adaptability	Hardware environmental adaptability	6.1 Adaptability	6 Portability
		System software environmental adaptability	System software environmental adaptability		
		Organisational environment adaptability	Organisational environment adaptability		
	7.2 Installability	Ease of installation	Ease of installation	6.2 Installability	
	7.3 Replaceability	Functional inclusiveness	Function inclusiveness	6.4 Replaceability	
8 Maintainability	8.3 Analysability	Audit trail capability	Audit trail capability	5.1 Analysability	5 Maintainability
		Diagnosis function sufficiency	Diagnostic function support		
	8.4 Modifiability	Modification complexity	Modification complexity	5.2 Changeability	
	8.5 Testability	Test restartability	Test restartability	5.4 Testability	

Notes: grey colour – partial compliance of the metrics (metrics of the standards [20] and [19]);
(*) – the metrics of the standard [20] which correspond to metrics group of the standard [19].

– some groups of the metrics of the standard [19] was merged in one metric of the standard [20] (such metrics are marked by sign «*» in Table 5).

4.2 Metrics of Reliability and Greenness

Lets analyse metrics evolution for «Greenness measures» and «Reliability measures» . We noticed that the semantically closest concept to «greenness measures» is «performance efficiency» in frameworks of analysis.

Main conclusions are the following for metrics regarding «Greenness measures» :

– general number of the metrics in the standards [20] and [19] equal 9 and 17 respectively;

Table 6. Quantitative results of software quality metrics analysis.

ISO/IEC 25023					ISO/IEC 9126-2
Characteristics measures	Sub-characteristics measures	General number of metrics	Number of full compliances	Number of partial compliances	General number of metrics
1. Functional suitability	1.1 Functional completeness	1	–	–	–
	1.2 Functional correctness	2	1	0	2
	1.3 Functional appropriateness	2	–	–	–
2. Performance efficiency	2.1 Time behavior	3	3(*)	0	4
	2.2 Resource utilization	3	1	1	13
	2.3 Capacity	3	–	–	–
3. Compatibility	3.1 Co-existence	1	1	0	1
	3.2 Interoperability	2	1(*)	1	1
4. Usability	4.1 Appropriateness recognizability	2	–	–	–
	4.2 Learnability	1	0	1	6
	4.3 Operability	3	2	1	12
	4.4 User error protection	2	–	–	–
	4.5 User interface aesthetics	1	1	0	2
	4.6 Accessibility	1	–	–	–
5. Reliability	5.1 Maturity	3	3	0	8
	5.2 Availability	2	–	–	–
	5.3 Fault tolerance	2	1	0	3
	5.4 Recoverability	1	1	0	6
6. Security	6.1 Confidentiality	2	1	0	1
	6.2 Integrity	1	1	0	1
	6.3 Non-repudiation	1	–	–	–
	6.4 Accountability	1	1	0	1
	6.5 Authenticity	1	–	–	–
7. Portability	7.1 Adaptability	3	3	0	5
	7.2 Installability	2	1	0	2
	7.3 Replaceability	3	1	0	3

(*Continued*)

Table 6. (*Continued*)

ISO/IEC 25023					ISO/IEC 9126-2
Characteristics measures	Sub-characteristics measures	General number of metrics	Number of full compliances	Number of partial compliances	General number of metrics
8. Maintainability	8.1 Modularity	1	–	–	–
	8.2 Reusability	1	–	–	–
	8.3 Analysability	2	1	1	4
	8.4 Modifiability	3	1	0	5
	8.5 Testability	3	1	0	3
Sum:		**59**	**26**	**5**	**83**

«-» - the metrics of the standard ISO/IEC 25023 do not correspond to the metrics of the standard ISO/IEC 9126-2;
(*) – the metrics of the standard ISO/IEC 25023 correspond to metrics group of the standard ISO/IEC 9126-2.

– number of full compliances of the metrics in the standards equal 3 and number of partial compliances equal 1.

Main conclusions are the following for metrics regarding «Reliability measures» :

– general number of the metrics in the standards [20] and [19] equal 8 and 17 respectively;
– number of full compliances of the metrics in the standards equal 5.

Hence, tendencies and reasons for changing software metrics sets are the following:

– reason for decreasing general number of the metrics in the standard [20] is their jointing in comparing with the standard [19]. Some groups of the metrics from [20] was merged in one metric in the standard [19]; on the other side, set of characteristics and subcharacteristics of the last standard ISO/IEC 25010 [2] became wider than in the standard [19];
– changing of metrics compliance for the standards [19] and [20] caused by modification of characteristics (subcharacteristics) nomenclature in the standard [2].

5 Conclusion

In compliance with technique of SWQM structural and semantic analysis we have researched software quality models by an evolutionary perspective and also the standards ISO/IEC 9126 and 25010 in context of reliability and greenness attributes. Using this technique, a relationship between the year of the SWQM appearance and the value of cumulative matching characteristics metric was obtained and analyzed. Besides, we have calculated the CMCM values for the green software characteristics of the next SWQM, the output of which may be expected in 2020.

We also obtained the value of metric - cumulative software quality models comparison metric for SWQM of 2020, which exceeds the value of this indicator for SWQM ISO/IEC 25010 (Fig. 4). It may be explained by possible inclusion of green software characteristics in SWQM explicitly.

According with the results of this analysis we can conclude that:

- since the first SWQMs the characteristics/ subcharacteristics related to green attributes show increasing dynamics;
- weights of green and reliability characteristics became equal in the SWQM provided by the standard ISO/IEC 25010;
- it is predicted faster increasing of number of green characteristics comparing with other more conservative characteristics.

However, implementation of green characteristics in future quality models should be harmonized with basic attributes such as reliability.

Changing of software quality metrics set for the 12 years (2003-2015) in the standards ISO/IEC 9126-2 and ISO/IEC 25023 is directly connected with evolution of software characteristics (subcharacteristics). Decreasing number of the metrics in the last standard [20] is caused by merging of the metrics in comparing with the standard [19].

In the future we plan to investigate all SWQM characteristic separately. The data obtained in this case will provide development of a prototype of new software quality model standard.

References

1. NATO Science Committee Report: Software engineering. In: Report on a Conference Sponsored by the NATO Science Committee, p. 136, Germany, Garmisch (1968)
2. International Standard ISO/IEC 25010: Systems and software engineering – Systems and software Quality Requirements and Evaluation (SQuaRE) – System and software quality models, ISO/IEC JTC1/SC7/WG6 (2011)
3. Dubey, S.K., Ghosh, S., Rana, A.: Comparison of software quality models: an analytical approach. Int. J. Emerg. Technol. Adv. Eng. **2**(2), 111–119 (2012)
4. Schiavone, G.: A life cycle software quality model using bayesian belief networks. University of Central Florida, Orlando (2006)
5. Jacobson, I., Booch, G., Rumbaugh, J.: The Unified Software Development Process. Addison Wesley Longman Inc., Boston (1999)
6. Lincke, R., Gutzmann, T., Löwe, W.: Software quality prediction models compared. In: International Conference on Quality Software, pp. 82–91 (2010)
7. Stavrinoudis, X.: Comparing internal and external software quality measurements. In: Proccedings of the 8th Joint Conference on Knowledge-Based Software Engineering, pp. 115–124. IOS Press (2008)
8. Sharma, A., Dubey, S.K.: Comparison of software quality metrics for object-oriented system. Spec. Issue Int. J. Comput. Sci. Manage. Stud. **12**, 12–24 (2012)
9. Wagner, S.: Software Product Quality Control. Springer, Berlin (2013)

10. Lami, G., Fabbrini, F., Fusani, M.: Software sustainability from a process-centric perspective. In: Winkler, D., O'Connor, R.V., Messnarz, R. (eds.) EuroSPI 2012. CCIS, vol. 301, pp. 97–108. Springer, Heidelberg (2012)
11. Gordieiev, O., Kharchenko, V., Fominykh, N., Sklyar, V.: Evolution of software quality models in context of the standard ISO 25010. In: Zamojski, W., Mazurkiewicz, J., Sugier, J., Walkowiak, T., Kacprzyk, J. (eds.) Proceedings of the Ninth International Conference on DepCoS-RELCOMEX. AISC, vol. 286, pp. 223–232. Springer, Heidelberg (2014)
12. Radulovic, F.: A software quality model for the evaluation of semantic technologies. Master thesis, Universidad Politecnica de Madrid Facultad de Informatica (2011)
13. Al-Qutaish, R.E.: Quality models in software engineering literature: an analytical and comparative study. J. Am. Sci. **6**(3), 166–175 (2010)
14. Malhotra, N., Pruthi, S.: An efficient software quality models for safety and resilience. Int. J. Recent Technol. Eng. (IJRTE) **1**(3), 66–70 (2012)
15. Murugesan, S., Gangadharan, G.R.: Harnessing Green IT. Principles and Practices. Wiley, Chichester (2012)
16. Kharchenko V., Sklyar V., Gorbenko A., Phillips C.: Green computing and communications in critical application domains: challenges and solutions. In: Proceedings of the 9th International Conference on Digital Technologies, 29–31 May 2013, Žilina, Slovakia, pp. 24–29 (2013)
17. Kharchenko, V. (ed.): Green IT-Engineering. 2 volumes: Principles, Components and Models, vol.1, p. 593. Systems, Industry, Society, vol. 2, p. 628. National Aerospace University KhAI, Ukraine (2014) (In Russian)
18. International Standard ISO/IEC9126–1: Software engineering – Product quality – Part 1: Quality, p. 32 (2001)
19. International Standard ISO/IEC9126–2: Software engineering – Product quality – Part 2: External metrics, p. 96 (2003)
20. International Standard ISO/IEC 25023: Systems and software engineering – Systems and software Quality Requirements and Evaluation (SQuaRE) - Measurement of system and software product quality, ISO/IEC JTC1/SC7, p. 47 (2015)
21. Gordieiev, O., Kharchenko, V.: Software quality models evolution: technique and results of analysis in context standard ISO/IEC 25010. Inf. Process. Syst. J. **6**(113), 13–31 (2013). Ukraine. – 2013 (In Russian)
22. Gordieiev, O., Kharchenko, V., Fusani, M.: Evolution of software quality models: usability, security and greenness issues. In: Proceedings of the 19-th International Conference on Computers (part of CSCC 15), 16–20 July 2015, Zakynthos Island, Greece, pp. 519–523 (2015)

The New Method of Building a Safety Model for Quantitative Risk Assessment of Complex Technical Systems for Critical Application

Bohdan Volochiy, Bohdan Mandziy, and Leonid Ozirkovskyy(✉)

Department of Theoretical Radio Engineering and Radio Measurement,
Lviv Polytechnic National University, 12 Bandera Street, Lviv 79013, Ukraine
bvolochiy@ukr.net, bmandziy@lp.edu.ua, l.ozirkovsky@gmail.com

Abstract. In the presented work the idea of improvement the state space method for building safety models of complex technical systems for critical application is proposed. Result of the this improvement one single model is developed on which due to the split state of critical failure state quantitative reliability and safety quantitative indicators of the system can be obtained. Unlike traditional models as in a fault trees, dynamic tree failures and FMEA/ FMECA-models the proposed model to allow to take into account independencies between accidental situations. This model allows to investigate the trend of risk indicators accidental situations variance from increasing system reliability through the use of fault-tolerant configurations and maintenance usage.

Keywords: Safety · Reliability · Reliability engineering · Modeling · Complex system for critical application

1 Introduction

In designing complex technical systems for critical application (CTSCA) developer must ensure a high level of reliability and safety of those systems. Safety increasing could be done by introducing additional subsystem protection, blocking, emergency stop and etc. which reduces the reliability. Thus developer must resolve the contradiction between reliability and safety. Moreover system complexity reduce system reliability. Increasing of CTSCA reliability by using fault-tolerant configurations not always improves its safety. At the same time using maintenance always increases the reliability and safety. This task could be resolved on design stage by multivariate mathematical modeling of CTSCA with comparing analysis of alternative variants and selecting of better.

In the general approach for forming reliability models these models are formalized and describe the interaction of elements of the system element's from the reliability position. These models reflect the degree of each element influence on the reliability in the whole.

The study of safety includes, in addition, the analysis of the transition of system failures due to accident and determines the qualitative (risk priority number) and quantitative (minimal cut sets) characteristics of accidents.

V. Yakovyna et al. (Eds.): ICTERI 2015, CCIS 594, pp. 56–70, 2016.
DOI: 10.1007/978-3-319-30246-1_4

Due to complexity of modern technical systems the multivariate analysis without automation of model building and estimation of reliability and safety indexes on its basis are not available in many cases. So often, especially for safety estimation, it is replaced by building one variant of the model followed by the combination of obtained results with expert evaluation of safety and recommendations to bring them up to acceptable values (FMEA).

Nowadays reliability behavior modeling of CTSCA and its safety modeling are carried out independently of each other, using different types of models, which in the case of reliability take into account some properties of the system, but in the case of safety – completely different, although in reality these properties are interrelated and can't be separated.

This approach is explained by the reliability models complexity as well as safety models and respectively by huge time costs for their building and by significant computational costs for their analysis when taking into account the important nuances of CTSCA behavior. The dimension of reliability models of modern systems can reach hundreds and thousands of equations. The safety model is, unlike the reliability model, complex logical function that contains hundreds and thousands of arguments. Experience shows that the "manual" building of reliability models of fault-tolerant systems even with small number of elements (10) without software usage requires time-consuming procedure of dozen hours. If you change the parameters of the state graph you need to rebuild the new one and the probability of making errors in the model is very high when the chances of detecting them is very low, also the time of restructuring the state graph is comparable with the time of construction its first version. Manual building of safety models as fault tree and the risk indexes estimation on its basis (minimal cut set) is comparable to the complexity of the building the reliability models as graph of states and transitions.

The actual task is the improvement and development of modeling methods of CTSCA reliability behavior which are focused on reliability and safety indexes estimation.

2 Approaches Analysis of Complex Technical Systems Critical Application Safety and Reliability Modeling

For reliability estimation of CTSCA nowadays there are enough formal and in some cases software implemented approaches, but for safety estimation there are only partially formalized methodologies which involve manual building of logical and probabilistic models in GUI. These models provide the automated determination of selected safety indexes - quantity indexes such as Minimal Cut Sets or quality indexes such as Risk Priority Number.

Well-known software suites such as RAM Commander (ALD, Israel) [3], PTC Windchill QualitySolutions (PTC, USA) [4], ReliaSoft Synthesis Master Suite (ReliaSoft USA) [5], Item Toolkit (Item Software, USA, UK) [6], Reliability Workbench (Isograph, US, UK) [7] allow building reliability models as reliability block diagrams (RBD) with the automated estimation of reliability. Models as graph of states and transitions are built manually with further automation of reliability analysis.

For safety estimation these software suites have graphical tools for forming fault trees in manual mode with the automated determination of minimum cut sets and special tools to carry out FMEA/FMECA analysis. The main advantage of these software suites is that they contain integrated frameworks of elements models (electronic, electromechanical, mechanical, etc.) in accordance with international standards: MIL-HDBK-217, Telcordia SR-332, IEC TR 62380, 217Plus, FIDES, which are required for reliability and safety analysis.

In work [7] are given the general principles of automation of building reliability models as matrix of states and transitions and matrix with subsequent transition to the graph of states and transitions as guidelines and recommendations. Also, this approach does not have tools to analyze safety. In monograph [5] the fundamental principles of logical and probabilistic models as fault trees for the reliability and safety estimation are provided. Actually, this approach is widely used to analyze safety indexes, namely, risk by the minimal cut sets determination. However, this approach isn't formalized and in the case of CTSCA it requires significant time costs for building the fault tree and computational costs for the analysis of safety indexes. In addition, any changes in the structure of the system require the construction of its new model. Therefore, for multivariate analysis at the design stage this approach is rarely used, it is usually provided for certification, when the structure of CTSCA is established.

For qualitative CTSCA safety assessment most used technology is FMEA-analysis. It provides a detailed safety performance assessment presented as risk priority number. But it should be noted that safety and risk indicators are qualitative and obtained by review of specialists which introduces subjectivity in the analysis results. Especially this subjectivity is significant when it is necessary to reduce the value of risk level as full rebuilding of model is not provided and safety indicator reduce is obtained only by expert estimates.

At the present time the most powerful method for reliability models of CTSCA building is the state space method. It allows us to adequately reflect the functional and reliability behavior of CTSCA. Generated by this method model is represented by the system of linear differential equations of Chapman-Kolmogorov which adequately describes all the features of system behavior that allows us to obtain standardized and non-standardized reliability indexes, which are required by developer at design stage. However, for the analysis of safety and risk, in particular, this mathematical tool is not used in practice, although there are attempts to use it for building dynamic fault trees [2]. Practical use of state space method [3] is limited at the design stage, due to cumbersome models, the phase space of which is equal to 10^3 .. 10^4 equations, and for multivariate analysis, in most cases, it is replaced by simplified evaluation using standard models.

In work [14] the method of automated generation of state space for behavior analysis of CTSCA basing on formalized description of the designed object in the form of structural-automatic model is described. Structural-automatic model allows to automate the process of reliability models building and to significantly reduce the time costs of multivariate analysis.

Time-costs for build the SAM by experienced developer are 1–30 h, depending on the complexity of the system. These costs justifies itself in multivariate analysis of fault-tolerant systems, because the next correction of the model, even with significant changes in the structure of the system takes time from tens of minutes to several hours.

This approach is implemented in ASNA software [3, 14]. Input data about the researched object for software module ASNA should be submitted in the form of SAM, which is formalized description of the structure and reliability behavior of system (the rules of transition from one state to another during the failure and recovery of elements). Basing on SAM software module ASNA generates the list of all possible states of the system, the table of transitions from one state to another, which is transformed into the matrix of intensities of transitions when entering numerical values of intensities of failures and recovery of the system. Therefore, basing on the matrix of intensities ASNA module automatically forms the system of differential Chapman-Kolmogorov equations and solves it by Runge-Kutta-Merson method. As a result the user gets the time dependences of probabilities of system being in each of the possible states. Basing on this information, the user can define standardized reliability indexes of system (availability function, probability of failure, failure flow parameter, MTTF, etc.), and arbitrary parameters that may be needed for the "thin" study of the system (probability of downtime, probability of having at least N employable elements when using a certain number of renewals, etc.). This approach focuses on estimation reliability indexes for reliability design and efficiency indexes for functional design. To use this approach to the safety indexes estimation the improvement

Table 1. Comparison of reliability and safety estimating methods.

Reliability and safety estimating methods / Method features	FTA	FMEA/ FMECA	SSM	SAM
Independencies between accidental situations	-/+	-	+	+
Multivariate analysis	-	-	-	+
Fault tree building	+	-	-	-/+
Taking into account reliability and functional behavior	-	-	+	+
Taking into account maintenance	-/+	-	+	+
Taking into account embedded control and diagnostics	+	+	+	+
Taking into account system downtime	+	+	+	+
Safety indexes estimation	+	+	-	-

both the graph states and transitions (to display emergency situations) and description of the state vector and principles of SAM building is needed.

Comparing results of existing methods for reliability and safety estimating which are suitable for use in the design phase CTSCA is presented in Table 1.

The next conventional signs are used in Table 1:

+ Method is provides the feature.

– Method isn't provides the feature.

+/– Method can provide the feature, if it will improve.

Disadvantages all without exception approaches to safety assessment are the following - among the known approaches there were not found ones which allow determining the reliability and safety indexes for the same behavior model of CTSCA with taking into account all behavior features of the system while disability, accidents, downtime, etc. Hence the task of updating SAM and state space method for their adaptation to the problems of multivariate analysis and safety indexes estimation.

3 Improvement of the State Space Method and Its Formalization for Safety Models Building

An analysis of existing safety estimation technologies showed that there is a need to develop a complex of techniques and tools which would allow to build a single model. And this model which will take into account the interdependence of fault events in the system, their consequences, maintenance and repair of individual elements or subsystems, diagnostics, downtime, system reliability and functional behavior.

As already noted the state space method combining with formalized description of the systems in the form of SAM is the powerful tool for the study of both functional and reliability indexes of CTSCA STSVP that allows us to perform multivariate analysis with minimal time-cost. Significant advantages of the state space method is that it provides the set of all states of CTSCA and determine the probability rates getting in or staying in any of them. This property is particularly relevant when the operation of the system allows the states of reduced functionality or partial disability. In addition, you can see the quantity of reliability increase when entering certain types of redundancy and their cost. These properties make it possible not only to investigate the reliability of CTSCA when carrying in redundancy or changing its behavior algorithm, but also to analyze the impact of these actions on safety, which we understand as the risk of emergency in case of failure of each element of system.

This index according to [4, 15] is called minimal cut set. Minimal cut set (MCS) – is a minimal combination of events which lead to catastrophic system failure. If when any of event is removed from the MCS the remaining events collectively cannot cause to catastrophic system failure [4].

Thus, when designing CTSCA we must have a single model that is based on the state space method and provides:

- adequate reflection of system behavior while disability;
- consideration of strategies for maintenance and repair;
- consideration of controls and diagnostics;

- possibility of obtaining reliability indexes (probability of faultless work, availability, MTTF, MTBF);
- possibility of obtaining safety indexes (MCS);
- consideration of system downtime;
- the opportunity to obtain indexes of economic efficiency;
- to carry out the multivariate analysis.

To achieve this goal it is necessary to make a number of modifications of the state space method, as described below.

The behavior of CTSCA is described by graph of states and transitions. Vertices of graph are the states in which the system can be. These states are characterized by probabilities. Edges of the graph are the possible transitions from state to state and are characterized by the transition intensities.

In all known methods the catastrophic failure condition is a combination of all inoperable states, which are united in one state. This is used, on the one hand, to obtain the required reliability indexes when only operable states are used, on the other hand, inoperable states significantly increase the phase space, dimensionality of which is great.

Idea for space state method modification for safety indexes estimation (MCS), is based on splitting the state of catastrophic failure (CF) in separate states.

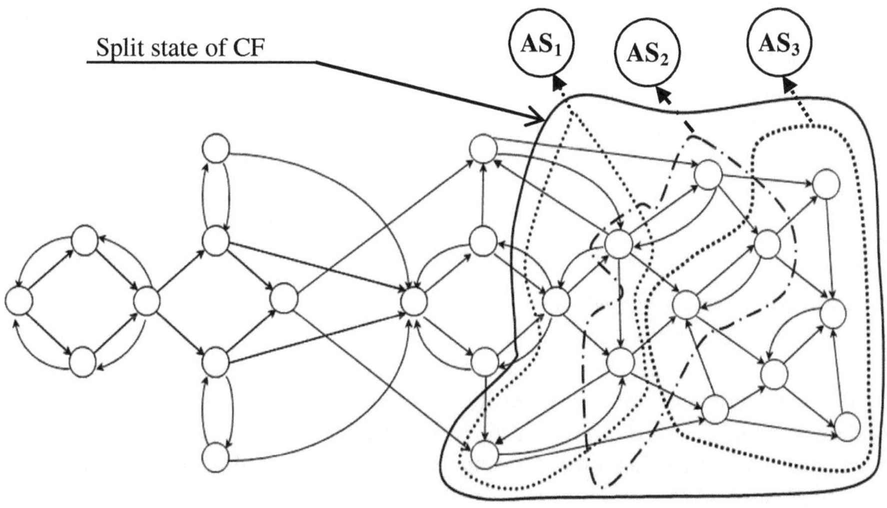

Fig. 1. Graph of state and transitions with split state of catastrophic failure

Thus, the set of inoperable states contains a subset of accidents (AS1, …, ASi, …), accordingly to CTSCA (Fig. 1). Each of these accidents can be represented by the corresponding fault tree.

In this case accidents are not isolated as the fault tree building as part of the states that form the emergency AS2 is included in other accidents such as AS1 and AS3. This is a characteristic of this method which will take into account not only the risk of an accidents but also cross-correlation between accidents. Such cross-correlation between accident situations is characteristic of CTSCA. But other methods such as fault tree analysis, dynamic fault tree analysis and FMEA-analysis does not allow this taking into account. The modified method of state space other than risk indicators gives a possibility to evaluate the severity of accidents which puts it on par with FMECA-analysis.

For safety indicators estimation - namely quantitative risk value the filtering from the resulting probability distribution of operable and inoperable states using the modified method of state space must be done. Filter is in this case the condition of critical failure. As a result of filtration, we obtain a set of probability of CTSCA being in operable states {Pi (t)} and the set of probability of CTSCA being in inoperable states {Qj (t)}, where i is the serial number for operable states and j is the serial number for inoperable states.

From the resulting set of operable states the necessary reliability indexes are formed and from the set of inoperable states the MCS – combination of inoperable states, when the critical failure definitely will occur – are obtained.

For minimal cut sets automated receiving were developed the search algorithm of all inoperable states combinations in which a critical system failure is occurred [13]. This means that this element is one of the most critical parts of the system. In the case of fault-tolerant systems, CTSCA is just that, the combination of several elements is possible.It is considered that as more inoperable states are included in MCS so the less vulnerable system is and so the effects of its failure will not be catastrophic for human life and health and the environment.

If vulnerable elements, which form inoperable states, which are included in MCS, are replaced by more reliable or reserved, the risk of accident is reduced in times. Thus, the MCS are necessary for designer to make reasonable redundancy in a new version of designed CTSCA. So due to the effect of redundancy input we can quantify the rate of risk reduction:

$$K_{rr} = C_m / C_n \tag{1}$$

where

Cm – MCS before redundancy input;

Cn – MCS after redundancy input;

Generalized diagram of technique of estimation of safety and reliability indexes basing on the graph of states and transitions with the split failure state and using SAM is shown in Fig. 2. According to it, the automated algorithm for obtaining MCS was developed. The input data for the algorithm is the set of inoperable states (MCS), derived from the binary SAM.

The binary SAM is the SAM of the CTSCA, in which all elements of structure are displayed by individual SV components and can take only of two values: zero and one. The binary SAM, which, unlike to original SAM [14], makes a possibility to describe the structure and behavior of CTS without unification of states of its structure elements. In addition, the binary SAM allows obtaining split failure state, in which states of CTSCA subsystems failures can be discerned with the given level of detail representation.

Procedure of filtering inoperable states from whole phase space is carried out by the analysis of the state vector component, comparing them with the critical failure condition. If the element is operable, the value of its corresponding SV component is greater than zero. If the element failed and led to accident, the component will be equal to zero.

Minimal cut sets are formed on the third stage from the filtered inoperable states. For this the automated algorithm of minimal cut sets (MCS) receiving were developed [13]. The input data for the algorithm is the set of inoperable states which were obtained from the binary SAM.

While the algorithm development it is taken into account that:

- at least one MCS is presented in the sysytem;
- cut set of the system is inoperable state, when system falls into catastrophic failure condition;
- MCS of the system is the state, when the system is in catastrophic failure but taking off at least one of the elements that are failed in this MCS, the catastrophic failure of the system can not occur at all.

Definition of MCS is provided in two stages: stage of MCS obtaining and stage of estimation their probability values.

Stage I. For MCS finding the following procedures are used: MCS sorting; MCS determination.

At this step it is necessary to sort obtained array of inoperable states of the system on the feature of the smallest number of events that led to the accident of the system. Further, basing on sorted array of inoperable states the MCS are defined. As a result of the proposed procedures the array of MCS is presents as a matrix.

Stage II. Determination of MCS probability is performed by the following procedures: determination of MCS from all cut sets; sum of MCS probabilities; forming of array of MCS and their probability values.

According to this stage we must create a matrix that consists of four columns – the first column is a serial number of MCS – N; the second column is SV component and its value; in the third column the numbers of states, which are attended by the corresponding MCS, are recorded. So in the fourth column there are recorded obtained probabilities of MCS as a result of this procedure. Also at this stage procedure of comparison of the system states is used.

The procedure for obtaining probability values of MS is the sum of probability values of being in respective states, whose numbers were found in the previous procedure, i.e., in the states that are recorded in the third column corresponding to the MCS matrix. As a result, the fourth column is filled with appropriate MCS probabilities value.

Obtained MCS are ranked in descending order of occurrence probability. Also is possible to calculate the percentage contribution of each MCS in an accident situation. From the MCS is evident weakness of the system.

To reduce the risk of accident must be reserved the weakest points of CTSCA and thus reduce the value of probability MCS.

Thus the MCS could be obtained from the graph of states and transitions without fault tree building.

4 An Example of the Usage of Developed Method of MCS Definition

Fault-tolerant system consists of six modules A, B, C, D, E and F. The modules A and B are the main operable configuration that provides performance of system functions. The modules C, D and E, F are whole-system redundancy modules. All modules have the same failure intensity $\lambda = 0{,}005$ and the observation period is $T = 50$ h. The reliability block diagram (RBD) of the fault-tolerant system is shown in Fig. 2.

In result of automatic method of generating [14] and solving a mathematical model of the system as a system of Chapmen - Kolmogorov differential equations the probability of being in every possible state was obtained. Probability of system being in operable state is 0,9391, and the probability of failure is equal to:

$$Q = 1 - 0,9391 = 0,0609$$

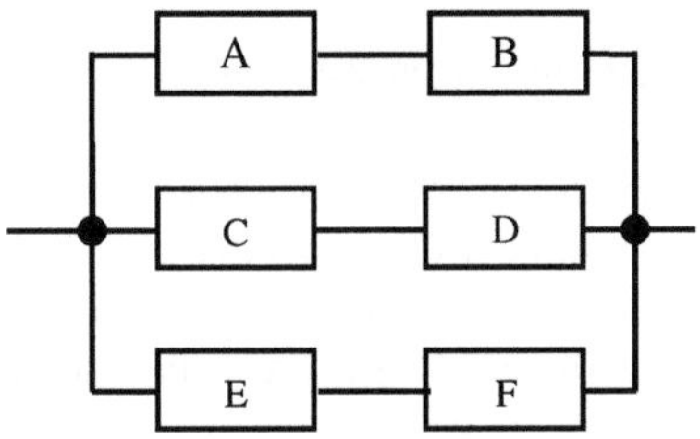

Fig. 2. The RBD of the fault-tolerant system

For reliability block diagram (Fig. 2) were build the binary structural-automaton model. Structural-automaton model (SAM) consists of three sets of data. The first set is a form of the state vector (VS), which enables a formalized description all the conditions for using variables - VS components. The components VS are variables that describe the state of the system. State vector can contain additional components that are used to detect the status of additional features such as counter current number of repairs each

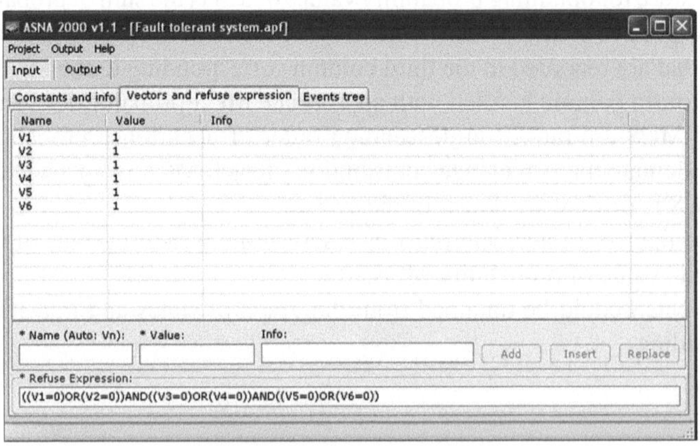

Fig. 3. The set state vector

item counting all repairs, meter total number of items that are out of order and so on. In this case system consists of 6 modules and therefore state vector will have six components. Module A component corresponds BC - V1, the module complies component - V2 etc. The set state vector introduced in the software module ASNA, shown in Fig. 3.

The second SAM set is a constant - set of formal parameters that characterize the structure of the system and its properties. Namely the number of parts on the system configuration, the number of reserve elements, their failure rate and intensity of renewals, limiting the number of renewals and so on. In this case it contains a set of formal parameters and module failure rate is shown in Fig. 4.

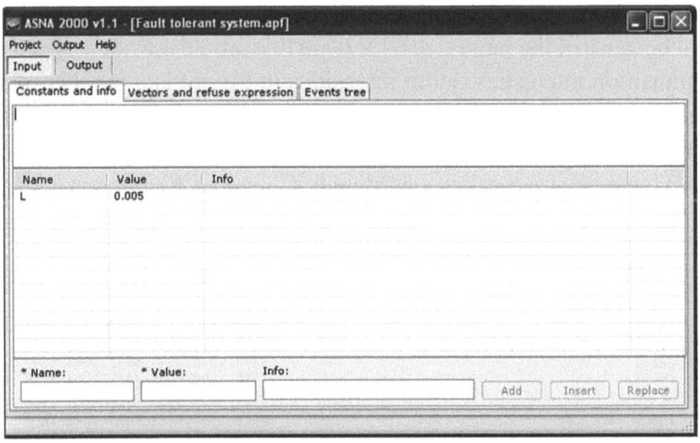

Fig. 4. The set of formal parameters

The third set of rules is tree of modification rules (TMR) of state vector which is given in tabular form and reflects the consequences that come after the failure or repair of individual elements under certain conditions. The components of TMR are events that can occur with elements (refusal or item recovery, connect reserve etc.), the set logic

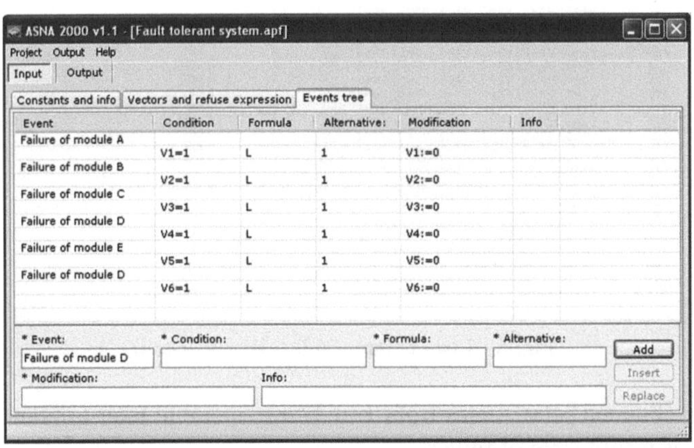

Fig. 5. The tree of modification rules of state vector

conditions that determine the combination of the values of the state vector components, which can take place at this event and the rules for modification VS. Each condition corresponds to the formula for calculating the intensity transition.

The consequence is the change VS events components and systems transition from one state to another according to the rules of transition. If certain elements inherent in more than one type of failures (such as breakage and short circuit), in such cases use a set of formulas for calculating probabilities of alternative transitions. Each of which uses a separate set of transition rules TRM of state vector. The set of formal parameters is shown in Fig. 5.

All three sets were introduced in software module ASNA as a result of his work graph of states and transitions was received as a list of states (Fig. 6) and matrix of transition intensities that because of the large size 64 × 64 in this article are not reduced. First column of matrix of transition intensities (jump intensities in Fig. 6) is a number of state whereto been done the transition. Second column is a number of state wherefrom been done the transition. Third column is a value of transition intensity. The diagonal elements of matrix (11, 22, 33, 44) have negative value according to Chapman-Kolmogorov rules.

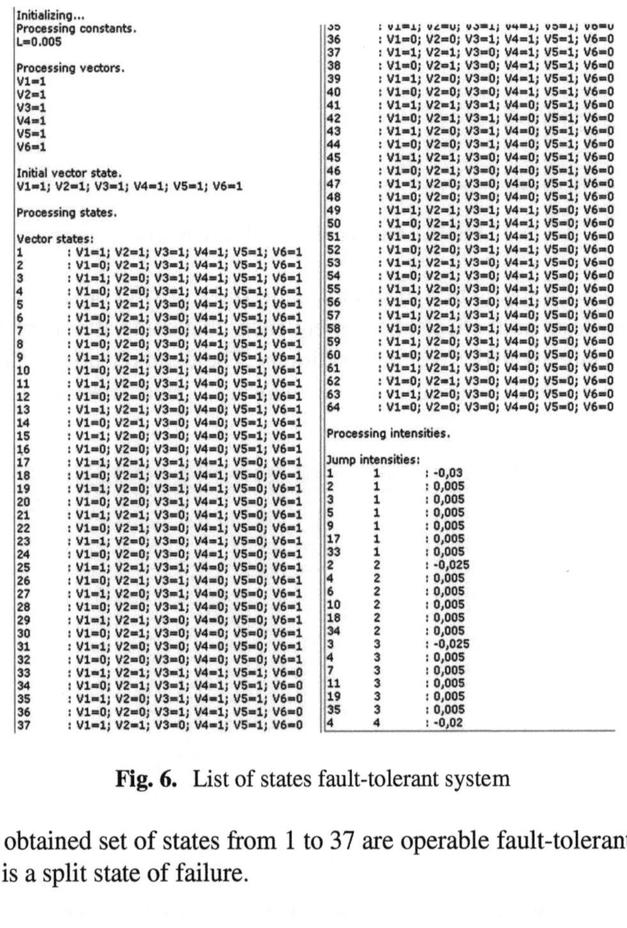

```
Initializing...
Processing constants.
L=0.005

Processing vectors.
V1=1
V2=1
V3=1
V4=1
V5=1
V6=1

Initial vector state.
V1=1; V2=1; V3=1; V4=1; V5=1; V6=1

Processing states.

Vector states:
1    : V1=1; V2=1; V3=1; V4=1; V5=1; V6=1
2    : V1=0; V2=1; V3=1; V4=1; V5=1; V6=1
3    : V1=1; V2=0; V3=1; V4=1; V5=1; V6=1
4    : V1=0; V2=0; V3=1; V4=1; V5=1; V6=1
5    : V1=1; V2=1; V3=0; V4=1; V5=1; V6=1
6    : V1=0; V2=1; V3=0; V4=1; V5=1; V6=1
7    : V1=1; V2=0; V3=0; V4=1; V5=1; V6=1
8    : V1=0; V2=0; V3=0; V4=1; V5=1; V6=1
9    : V1=1; V2=1; V3=1; V4=0; V5=1; V6=1
10   : V1=0; V2=1; V3=1; V4=0; V5=1; V6=1
11   : V1=1; V2=0; V3=1; V4=0; V5=1; V6=1
12   : V1=0; V2=0; V3=1; V4=0; V5=1; V6=1
13   : V1=1; V2=1; V3=0; V4=0; V5=1; V6=1
14   : V1=0; V2=1; V3=0; V4=0; V5=1; V6=1
15   : V1=1; V2=0; V3=0; V4=0; V5=1; V6=1
16   : V1=0; V2=0; V3=0; V4=0; V5=1; V6=1
17   : V1=1; V2=1; V3=1; V4=1; V5=0; V6=1
18   : V1=0; V2=1; V3=1; V4=1; V5=0; V6=1
19   : V1=1; V2=0; V3=1; V4=1; V5=0; V6=1
20   : V1=0; V2=0; V3=1; V4=1; V5=0; V6=1
21   : V1=1; V2=1; V3=0; V4=1; V5=0; V6=1
22   : V1=0; V2=1; V3=0; V4=1; V5=0; V6=1
23   : V1=1; V2=0; V3=0; V4=1; V5=0; V6=1
24   : V1=0; V2=0; V3=0; V4=1; V5=0; V6=1
25   : V1=1; V2=1; V3=1; V4=0; V5=0; V6=1
26   : V1=0; V2=1; V3=1; V4=0; V5=0; V6=1
27   : V1=1; V2=0; V3=1; V4=0; V5=0; V6=1
28   : V1=0; V2=0; V3=1; V4=0; V5=0; V6=1
29   : V1=1; V2=1; V3=0; V4=0; V5=0; V6=1
30   : V1=0; V2=1; V3=0; V4=0; V5=0; V6=1
31   : V1=1; V2=0; V3=0; V4=0; V5=0; V6=1
32   : V1=0; V2=0; V3=0; V4=0; V5=0; V6=1
33   : V1=1; V2=1; V3=1; V4=1; V5=1; V6=0
34   : V1=0; V2=1; V3=1; V4=1; V5=1; V6=0
35   : V1=1; V2=0; V3=1; V4=1; V5=1; V6=0
36   : V1=0; V2=0; V3=1; V4=1; V5=1; V6=0
37   : V1=1; V2=1; V3=0; V4=1; V5=1; V6=0
```

```
35   : V1=1; V2=0; V3=1; V4=1; V5=1; V6=0
36   : V1=0; V2=0; V3=1; V4=1; V5=1; V6=0
37   : V1=1; V2=1; V3=0; V4=1; V5=1; V6=0
38   : V1=0; V2=1; V3=0; V4=1; V5=1; V6=0
39   : V1=1; V2=0; V3=0; V4=1; V5=1; V6=0
40   : V1=0; V2=0; V3=0; V4=1; V5=1; V6=0
41   : V1=1; V2=1; V3=1; V4=0; V5=1; V6=0
42   : V1=0; V2=1; V3=1; V4=0; V5=1; V6=0
43   : V1=1; V2=0; V3=1; V4=0; V5=1; V6=0
44   : V1=0; V2=0; V3=1; V4=0; V5=1; V6=0
45   : V1=1; V2=1; V3=0; V4=0; V5=1; V6=0
46   : V1=0; V2=1; V3=0; V4=0; V5=1; V6=0
47   : V1=1; V2=0; V3=0; V4=0; V5=1; V6=0
48   : V1=0; V2=0; V3=0; V4=0; V5=1; V6=0
49   : V1=1; V2=1; V3=1; V4=1; V5=0; V6=0
50   : V1=0; V2=1; V3=1; V4=1; V5=0; V6=0
51   : V1=1; V2=0; V3=1; V4=1; V5=0; V6=0
52   : V1=0; V2=0; V3=1; V4=1; V5=0; V6=0
53   : V1=1; V2=1; V3=0; V4=1; V5=0; V6=0
54   : V1=0; V2=1; V3=0; V4=1; V5=0; V6=0
55   : V1=1; V2=0; V3=0; V4=1; V5=0; V6=0
56   : V1=0; V2=0; V3=0; V4=1; V5=0; V6=0
57   : V1=1; V2=1; V3=1; V4=0; V5=0; V6=0
58   : V1=0; V2=1; V3=1; V4=0; V5=0; V6=0
59   : V1=1; V2=0; V3=1; V4=0; V5=0; V6=0
60   : V1=0; V2=0; V3=1; V4=0; V5=0; V6=0
61   : V1=1; V2=1; V3=0; V4=0; V5=0; V6=0
62   : V1=0; V2=1; V3=0; V4=0; V5=0; V6=0
63   : V1=1; V2=0; V3=0; V4=0; V5=0; V6=0
64   : V1=0; V2=0; V3=0; V4=0; V5=0; V6=0

Processing intensities.

Jump intensities:
1    1    : -0,03
2    1    : 0,005
3    1    : 0,005
5    1    : 0,005
9    1    : 0,005
17   1    : 0,005
33   1    : 0,005
2    2    : -0,025
4    2    : 0,005
6    2    : 0,005
10   2    : 0,005
18   2    : 0,005
34   2    : 0,005
3    3    : -0,025
4    3    : 0,005
7    3    : 0,005
11   3    : 0,005
19   3    : 0,005
35   3    : 0,005
4    4    : -0,02
```

Fig. 6. List of states fault-tolerant system

From the obtained set of states from 1 to 37 are operable fault-tolerant system, and states 38–64 is a split state of failure.

As a result of software module ASNA probability distribution system stays in each state were received. As a result of the summation of probabilities stay in working condition was obtained dependence of probability of failure of the fault-tolerant system from the time (Fig. 7). On the basis of inoperable system it was determined that the system as a whole fails at six different MCS.

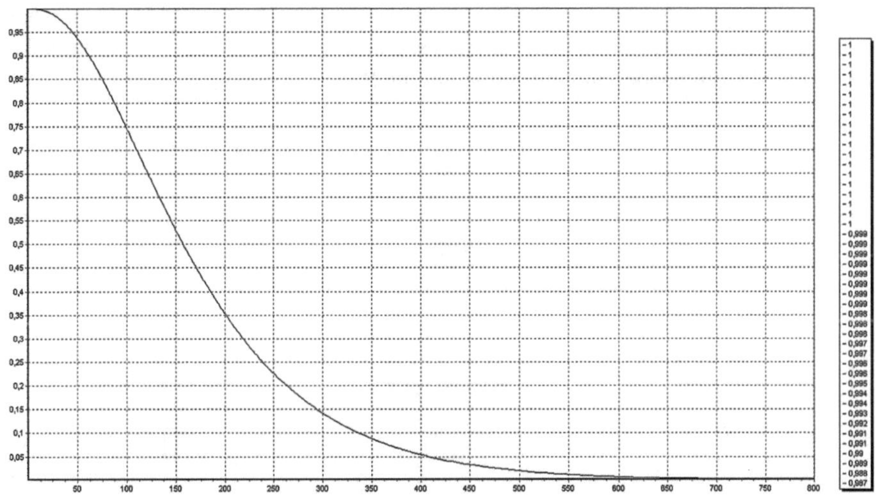

Fig. 7. Dependence of the probability of failure of the refusal stable system of time

Obtained MCS are shown in Table 2.

Table 2. Minimal cut sets based on Markov model

№	Modules failed	Quality	Quantity MCS	Contribution of MCS %
1	A, C, E	3	0,0108	12,5
2	A, D, E	3	0,0108	12,5
3	B, C, E	3	0,0108	12,5
4	B, D, E	3	0,0108	12,5
5	A, C, F	3	0,0108	12,5
6	A, D, F	3	0,0108	12,5
7	B, C, F	3	0,0108	12,5
8	B, D, F	3	0,0108	12,5

4.1 Validation of the Developed Method

To validate the developed method a fault tree was implemented for the system (Fig. 3) according to the approach [5] and the values of the probability of failures for each MCS were calculated. It was considered that the results obtained by fault tree are accurate and they were compared with results which are shown in Table 1.

The validation was performed using specialized software suite RAM Commander by ALD Service. For RBD the fault tree was set up (Fig. 8) and MCS were obtained by tools of RAM Commander and are shown in Fig. 9.

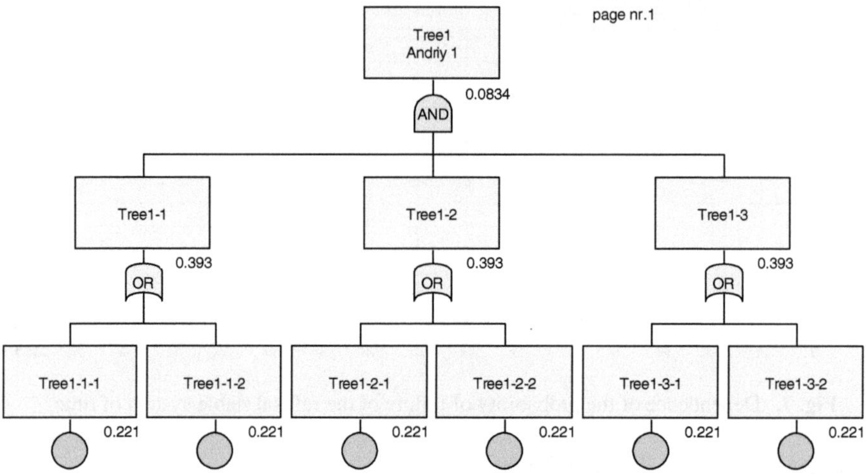

Fig. 8. Fault tree

2	FTA - Minimum Cut Sets						
3							
4	Project name: MASCHAK						
5	FTA: Andriy_1						
6	Top event: Tree1 Andriy 1						
7	Q mean=0.0833748						
8	MCS count: 8; MCS min.order: 3; MCS max.order: 3						
9							
10	N	Q mean	%	Order	Event 1	Event 2	Event 3
11	1	0.0108	12,50	3	Tree1-1-2	Tree1-2-2	Tree1-3-2
12	2	0.0108	12,50	3	Tree1-1-1	Tree1-2-2	Tree1-3-2
13	3	0.0108	12,50	3	Tree1-1-2	Tree1-2-1	Tree1-3-2
14	4	0.0108	12,50	3	Tree1-1-1	Tree1-2-1	Tree1-3-2
15	5	0.0108	12,50	3	Tree1-1-2	Tree1-2-2	Tree1-3-1
16	6	0.0108	12,50	3	Tree1-1-1	Tree1-2-2	Tree1-3-1
17	7	0.0108	12,50	3	Tree1-1-2	Tree1-2-1	Tree1-3-1
18	8	0.0108	12,50	3	Tree1-1-1	Tree1-2-1	Tree1-3-1
19							
20							
21	Minimal Cut Sets distribution by order						
22	Order	Number of MCS					
23	3	8					

Fig. 9. Minimal cut sets based on FTA model

The comparison shows that the calculated values of MCS, which were obtained from fault tree using software suite RAM Commander coincide with the values obtained from the graph of states and transitions with the split failure state using binary SAM. The developed approach (Fig. 2) allows us to get the MCS in automatic mode without fault tree construction.

5 Conclusions

1. Split of critical failure state in graph of states and transitions, in contrast to the known approaches, allows estimation of reliability and safety indexes, that allows the impact of maintenance strategies on safety and reliability and the impact of the fault tolerance on safety to be considered. This will increase the accuracy (certainty) of efficiency indexes estimation of complex technical systems for critical application.
2. Minimal cut sets obtaining on the basis of the graph of states and transitions allows taking into account the interrelations of accidents directly from the analysis of system states for identification weaknesses. It gives to use only efficient means for providing fault tolerance that reasonably reduces the cost of improving the system.
3. Using binary structural-automatic model allows automated obtaining of split critical failure state and reducing time costs for building the graph of states and transitions.
4. Risk reduction factor was introduced for quantitatively assessment of the efficiency of improving safety by improving reliability by introducing redundancy in critical elements of complex technical systems for critical application.
5. Fault tree building from the graph of states and transitions basing on minimal cut sets takes into account the behavior of complex system that is not available when using static and dynamic fault trees.

References

1. Verma, A.K., Ajit, S., Karanki, D.R.: Reliability and Safety Engineering. Springer Science & Business Media, London (2010)
2. Birolini, A.: Reliability Engineering: Theory and Practice, 6th edn. Springer, Heidelberg (2010)
3. Volochiy, B., Mandziy, B., Ozirkovskyi, L.: Extending the features of software for reliability analysis of fault-tolerant systems. Computational Problems of Electrical Engineering **2**(2), 113–121 (2012)
4. Yang, G.: Life Cycle Reliability Engineering. Wiley, Hoboken (2007)
5. Henley, E.J., Kumamoto, H.: Probabilistic Risk Assessment: Reliability Engineering, Design and Analysis, 2nd edn. Wiley-IEEE Press, New York (2000)
6. Mandziy, B.A., Ozirkovskyi, L.D.: Automation of building reliability models of redundant restorable complex technical systems. Eastern-Eur. J. Enterp. Technol. **2**(4(62)), pp. 44–49 (2013) (in Ukrainian)
7. Polovko, A.M., Gurov, S.V.: Basics of Reliability Theory. BHV Peterburg Publ., Saint Petersburg (2006) (in Russian)
8. PTC Windchill. http://ru.ptc.com/product/windchill/quality

9. RAMS (Reliability, Availability, Maintainability and Safety) Software. http://aldservice.com/en/reliability-products/rams-software.html
10. ReliaSoft Synthesis Master Suite. http://www.reliasoft.com/products.htm
11. Reliability Engineering Software. Products. http://www.itemsoft.com/products.html
12. Reliability Workbench. http://www.isograph.com/software/reliability-workbench/
13. Volochiy, B.Y., Ozirkovskyi, L.D., Mashchak, A.V., Shkiliuk, O.P.: Fault tree build automation for safety estimation of complex technical system. In: PREDT-2014 Proceedings of IV International Conference on Physical and Technological Problems of Wireless Devices, Telecommunications, Nano-and Microelectronics, pp. 102–103 (2014) (in Ukrainian)
14. Bobalo, Y., Volochiy, B., Lozynskyy, O., Mandziy, B., Ozirkovskyy, L., Fedasyuk, D., Shcherbovskykh, S., Yakovyna, V.: Mathematical Models and Methods of Analysis of Radioelectronic, Electromechanic and Software Systems. Lviv Polytechnic National University Publ., Lviv (2013) (in Ukrainian)
15. Zentis, T., Schmitt, R.: Technical risk management for an ensured and efficient product development on the example of medical equipment. In: Proceedings of the 23rd CIRP Design Conference on Smart Product Engineering, Bochum, pp. 387–398. 11–13 March 2013

Formal Frameworks

Main Steps in Defining Finitely Supported Mathematics

Andrei Alexandru and Gabriel Ciobanu(✉)

Romanian Academy, Institute of Computer Science, Iaşi, Romania
andrei.alexandru@iit.academiaromana-is.ro, gabriel@info.uaic.ro

Abstract. This paper presents the main steps in defining a Finitely Supported Mathematics by using sets with atoms. Such a mathematics generalizes the classical Zermelo-Fraenkel mathematics, and represents an appropriate framework to work with (infinite) structures in terms of finitely supported objects. We focus on the techniques of translating the Zermelo-Fraenkel results into this Finitely Supported Mathematics over infinite (possibly non-countable) sets with atoms. Two general methods of proving the finite support property for certain algebraic structures are presented. Finally, we provide a survey on the applications of the Finitely Supported Mathematics in experimental sciences.

Keywords: Fraenkel-Mostowski set theory · Invariant sets · Finite support principle · Finitely Supported Mathematics

1 Introduction

Since the experimental sciences are mainly interested in quantitative aspects, and since there exists no evidence for the presence of infinite structures, it becomes useful to develop a mathematics which deals with a more relaxed notion of (in)finiteness. We present our attempt of building the necessary concepts and structures for a finitely supported mathematics. What we call Finitely Supported Mathematics is a mathematics which is consistent with the axioms of the Fraenkel-Mostowski (FM) set theory. The FM axioms represents an "axiomatization" of the FM permutation model of the Zermelo-Fraenkel set theory with atoms; in this way, these axioms transform this model into an independent set theory. The axioms of the FM set theory are precisely the Zermelo-Fraenkel with atoms (ZFA) axioms over an infinite set of atoms [24], together with the special property of finite support which claims that for each element x in an arbitrary set we can find a finite set supporting x. Therefore, in the FM universe only finitely supported objects are allowed. The original purpose of the FM set theory was to provide a mathematical model for variables in a certain syntax. Since they have no internal structure, atoms can be used to represent names. The finite support axiom is motivated by the fact that syntax can only involve finitely many names. The FM framework provides a balance between rigorous formalism and informal reasoning. This is discussed in [34], where principles of structural recursion and

V. Yakovyna et al. (Eds.): ICTERI 2015, CCIS 594, pp. 73–90, 2016.
DOI: 10.1007/978-3-319-30246-1_5

induction are explained in such a framework. We can use this theory in order to manage infinite structures in a finitary manner; namely, in the FM framework we try to model the infinite using a more relaxed notion of finite, i.e. the notion of finite support.

Although a set of axioms for describing sets with atoms (or FM-sets) was introduced in [24], an earlier idea of using atoms in computer science belongs to Gandy [25]. Gandy proved that any machine satisfying four physical 'principles' is equivalent to some Turing machine. Gandy's four principles define a class of computing machines, namely the 'Gandy machines'. Gandy machines are represented by classes of 'states' and 'transition operations between states'. States are represented by hereditary finite sets built up from an infinite set U of atoms, and transformations are given by restricted operations from states to states. The class HF of all hereditary finite sets over U introduced in Definition 2.1 from [25] is described quite similar to the von-Neumann cumulative hierarchy of FM-sets, FM_A presented in [24]. The single difference between these approaches is that each HF_{n+1} is defined inductively involving '*finite* subsets of $U \cup HF_n$', whilst each $FM_{\alpha+1}(A)$ is defined inductively by using 'the disjoint union between A and the *finitely supported* subsets of $FM_\alpha(A)$'; HF is the union of all HF_n (with the mention that the empty set is not used in this construction), and the family of all FM-sets is the union of all FM_α from which we exclude the set A of atoms. The support of an element x in HF, obtained according to Definition 2.2(1) of [25], coincides with $supp(x)$ (with notations from Definition 2(4)) if we see x as an FM-set. Also, the effect of a permutation π on a structure x described in Definition 2.3 from [25] is defined analogue as the application of the S_A-action on FM_A to the element $(\pi, x) \in S_A \times FM_A$. Obviously, the Gandy's principles can also be presented in the FM framework because any finite set is well defined in FM; however, an open problem regards the consistency of Gandy's principles when 'finite' is replaced by 'finitely supported'.

The construction of the universe of all FM-sets [24] is inspired by the construction of the universe of all admissible sets over an arbitrary collection of atoms [13]. The hereditary finite sets used in [25] are particular examples of admissible sets. The FM-sets represent a generalization of hereditary finite sets because any FM-set is an hereditary finitely supported set.

2 Subdivisions of the Fraenkel-Mostowski Framework

In the literature there exist various approaches regarding the FM framework. We try to clarify the differences between these approaches.

- **The FM permutation model of the ZFA set theory.** The original motivation for developing such a permutation model is related to establishing the independence of the axiom of choice (**AC**) from the other axioms of the ZFA set theory. Informally, **AC** claims that given any family of non-empty sets $\mathcal{F}$, it is possible to select a single element from each member of $\mathcal{F}$. This statement is equivalent to the assertion that for any family of non-empty sets $\mathcal{F}$ there exists at least one choice function on $\mathcal{F}$, where a choice function on $\mathcal{F}$ is a function f with domain $\mathcal{F}$ such that, for each non-empty set X in $\mathcal{F}$, $f(X)$ is an element of X. Since its first formulation **AC** leads to some controversies. The first controversy is about the meaning of the word "exists". Some mathematicians believe that a set exists only if each of its elements can be designated specifically or at least if there is a law by which each of its elements can be constructed. Another controversy is represented by a geometrical consequence of **AC** known as Banach and Tarski's paradoxical decomposition of the sphere. In [12] they showed that any solid sphere can be split into finitely many subsets which can themselves be reassembled to form two solid spheres, each of the same size as the original. Questions about the **AC**'s independence of the systems of set-theoretic axioms appeared naturally. In 1922 Fraenkel introduces the permutation method to establish the independence of **AC** from a system of set theory with atoms [22]. Fraenkel constructed a model in which the axioms of set theory excluding the axiom of choice are satisfied but this model contains a set which does not satisfy the axiom of choice. Fraenkel's model was refined and extended by Lindenbaum and Mostowski [31] to what we call the FM permutation model of the ZFA set theory. There also exist some other permutation models of ZFA presented in [29] which are defined by using countable infinite sets of atoms.

It is worth noting that the FM permutation method was not sufficient to prove the independence of the axiom of choice from the axioms of the Zermelo-Fraenkel (ZF) set theory. In [26] Gödel proved that the axiom of choice is consistent with the other axioms of set theory (von Neumann-Bernays-Gödel set theory). He proved that given a model for set theory in which there are no atoms and the axiom of foundation is true, there exists a model in which, in addition, the axiom of choice is true. Moreover, if Gödel's model is modified so that either atoms exist or the axiom of foundation is false, the validity of the axiom of choice is not disturbed. Fraenkel showed that the collections of sets of atoms need not necessarily have choice functions [22]. However, at that time he was unable to establish the same fact for the usual sets of mathematics, for example the set of real numbers. This problem remained unsolved until 1963 when Cohen proved the independence of **AC** (and of the axiom of countable choice) from the standard axioms of ZF set theory [21]. Cohen's independence proof (known as the method of *forcing*) also made use of permutations in essentially the form in which Fraenkel had originally employed them.

- **The FM axiomatic set theory.** This set theory was presented by Gabbay and Pitts [24] in order to provide a new formalism for managing fresh names and bindings. An advantage of modeling syntax in a model of FM set theory is that datatypes of syntax modulo α-equivalence can be modeled inductively. This is because the FM set theory provides a model of variable symbols and α-abstraction. The FM axiomatic set theory is inspired by both the FM permutation model of the ZFA set theory and the theory of admissible sets [13]. However, the FM set theory, the ZFA set theory and the ZF set theory are independent axiomatic set theories. All of these theories are described by axioms, and all of them have models. For example, the Cumulative Hierarchy

Fraenkel-Mostowski universe FM_A presented in [24] is a model of the FM set theory, while some models of the ZF set theory can be found in [28], and the permutation models of the ZFA set theory can be found in [29]. The sets defined using the FM axioms are called FM-sets. A ZFA set is an FM-set if and only if all its elements have hereditary finite supports. Note that the infinite set of atoms in the FM set theory does not necessary be countable. The Fraenkel-Mostowski set theory is consistent whether the infinite set of atoms is countable or not. In [24] it is used a countable set of atoms in order to define a model of the Fraenkel-Mostowski set theory for new names in computer science, while in [14] there are described FM-sets over a set of atoms which do not represent a homogeneous structure. Also, in [19] the authors use non-countable sets of atoms (like the set of real numbers) in order to study the minimization of deterministic timed automata.

- **Nominal sets.** The theory of nominal sets represents an alternative to the FM set theory. These sets can be defined both in the ZF framework [35] and in the FM framework [24]. In ZF, a fixed infinite set A is considered as a set of names. A nominal set is defined as a usual ZF set endowed with a particular group action of the group of permutations over A that satisfies a certain finiteness property. Such a finiteness property allows us to say that nominal sets are well defined according to the axioms of the FM set theory whenever the set of names is the set of atoms in the FM set theory. There exists also an alternative definition for nominal sets in the FM framework. They can be defined as sets constructed according to the FM axioms with the additional property of being empty supported (invariant under all permutations). These two ways of defining nominal sets finally lead to similar properties. According to the previous remark we use the terminology "invariant" for "nominal" in order to establish a connection between approaches in the FM framework and in the ZF framework. Moreover, we can say that any set defined according to the FM axioms (any FM-set) can be seen as a subset of the nominal (invariant) set FM_A. However, an FM-set is itself a nominal set only if it has an empty support. The theory of nominal sets makes sense even if the set of atoms is infinite but not countable. Informally, since the ZFA set theory collapses into the ZF set theory when the set of atoms is empty, we can say that the nominal sets represent a natural extension of the usual sets. In computer science, nominal sets offer an elegant formalism for describing λ-terms modulo α-conversion [24]. They can also be used in algebra [3,6], in proof theory [40], in domain theory [39], in topology [33], semantics of process algebras [5,23] and programming [37]. A survey on the applications of nominal sets in computer science emphasizing our contributions can be found in [4].
- **Generalized nominal sets.** The theory of nominal sets over a fixed set A of atoms is generalized in [17] to a new theory of nominal sets over arbitrary (unfixed) sets of data values. This provides the generalized nominal sets. The notion of 'S_A-set' (Definition 2) is replaced by the notion of 'set endowed with an action of a subgroup of the symmetric group of $\mathbb{D}$' for an arbitrary set of data values $\mathbb{D}$, and the notion of 'finite set' is replaced by the notion of 'set with a finite number of orbits according to the previous group action

(orbit-finite set)'. This approach is useful for studying automata on data words [17], languages over infinite alphabets [15], or Turing machines that operate over infinite alphabets [18]. Computations in these generalized nominal sets are presented in [16,20].

As their names say, the nominal sets are used to manage notions like renaming, binding or fresh name. However, this theory could be studied deeper from an algebraically viewpoint, and it could be used in order to characterize some infinite structures in terms of finitely supported objects.

Finitely Supported Mathematics (FSM) is introduced to prove that many finiteness ZF properties still remain valid if we replace the term 'finite' with 'infinite, but with finite support'. Such results have already been presented in [6] where we proved that a class of multisets[1] over infinite alphabets (interpreted in the nominal framework) has similar properties to the classical multisets over finite alphabets. FSM is the mathematics developed in the world of finitely supported objects where the set of atoms has to be infinite (countable or not countable). Informally, FSM extends the framework of the ZF set theory without choice principles; ZF set theory is actually the Empty Supported Mathematics. In FSM, we use either 'invariant sets' or 'finitely supported sets' instead of 'sets'. FSM is not at all the theory of nominal sets from [35] presented in a different manner. The theory of nominal sets [35] could be considered as a tool for defining FSM which is, informally, a theory of 'invariant algebraic structures'.

We do not employ axioms in order to describe FSM because FSM is already consistent to the ZF axioms. However, we describe FSM by using principles. The principles of constructing FSM have historical roots in the definition of 'logical notions' in Tarski's view [38]. The general principle of constructing FSM is that all the structures have to be invariant or finitely supported. As a general rule, we are not allowed to use in the proofs of the results of FSM any construction that does not preserve the property of finite support. This means we cannot obtain a property in FSM only by employing a ZF result without an appropriate proof presented according the finite support requirement.

Since the invariant sets can also be defined in the ZFA framework similarly as in the ZF framework (see the first paragraph in Sect. 3), the construction of FSM also makes sense over the ZFA axioms.

3 Sets with Atoms

Let A be a fixed infinite (countable or non-countable) ZF-set. The following results make also sense if A is considered to be the set of atoms in the ZFA framework (characterized by the axiom "$y \in x \Rightarrow x \notin A$") and if 'ZF' is replaced by 'ZFA' in their statements. Thus, we mention that the theory of invariant sets makes sense both in ZF and in ZFA. Several results of this section are similar to those in [35], but without assuming the set of atoms to be countable.

[1] A *multiset* on an alphabet Σ is a function from Σ to $\mathbb{N}$ where each element in Σ has associated its multiplicity.

Definition 1. *A* transposition *is a function* $(a\,b) : A \to A$ *defined by* $(a\,b)(a) = b$, $(a\,b)(b) = a$, *and* $(a\,b)(n) = n$ *for* $n \neq a, b$. *A* permutation *of A is generated by composing finitely many transpositions.*

Definition 2. *Let* S_A *be the set of all permutations of A.*

1. *Let X be a ZF set. An* S_A-action *on X is a function* $\cdot : S_A \times X \to X$ *having the properties that* $Id \cdot x = x$ *and* $\pi \cdot (\pi' \cdot x) = (\pi \circ \pi') \cdot x$ *for all* $\pi, \pi' \in S_A$ *and* $x \in X$. *An* S_A-set *is a pair* $(X, \cdot)$ *where X is a ZF set, and* $\cdot : S_A \times X \to X$ *is an* S_A*-action on X.*
2. *Let* $(X, \cdot)$ *be an* S_A*-set. We say that* $S \subset A$ supports x *whenever for each* $\pi \in Fix(S)$ *we have* $\pi \cdot x = x$, *where* $Fix(S) = \{\pi \,|\, \pi(a) = a, \forall a \in S\}$.
3. *Let* $(X, \cdot)$ *be an* S_A*-set. We say that X is an* invariant set *if for each* $x \in X$ *there exists a finite set* $S_x \subset A$ *which supports x. Invariant sets are also called* nominal sets *if we work in the ZF framework [35], or* equivariant sets *if they are defined as elements in the cumulative hierarchy* FM_A *[24].*
4. *Let X be an* S_A*-set and let* $x \in X$. *If there exists a finite set supporting x, then there exists a least finite set supporting x [24] which is called* the support of x *and is denoted by* $supp(x)$. *An element supported by the empty set is called equivariant.*

Proposition 1. *Let* $(X, \cdot)$ *be an* S_A*-set and* $\pi \in S_A$. *If* $x \in X$ *is finitely supported, then* $\pi \cdot x$ *is finitely supported, and* $supp(\pi \cdot x) = \pi(supp(x))$.

Example 1

1. The set A of atoms is an S_A-set with the S_A-action $\cdot : S_A \times A \to A$ defined by $\pi \cdot a := \pi(a)$, $\forall \pi \in S_A, a \in A$. Moreover, $supp(B) = B$, $\forall B \subset A$, B finite.
2. Any ordinary ZF set X (like $\mathbb{N}$ or $\mathbb{Z}$) is an S_A-set with the trivial S_A-action $\cdot : S_A \times X \to X$ defined by $\pi \cdot x := x$ for all $\pi \in S_A$ and $x \in X$.
3. If $(X, \cdot)$ is an S_A-set, then $\wp(X) = \{Y \,|\, Y \subseteq X\}$ is also an S_A-set with the S_A-action $\star : S_A \times \wp(X) \to \wp(X)$ defined by $\pi \star Y := \{\pi \cdot y \,|\, y \in Y\}$ for all $\pi \in S_A$, and all subsets Y of X. For each invariant set $(X, \cdot)$ we denote by $\wp_{fs}(X)$ the set formed from those subsets of X which are finitely supported according to the action $\star$. $(\wp_{fs}(X), \star|_{\wp_{fs}(X)})$ is an invariant set, where $\star|_{\wp_{fs}(X)}$ represents the action $\star$ restricted to $\wp_{fs}(X)$.
4. Let $(X, \cdot)$ and $(Y, \diamond)$ be S_A-sets. The Cartesian product $X \times Y$ is also an S_A-set with the S_A-action $\star : S_A \times (X \times Y) \to (X \times Y)$ defined by $\pi \star (x, y) = (\pi \cdot x, \pi \diamond y)$ for all $\pi \in S_A$ and all $x \in X$, $y \in Y$. If $(X, \cdot)$ and $(Y, \diamond)$ are invariant sets, then $(X \times Y, \star)$ is also an invariant set.
5. The FM cumulative hierarchy FM_A described in [24] is an invariant set with S_A-action $\cdot : S_A \times FM_A \to FM_A$ defined inductively by $\pi \cdot a := \pi(a)$ for all atoms $a \in A$ and $\pi \cdot x := \{\pi \cdot y \,|\, y \in x\}$ for all $x \in FM_A \setminus A$. An FM-set is a finitely supported element in FM_A; additionally an FM-set has the recursive property that all its elements are also FM-sets. An FM-set which is empty supported as an element in FM_A is an invariant set.

Definition 3. *Let $(X, \cdot)$ be an invariant set. A subset Z of X is called* finitely supported *if and only if $Z \in \wp_{fs}(X)$ with the notations of Example 1 (3).*

A function $f : X \to Y$ is a particular relation on $X \times Y$, namely a function $f : X \to Y$ is a subset f of $X \times Y$ characterized by the property that for each $x \in X$ there is exactly one $y \in Y$ such that $(x, y) \in f$. Using Definition 3, the finitely supported functions are defined in FSM in the following way.

Definition 4. *Let X and Y be invariant sets, and Z be a finitely supported subset of X. A function $f : Z \to Y$ is* finitely supported *if $f \in \wp_{fs}(X \times Y)$.*

Proposition 2. *[6] Let $(X, \cdot)$ and $(Y, \diamond)$ be invariant sets, and let Z be a finitely supported subset of X. The function $f : Z \to Y$ is finitely supported in the sense of Definition 4 if and only if there exists a finite set S of atoms such that for all $x \in Z$ and all $\pi \in Fix(S)$ we have $\pi \cdot x \in Z$ and $f(\pi \cdot x) = \pi \diamond f(x)$.*

4 Reformulating the Classical ZF Results in FSM

The main idea of translating a classical ZF result (depending on sets and relations) into FSM is to analyze if there exists a valid result obtained by replacing "set" with "invariant/finitely supported set" and "relation" with "invariant/finitely supported relation" in the ZF result. If this is possible, then things go smoothly; however, this is not always so simple.

Every ZF set is a particular invariant set equipped with a trivial permutation action (Example 1(2)). Therefore, the general properties of invariant sets lead to valid properties of ZF sets. The converse is not always valid, namely not every ZF result can be directly rephrased in the world of invariant sets, terms of finitely supported objects according to arbitrary permutation actions. This is because, given an invariant set X, there could exist some subsets of X (and also some relations or functions involving subsets of X) which fail to be finitely supported. A classical example (presented also in Subsect. 2.2.3.6 of [39]) is represented by the powerset of the invariant set A. A subset of A which is in the same time infinite and coinfinite could be defined in some models of ZF (or of ZFA is we consider A to be the set of atoms in ZFA), but it can not be defined in FSM because it is not finitely supported. Therefore, the remark that everything that can be done in ZF can also be done in FSM is not valid. This means there may exist some valid results depending on several ZF structures which fail to be valid in FSM if we simply replace "ZF structure" with "FSM structure" in their statement.

We present few examples regarding these aspects. There exist some valid ZF results that cannot be translated into FSM. According to Remark 1, the following examples are particularly interesting because they do not overlap neither on some known properties of permutative models of ZFA, nor on some properties of nominal sets [35].

Example 2

- There exist models of ZF without choice that satisfy the ordering principle **OP**: "Every set can be totally ordered". More details about such models are in [28], where there are mentioned Howard-Rubin's first model N38 and Cohen's first model M1. Therefore, the ordering principle is independent from the axioms of the ZF set theory.
- In FSM the following result fails "For every invariant set X there exists a finitely supported total order relation on X". Therefore, the ordering principle is inconsistent with the principles of defining FSM. Indeed, suppose that there exists a finitely supported total order $<$ on the invariant set A. Let $a, b, c \notin supp(<)$ with $a < b$. Since $(a\,c) \in Fix(supp(<))$, we have $(a\,c)(a) < (a\,c)(b)$, that is $c < b$. However, we also have $(a\,b), (b\,c) \in Fix(supp(<))$, and so $((a\,b) \circ (b\,c))(a) < ((a\,b) \circ (b\,c))(b)$, that is $b < c$. We get a contradiction, and so the translation of the ordering principle in FSM realized by replacing "structure" with "finitely supported structure" leads to a false statement.

Example 3

- There exist models of ZF without choice that satisfy the partial countable choice principle **PCC**: "Given any countable family (sequence) of non-empty sets $\mathcal{F} = (X_n)_{n \in \mathbb{N}}$, there exists an infinite subset M of the set of all positive integers $\mathbb{N}$ such that it is possible to select a single element from each member of the family $(X_m)_{m \in M}$, i.e. there exists a choice function on $(X_m)_{m \in M}$". More details about such models are in [28], where there are mentioned Pincus-Solovay's First Model M27, Shelah's Second Model M38 and Howard-Rubin's first model N38. Therefore, the partial countable choice principle is independent from the axioms of the ZF set theory.
- In FSM the following result fails: "Given any invariant set X, and any countable family $\mathcal{F} = (X_n)_{n \in \mathbb{N}}$ of subsets of X such that the mapping $n \mapsto X_n$ is finitely supported, there exists an infinite subset M of $\mathbb{N}$ with the property that there is a finitely supported choice function on $(X_m)_{m \in M}$". Therefore, the partial countable choice principle is inconsistent with the principles of defining FSM. Indeed, for the invariant set A we consider the countable family $(X_n)_n$ where X_n is the set of all injective n-tuples from A. Since A is infinite, it follows that each X_n is non-empty. In the FSM framework, each X_n is equivariant because A is an invariant set and each permutation is a bijective function. Therefore, the family $(X_n)_n$ is equivariant, and the mapping $n \mapsto X_n$ is also equivariant. Suppose that there exists an infinite subset M of $\mathbb{N}$ and a finitely supported choice function f on $(X_m)_{m \in M}$. Let $f(X_m) = y_m$ with each $y_m \in X_m$. Let $\pi \in Fix(supp(f))$. According to Proposition 2, and because each element X_m is equivariant according to its definition, we obtain that $\pi \cdot y_m = \pi \cdot f(X_m) = f(\pi \cdot X_m) = f(X_m) = y_m$. Therefore, each element y_m is supported by $supp(f)$, and so $supp(y_m) \subseteq supp(f)$ for all $m \in M$. Since y_m is a finite tuple of atoms which has exactly m elements for each $m \in M$, we have that $supp(y_m) = y_m$, $\forall m \in \mathbb{N}$ (see Example 1(1)). Thus, $y_m \subseteq supp(f)$ for all $m \in M$. However, because M is infinite, we contradict the finiteness of

supp(f). Therefore, the translation of the partial countable choice principle in FSM realized by replacing "structure" with "finitely supported structure" leads to a false statement.

Remark 1. Examples 2 and 3 show us that there exist some choice principles (namely **OP** and **PCC**) which are independent from the axioms of the ZF set theory, but inconsistent in FSM. Since FSM is consistent even if the set of atoms is not countable, such results do not overlap on some related properties in the basic or in the second Fraenkel modes of the ZFA set theory (which are defined using countable sets of atoms) [29]. Also, the previous results do not follow immediately from [35] because the nominal sets are defined over countable sets of atoms, while we define invariant sets over possible non-countable sets of atoms; in [35] where the set of atoms is countable, Example 3 would be trivial. Moreover, we claim that all the choice principles from [27] (generally denoted in the related reference by **DC**, **ZL**, **CC**, **PCC**, **AC(fin)**, **Fin**, **PIT**, **UFT**, **OP**, **KW**, and **OEP**), rephrased in terms of invariant sets, are all inconsistent in FSM for any set of atoms. We also conjecture that, in the particular case when the set of atoms is countable, the choice principle generally denoted by **CC(fin)** is also inconsistent in FSM. Note that it is not easy to prove such a result in FSM, even if various relationship results between several forms of choice hold in the ZF framework. This is because nobody guarantees that ZF results remain valid in FSM. Therefore, all the possible relationship results between various choice principles in FSM have to be independently proved in terms of finitely supported object. Details regarding the consistency of various choice principles in the world of invariant sets defined over possibly non-countable sets of atoms will be presented in another paper.

Other results which fail in FSM are given by the Stone duality [33], by the determinization of finite automata and by the equivalence of two-way and one-way finite automata [17]. There also exist some valid ZF results that can be translated into FSM only in a weaker form (in the sense of Remark 2).

Example 4. We define an invariant complete lattice as an invariant set $(L, \cdot)$ together with an equivariant order relation $\sqsubseteq$ on L satisfying the property that every finitely supported subset $X \subseteq L$ has a least upper bound with respect to the order relation $\sqsubseteq$.

- Let L be a ZF complete lattice and $f : L \to L$ a ZF monotone function. Then there exists a greatest $e \in L$ such that $f(e) = e$ and a least $e \in L$ such that $f(e) = e$ (weak form of Tarski theorem).
- Let $(L, \sqsubseteq, \cdot)$ be an invariant complete lattice and $f : L \to L$ a finitely supported monotone function. Then there exists a greatest $e \in L$ such that $f(e) = e$, and a least $e \in L$ such that $f(e) = e$ (the proof is similar to Theorem 3.2 in [1]).

These results show that the weak form of the Tarski theorem can be naturally translated into FSM. However, as it is presented below, the strong form of the Tarski theorem cannot be naturally translated into FSM; it holds in FSM only for a particular class of finitely supported monotone functions, i.e. the equivariant monotone functions.

- Let L be a ZF complete lattice and $f : L \to L$ a ZF monotone function over L. Let P be the set of fixed points of f. Then P is a complete lattice (strong form of Tarski theorem).
- Let $(L, \sqsubseteq, \cdot)$ be an invariant complete lattice, $f : L \to L$ an equivariant monotone function over L and P be the set of fixed points of f. Then $(P, \sqsubseteq, \cdot)$ is an invariant complete lattice. This result does not hold if f is finitely supported (and not equivariant); the proof is similar to Theorem 3.3 in [1].

Remark 2. Note that the previous example does not present a case of a ZF result that completely fails in FSM. It suggests that it is a bit tricky to formalize a certain ZF result in FSM. What we call "weaker form" means that when translating a ZF result into FSM we have to be careful when choosing either "finitely supported" or "equivariant" in the statement of the desired FSM result. Actually the result mentioned in the second part of Example 4 works as expected. This is because the set of the fixed points of f is S-supported whenever f is S-supported. However, when translating a ZF result into FSM, one cannot just insert "equivariant" or "finitely supported" without a preliminary analysis about which of the previous terms is adequate for the desired FSM result.

5 Proving that Some Structures Are Finitely Supported

In order to translate a general ZF result into FSM, one must prove that several structures are finitely supported. There exist two general methods of proving that a certain structure is finitely supported. The first method is a constructive one: by using some intuitive arguments, we anticipate a possible candidate for the support and prove that this candidate is indeed a support. The second method is based on a general finite support principle which is defined using the higher-order logic. According to Theorem 3.5 in [34], we have the following equivariance/finite support principle which works over invariant sets.

Theorem 1

- *Any function or relation that is defined from equivariant functions and relations using classical higher-order logic is itself equivariant.*
- *Any function or relation that is defined from finitely supported functions and relations using classical higher-order logic is itself finitely supported.*

In applying this equivariance/finite support principle, one must take into account all the parameters upon which a particular construction depends. We think that the formal involvement of the equivariance/finite support principle, i.e. the precise verification if the conditions for applying the equivariance/finite support principle are properly satisfied is sometimes at least as difficult as a constructive proof. Moreover, in many cases we need to construct effectively the support, and it is not enough to prove only that a certain structure is finitely supported.

Example 5. An invariant monoid $(M, \cdot, \diamond)$ is an invariant set $(M, \diamond)$ endowed with an equivariant internal monoid law $\cdot : M \times M \to M$. If $(\Sigma, \diamond)$ is an invariant set, then the free monoid Σ^* on Σ is an invariant monoid [6].

1. For each monoid M and each function $f : \Sigma \to M$, there exists a unique homomorphism of monoids $g : \Sigma^* \to M$ with $g \circ i = f$, where $i : \Sigma \to \Sigma^*$ is the standard inclusion of Σ into Σ^* which maps each element $a \in \Sigma$ into the word a (ZF universality theorem for monoids).
2. (i) Let $(\Sigma, \diamond_\Sigma)$ be an invariant set. Let $i : \Sigma \to \Sigma^*$ be the standard inclusion of Σ into Σ^* which maps each element $a \in \Sigma$ into word a. If $(M, \cdot, \diamond_M)$ is an arbitrary invariant monoid and $\varphi : \Sigma \to M$ is an arbitrary finitely supported function, then there exists a unique finitely supported homomorphism of monoids $\psi : \Sigma^* \to M$ with $\psi \circ i = \varphi$.

   This result can be proved directly by involving the equivariance/finite support principle.

   (ii) Let $(\Sigma, \diamond_\Sigma)$ be an invariant set. Let $i : \Sigma \to \Sigma^*$ be the standard inclusion of Σ into Σ^* which maps each element $a \in \Sigma$ into the word a. If $(M, \cdot, \diamond_M)$ is an arbitrary invariant monoid and $\varphi : \Sigma \to M$ is an arbitrary finitely supported function, then there exists a unique finitely supported homomorphism of monoids $\psi : \Sigma^* \to M$ with $\psi \circ i = \varphi$. Moreover, if a finite set S supports φ, then the same set S supports ψ.

   The last sentence of this theorem cannot be proved by involving the equivariance/finite support principle in the form from [34] (it could be proved by using a stronger form of the finite support principle which will be mentioned in the paragraphs below).

Proof. If $(M, \cdot, \diamond_M)$ is an invariant monoid, then $(M, \cdot)$ is a monoid. From the general ZF theory of monoids, we can define a unique homomorphism of monoids $\psi : \Sigma^* \to M$ with $\psi \circ i = \varphi$.

In [6] we proved that the free monoid Σ^* on Σ is an invariant monoid whenever $(\Sigma, \diamond)$ is an invariant set. The S_A-action $\tilde{\star} : S_A \times \Sigma^* \to \Sigma^*$ is defined by $\pi \tilde{\star} x_1 x_2 \dots x_l = (\pi \diamond x_1) \dots (\pi \diamond x_l)$ for all $\pi \in S_A$ and $x_1 x_2 \dots x_l \in \Sigma^* \setminus \{1\}$, and $\pi \tilde{\star} 1 = 1$ for all $\pi \in S_A$.

In order to prove that ψ is finitely supported it is sufficient to apply Theorem 1 because ψ is defined from the finitely supported functions φ and i using the higher-order logic. However, Theorem 1 (without a specific refinement) is not sufficient to prove that if a finite set S supports φ, then the same set S supports ψ. In order to prove the previous statement we proceed as follows.

Let us consider $S = supp(\varphi)$. Thus, by Proposition 2 we have $\varphi(\pi \diamond_\Sigma x) = \pi \diamond_M \varphi(x)$ for all $x \in \Sigma$ and $\pi \in Fix(S)$. We have to prove that S supports ψ. Let $\pi \in Fix(S)$. According to Proposition 2 it is sufficient to prove that $\psi(\pi \tilde{\star} x_1 x_2 \dots x_n) = \pi \diamond_M \psi(x_1 x_2 \dots x_n)$ for each $x_1 x_2 \dots x_n \in \Sigma^*$. However, ψ is a monoid homomorphism between Σ^* and M, and $\psi \circ i = \varphi$. This means $\psi(x_1 x_2 \dots x_n) = \varphi(x_1) \cdot \varphi(x_2) \cdot \dots \cdot \varphi(x_n)$. Since $(M, \cdot, \diamond_M)$ is an invariant monoid we have $\pi \diamond_M \psi(x_1 x_2 \dots x_n) = \pi \diamond_M (\varphi(x_1) \cdot \varphi(x_2) \cdot \dots \cdot \varphi(x_n)) = (\pi \diamond_M \varphi(x_1)) \cdot (\pi \diamond_M \varphi(x_2)) \cdot \dots \cdot (\pi \diamond_M \varphi(x_n)) = \varphi(\pi \diamond_\Sigma x_1) \cdot \varphi(\pi \diamond_\Sigma x_2) \cdot \dots \cdot \varphi(\pi \diamond_\Sigma x_n)$.

However, $\pi\widetilde{\star}x_1x_2\ldots x_n = (\pi \diamond_\Sigma x_1)\ldots(\pi \diamond_\Sigma x_n)$ and $\psi(\pi\widetilde{\star}x_1x_2\ldots x_n) = \psi((\pi \diamond_\Sigma x_1)\ldots(\pi \diamond_\Sigma x_l)) = \varphi(\pi \diamond_\Sigma x_1)\cdot\varphi(\pi \diamond_\Sigma x_2)\cdot\ldots\cdot\varphi(\pi \diamond_\Sigma x_n)$. Hence $\psi(\pi\widetilde{\star}x_1x_2\ldots x_n) = \pi \diamond_M \psi(x_1x_2\ldots x_n)$ for each $\pi \in Fix(S)$, which means S supports ψ.

Example 5(2) shows us that by using the equivariance/finite support principle we can obtain a universality property for invariant monoids which is similar to the one described in Example 5(1). However, in order to prove that $supp(\psi) \subseteq supp(\varphi)$ in the second item of Example 5(2), we need to present a more constructive method of defining a set supporting ψ (see also Theorem 6 from [6]). Other related examples regarding the equivariance/finite support principle are Theorems 4, 9 and 11 from [6], or Theorem 3.7 from [3]. In these theorems we are able to prove a precise characterization for the support of some structures which could not be obtained by a direct application of the equivariance/finite support principle in the form from Theorem 1. In these results we do not prove only that some structures are finitely supported, but we also found a relationship between the supports of the related structures.

A more constructive method of defining the support is also necessary in order to assure that some structures are uniformly finitely supported (i.e. supported by the same finite set of atoms). Note that a chain is finitely supported if and only if all its elements are finitely supported and have the same support, i.e. all its elements are uniformly finitely supported. Therefore, in order to prove that a chain is finitely supported, we have to present, almost always, a constructive method of defining the support of its elements. More exactly, we cannot use the equivariance/finite support principle which would not assure the uniformity of the support of its elements. Suggestive examples regarding finitely supported chains are presented in Chapter 4 of [37].

We conclude that the equivariance/finite support principle is not so useful (in the form presented as Theorem 3.5 from [34]) when we want to obtain a relationship between the supports of several constructions (and we do not want only to prove that these constructions are finitely supported). This is because, in its actual form, the second part of Theorem 1 allows to prove that a certain structure is finitely supported, but it does not provide any information about the structure of the support. A concrete calculation for the supports of some structures is able to provide more informations about the related supports; we justify this viewpoint in Example 5. However, looking to direct method of constructing the related support in the proof Example 5(2), we could provide a refinement (stronger form) of the equivariance/finite support principle stating, informally, that for any finite set S of atoms, anything that is definable from S-supported structures using S-supported constructions is S-supported. This statement can be proved by refining the proof of the equivariance/finite support principle from [34]. However, it is worth noting that the related refinement of the equivariance/finite support principle is not carried out in [34] in this form. This stronger form of the finite support principle could be successfully applied in order to prove that some structures are uniformly supported and in order to establish some relationship results between several supports. However, we agree to employ a direct method for constructing the supports of some structures. This is because the general principles of equivariance and finite support are hard to apply formally, and in practice it is often easier and less error-prone to check equivariance by hand rather than try to formalize proofs in higher-order logic.

6 Applications of FSM in Experimental Sciences

The FM set theory is a more suitable framework for experimental sciences. Therefore, translating ZF properties of several algebraic structures into such a framework deserve a special attention. Rather than working with an alternative set theory we work in FSM, and express our results in terms of invariant sets.

6.1 Algebraic Structures in Finitely Supported Mathematics

Various algebraic structures involved in experimental sciences are presented in FSM emphasizing a strong connection between the FSM properties of these algebraic structures and their related ZF properties [1,3,6,8]. The general idea in these papers is to rephrase the classical ZF properties of some algebraic structures by replacing 'object' with 'finitely supported object', and to prove that the validity of the ZF properties of these algebraic structures is preserved in the new framework. Informally, this approach allow us to replace 'finite' with 'infinite but with finite support'.

In [6] we extend the notion of multiset over a finite alphabet by considering the notion of extended invariant multiset. An extended invariant multiset is actually an algebraically finitely supported multiset over a possibly infinite alphabet. We study the correspondence between some properties of multisets obtained in FSM where only finitely supported objects are allowed, and those obtained in the classical ZF framework. Analogously, the generalized multisets, i.e. the multisets with possibly negative multiplicities are translated in [8] into FSM, and presented in terms of finitely supported objects. Using the finite support property, many ZF properties of a generalized multisets on a finite alphabet still hold when the finite alphabet is replaced by an infinite alphabet with the mention that the generalized multisets have to be algebraically finitely supported. Several universality, order and embedding properties for extended multisets and extended generalized multisets, respectively, are presented in the related references.

An FSM theory for partially ordered sets has its roots in the developments from [35,37]. Its original purpose was to describe a denotational semantics for a functional programming language incorporating facilities for manipulating syntax involving names and binding operations. The solution of the Scott recursive domain equation $D \cong (D \to D)$ in the FM approach is presented in [37]; such a result also holds in FSM. However the Tarski-like theorem for invariant complete lattices is an original result (see Example 4). Using this fixpoint theorem and some equivariant Galois connections we are able to develop an FSM theory of abstract interpretation of programming languages [9], and we are also able to approximate finitely supported subsets of an possibly infinite invariant set in terms of invariant complete Boolean lattices [10]. Some calculability properties of the fixed points of a class of finitely supported functions are also proved in [9].

Invariant (nominal) groups are defined as groups which are also invariant sets and whose internal laws are equivariant. Several algebraic properties of invariant groups are presented in Sect. 3 from [3]. The classical correspondence and isomorphism theorems from the ZF groups theory are translated in FSM in terms of equivariant (empty supported) homomorphisms (see Sect. 4 from [3]). Also, uniform invariant groups (i.e. those groups with the property that all the elements are supported by the same finite set) are defined in Sect. 5 from [3], and several FSM embedding theorems valid for this class of groups are presented. The finitely supported subgroups of an invariant group are studied in terms of invariant lattices and invariant domains in [11]. Invariant groups are, actually, the natural extension of nominal monoids defined in [15]. However, the presence of the inverse elements in a group allows us to think to the study of reversibility in FSM terms. In [3] we present an algebraic framework from such a future development. The wreath product and one of its generalizations are used in the algebraic theory of automata in order to prove the Krohn-Rhodes theorem which states that any deterministic automaton is a homomorphic image of a cascade of some simple automata which realize either resets or permutations [30]. According to Theorem 3.20 in [3], the regular wreath product of two invariant groups is also invariant. The cascade product of two (invariant) automata can be studied in a similar way. We conjecture that a similar decomposition theorem for a class of invariant automata can be presented in FSM in terms of invariant wreath products.

6.2 Process Algebras in Finitely Supported Mathematics

Process algebras are used as a formal framework for the study of concurrent computation. In [2,5] we provide new FSM transition rules for several process algebras. We use the freshness quantifier И[2] introduced in [24] to "encode" the freshness conditions in the hypothesis of the transition rules of these process algebras, and we obtain some sets of compact transition rules (i.e. transition rules without side conditions) which defines the FSM semantics of the related process algebras. The central idea is to use *atoms* to represent variable symbols, and the *nominal abstraction* defined in [24] to represent the binding operators in various process algebras. A mixing of $\forall$ and И quantifiers is used to replace the side conditions in the transition rules of these process algebras. Finally, we are able to make a comparison between the expressive prower of the usual semantics and of the FSM semantics of the related process algebras. According to Theorem 4.20 in [5], the new FSM semantics of the monadic fusion calculus and the original semantics of the monadic fusion calculus presented in [32] have the same expressive power. The FSM transition rules of the πI-calculus defined

[2] Let P be a predicate on A. We say that И$a.P(a)$ if $P(a)$ is true for all but finitely many elements of A.

in [2] and the original transition rules of the πI-calculus presented in [36] provide the same transitions (see Theorem 4.11 in [2]).

7 Conclusion

This papers is an extended version of [7]. Our goal is to develop a mathematics for experimental science which deals with a more relaxed notion of finiteness. We call it the 'Finitely Supported Mathematics'. Informally, in Finitely Supported Mathematics we can model infinite structures after a finite number of observations. More precisely, we intend to restate some parts of algebra by replacing '(infinite) sets' with 'invariant sets'. This allows to model some infinite structures by using their finite supports. In order to sustain our viewpoint, we involve the axiomatic theory of FM-sets presented in [24]. Rather than using a non-standard set theory, we could alternatively work with invariant sets, which are defined within ZF as usual sets endowed with some group actions satisfying a finite support requirement. The properties of invariant sets are similar to those presented in [35], with the mention that we assume invariant sets to be defined over possible non-countable sets of atoms. Our paper presents the basic steps requested in order to provide an extension of the theory of invariant sets to a theory of invariant algebraic structures. Although the initial purpose of defining invariant sets was to formulate a semantics for syntax with variable binding, we consider that such sets can also be used from an algebraic perspective in order to characterize infinite structures modulo finite supports, and thus, in order to provide more informations about infinite objects.

The category of invariant sets has a very rich structure, and so the definitions of many structures given in the usual category of sets can be reformulated within the invariant sets framework. A natural question is which classical theorems about these structures hold internally in the world of invariant sets. Until now (or, more precisely, until we would be able to solve the open problem presented below), there does not exist a standard algorithm to translate any classical ZF result into FSM. This is because there may exist some subsets of an invariant set which fail to be finitely supported, and thus, there may exist some ZF results that fail in the universe of invariant sets. Related examples regarding the previous statement are presented in Sect. 4. Therefore, reformulating the ZF theorems into FSM should be done for each case separately. For example, the theory of monoids is studied in FSM in [6], the theory of groups is rephrased in FSM in [3], and the theory of posets and domains is reformulated within invariant sets framework in [35,37]. In order to prove that a structure is finitely supported, one could use either the finite support principle of [35] (e.g. Theorem 1), or a more "constructive" method. To employ such a "constructive method" means that we anticipate a possible candidate for a support, and then prove that this candidate is indeed a support. The benefit of this method is that we are able to obtain more informations about the related support than by using the finite support principle in the form from [34]. Related examples can be found in Sect. 5.

8 An Open Problem

The main task in order to define a finitely supported mathematics is to prove that certain subsets of an invariant set are finitely supported. We already know that given an invariant set X, there could exist some subsets of X which fail to be finitely supported. Some related examples are presented in [35,39]. However, all these examples are described by using choice principles or consequences of choice principles (like the assertion that the set A can be non-amorphous in ZF or in ZFA) in order to construct some structures which later fail to be finitely supported. We conjecture that all the choice principles presented in [27] are inconsistent in FSM. We did not find yet any example of a non-finitely supported subset of an invariant set defined without using a choice principle from [27] or a consequence of a form of choice (like the construction of an infinite and coinfinite subset of an infinite set). Therefore, the question regarding the validity of the following assertions naturally appears.

- If we consider the ZF set theory (or the ZFA set theory) without any choice principle, then every subset of an invariant set is finitely supported?
- For what kind of atoms the previous question has an affirmative answer?

If we get an affirmative answer (even for a particular set of atoms), then the mathematics developed in the ZF (or ZFA) set theory without any choice principle would be somehow equivalent to FSM, namely we could model any infinite structure by using its finite support.

References

1. Alexandru, A., Ciobanu, G.: Nominal event structures. Rom. J. Inf. Sci. Technol. **15**, 79–90 (2012)
2. Alexandru, A., Ciobanu, G.: Nominal techniques for πI-calculus. Rom. J. Inf. Sci. Technol. **16**, 261–286 (2013)
3. Alexandru, A., Ciobanu, G.: Nominal groups and their homomorphism theorems. Fundamenta Informaticae **131**(3–4), 279–298 (2014)
4. Alexandru, A., Ciobanu, G.: On the development of the Fraenkel-Mostowski set theory. Bull. Polytech. Inst. Jassy **LX**, 77–91 (2014)
5. Alexandru, A., Ciobanu, G.: A nominal approach for fusion calculus. Rom. J. Inf. Sci. Technol. **17**(3), 265–288 (2014)
6. Alexandru, A., Ciobanu, G.: Mathematics of multisets in the Fraenkel-Mostowski framework. Bulletin Mathematique de la Societe des Sciences Mathematiques de Roumanie **58/106**(1), 3–18 (2015)
7. Alexandru, A., Ciobanu, G.: Defining finitely supported mathematics over sets with atoms. In: Batsakis, S., Bobalo, Y., Ermolayev, V., Kharchenko, V., Kobets, V., Kravtsov, H., Mayr, H.C., Nikitchenko, M., Peschanenko, V., Spivakovsky, A., Yakovyna, V., Zholtkevych, G. (eds.) 4th International Workshop on Algebraic, Logical, and Algorithmic Methods of System Modeling, Specification and Verification, vol. 1356, pp. 382–395 (2015). http://CEUR-WS.org
8. Alexandru, A., Ciobanu, G.: Generalized multisets: from ZF to FSM. Comput. Inform. **34**(5), 1133–1150 (2015)

9. Alexandru, A., Ciobanu, G.: Static analysis in finitely supported mathematics. In: 17th International Symposium on Symbolic and Numeric Algorithms for Scientific Computing. IEEE Computer Society Press (2015, in press)
10. Alexandru, A., Ciobanu, G.: Pawlak approximations in the framework of nominal sets. J. Multiple-Valued Logic Soft Comput. **26**(3) (2016, in press)
11. Alexandru, A., Ciobanu, G.: Finitely supported subgroups of a nominal group. Mathematical Reports 18(2) (2016)
12. Banach, S., Tarski, A.: Sur la décomposition des ensembles de points en parties respectivement congruentes. Fundamenta Mathematicae **6**, 244–277 (1924)
13. Barwise, J.: Admissible Sets and Structures: An Approach to Definability Theory. Perspectives in Mathematical Logic, vol. 7. Springer, Berlin (1975)
14. Bojańczyk, M., Lasota, S.: Fraenkel-Mostowski sets with non-homogeneous atoms. In: Finkel, A., Leroux, J., Potapov, I. (eds.) RP 2012. LNCS, vol. 7550, pp. 1–5. Springer, Heidelberg (2012)
15. Bojanczyk, M.: Nominal monoids. Theor. Comput. Syst. **53**, 194–222 (2013)
16. Bojanczyk, M., Braud, L., Klin, B., Lasota, S.: Towards nominal computation. In: 39th ACM Symposium on Principles of Programming Languages, pp. 401–412 (2012)
17. Bojanczyk, M., Klin, B., Lasota, S.: Automata with group actions. In: 26th Symposium on Logic in Computer Science, pp. 355–364. IEEE Computer Society Press (2011)
18. Bojanczyk, M., Klin, B., Lasota, S., Torunczyk, S.: Turing machines with atoms. In: 28th Symposium on Logic in Computer Science, pp. 183–192. IEEE Computer Society Press (2013)
19. Bojanczyk, M., Lasota, S.: A machine-independent characterization of timed languages. In: 39th International Colloquium on Automata, Languages and Programming, pp. 92–103 (2012)
20. Bojanczyk, M., Torunczyk, S.: Imperative programming in sets with atoms. In: D'Souza, D., Kavitha, T., Radhakrishnan, J. (eds.) IARCS Annual Conference on Foundations of Software Technology and Theoretical Computer Science, vol. 18, pp. 4–15. LIPIcs (2012)
21. Cohen, P.J.: The Independence of the Axiom of Choice. Stanford University, Mimeographed (1963)
22. Fraenkel, A.: Zu den grundlagen der Cantor-Zermeloschen mengenlehre. Mathematische Annalen **86**, 230–237 (1922)
23. Gabbay, M.J.: The pi-calculus in FM. In: Kamareddine, F.D. (ed.) Thirty Five Years of Automating Mathematics. Applied Logic Series, vol. 28, pp. 247–269. Springer, The Netherlands (2003)
24. Gabbay, M.J., Pitts, A.M.: A new approach to abstract syntax with variable binding. Formal Aspects Comput. **13**, 341–363 (2001)
25. Gandy, R.: Church's thesis and principles for mechanisms. In: Barwise, J., Keisler, H.J., Kunen, K. (eds.) The Kleene Symposium, pp. 123–148. North-Holland, Amsterdam (1980)
26. Gödel, K.: The Consistency of the Axiom of Choice and of the Generalized Continuum-Hypothesis with the Axioms of Set Theory. Annals of Mathematics Studies. Princeton University Press, Princeton (1940)
27. Herrlich, H.: Axiom of Choice. Lecture Notes in Mathematics. Springer, Heidelberg (2006)
28. Howard, P., Rubin, J.E.: Consequences of the Axiom of Choice. Mathematical Surveys and Monographs, vol. 59. American Mathematical Society, Providence (1998)

29. Jech, T.J.: The Axiom of Choice. Studies in Logic and the Foundations of Mathematics. North-Holland, Amsterdam (1973)
30. Krohn, K., Rhodes, J.: Algebraic theory of machines: prime decomposition theorem for finite semigroups and machines. Trans. Am. Math. Soc. **116**, 450–464 (1965)
31. Lindenbaum, A., Mostowski, A.: Uber die unabhangigkeit des auswahlsaxioms und einiger seiner folgerungen. Comptes Rendus des Seances de la Societe des Sciences et des Lettres de Varsovie. **31**, 27–32 (1938)
32. Parrow, J., Victor, B.: The update calculus. In: Johnson, M. (ed.) Algebraic Methodology and Software Technology. LNCS, vol. 1349, pp. 409–423. Springer, Heidelberg (1997)
33. Petrisan, D.: Investigations into algebra and topology over nominal sets. Ph.D. thesis, University of Leicester (2011)
34. Pitts, A.M.: Alpha-structural recursion and induction. J. ACM **53**, 459–506 (2006)
35. Pitts, A.M.: Nominal Sets Names and Symmetry in Computer Science. Cambridge University Press, Cambridge (2013)
36. Sangiorgi, D.: π-calculus, internal mobility, and agent-passing calculi. Rapport INRIA no.2539 (1995)
37. Shinwell, M.R.: The fresh approach: functional programming with names and binders. Ph.D. thesis, University of Cambridge (2005)
38. Tarski, A.: What are logical notions? Hist. Philos. Logic **7**, 143–154 (1986)
39. Turner, D.: Nominal Domain Theory for Concurrency. Technical report no.751, University of Cambridge (2009)
40. Urban, C.: Nominal techniques in Isabelle/HOL. J. Autom. Reasoning **40**, 327–356 (2008)

Solving NP-complete Problems in Polynomial Time by Using a Natural Computing Model

Bogdan Aman(✉) and Gabriel Ciobanu

Romanian Academy, Institute of Computer Science, Blvd. Carol I no. 8, 700505 Iaşi, Romania
baman@iit.tuiasi.ro, gabriel@info.uaic.ro

Abstract. The first part of the paper is devoted to a polynomial solution of a well-known NP-complete problem (SAT problem) by using an unconventional computation model provided by P systems with active membranes (with neither polarization nor division rules). An important step of this semi-uniform solution is given by polynomial computing devices to build P systems that contain some exponential-size feature for which solving the SAT problem is easy. NP-complete problems are decision problems that can be solved in polynomial time on a non-deterministic Turing machine. Related to this step, in the second part we show how we can simulate polynomial space Turing machines by using a logarithmic space P system with active membranes, and employing a binary representation in order to encode the positions on the Turing machine tape.

Keywords: Natural computing · Membrane computing · Turing machines

1 Introduction

Membrane computing [15] is a branch of the natural computing inspired by the architecture and behaviour of living cells. Membrane systems (also called P systems) have been introduced by the computer scientist Gheorghe Păun, whose last name is the origin of the letter P in "P Systems". Membrane systems are characterized by three features: (i) a membrane structure consisting of a hierarchy of membranes (which are either disjoint or nested), with an unique top membrane called the *skin*; (ii) multisets of objects associated with membranes; (iii) rules for processing the objects and membranes. When membrane systems are seen as computing devices, two main research directions are usually considered: computational power in comparison with the classical notion of Turing computability (e.g., [2]), and efficiency in algorithmically solving NP-complete problems in polynomial time (e.g., [3]). Such efficient algorithms are obtained by trading space for time, with the space grown exponentially in a linear time by means of bio-inspired operations (e.g., membrane division). Thus, membrane systems define classes of computing devices which are both powerful and efficient.

V. Yakovyna et al. (Eds.): ICTERI 2015, CCIS 594, pp. 91–108, 2016.
DOI: 10.1007/978-3-319-30246-1_6

Related to the investigations of these research directions, there have been studied several applications of these systems; among them, modelling of various biological phenomena and the complexity and emergent properties of such systems presented in [7]. In [4] it is presented the detailed functioning of the sodium-potassium pump, while in [1] it is described and analyzed the immune system in the formal framework of P systems. Under the assumption that $\mathbf{P} \neq \mathbf{NP}$, efficient solutions to **NP**-complete problems cannot be obtained without introducing features which enhance the efficiency of the system ways to exponentially grow the workspace during the computation, non-determinism, and so on). For instance, some pre-computed resources are used in [9].

We show that P systems with active membranes [13] can provide simple semi-uniform solutions to the SAT problem without using neither polarization nor division, but using exponential size pre-computed initial configurations (either alphabet or structure). An important observation is that we specify how our pre-computed initial configurations are constructed in a polynomial number of steps by additional well-defined P systems (P systems with replicated rewriting and P systems with active membranes and membrane creation, respectively).

The semi-uniform solutions rely on constructing the system and the solution in polynomial time in order to avoid solving the problem during the evolution of the system. In this context, the initial (exponential) configuration is constructed by another (polynomial) system, and the problem is solved by combining these two systems. In this way, we propose a polynomial solution that uses a polynomial P system for constructing the initial configuration (that is exponential). Related to this step, we show that P systems with active membranes provide an interesting simulation of polynomial space Turing machines by using only logarithmic space and a polynomial number of read-only input objects.

The rest of this paper is organized as follows: Sect. 2 contains some preliminary notions used in this paper. Section 3 provides simple semi-uniform solutions to the SAT problem, while Sect. 4 provides a simulation of polynomial space Turing machines by using only logarithmic space P systems with active membranes. Conclusion and references end the paper.

2 Preliminaries

We consider P systems with active membranes extended with an input alphabet, and such that the input objects cannot be created during the evolution [17]. The original definition also includes division rules, rules that are not needed here. The version used in this paper is similar to evolution-communication P systems used in [6] with additional read-only input objects and polarities.

Definition 1. *A* P system with active membranes and input objects *is a tuple*

$$\Pi = (\Gamma, \Delta, \Lambda, \mu; w_1, \ldots, w_d, R)$$

Where:

- $d \geq 1$ *is the* initial degree*;*
- Γ *is a finite non-empty alphabet of* objects*;*

- Δ *is an* input alphabet *of objects such that* $\Delta \cap \Gamma = \emptyset$*;*
- Λ *is a finite* set of labels *for membranes;*
- μ *is a* membrane structure *(i.e., a rooted unordered tree, usually represented by nested brackets) in which each membrane is labelled by an element of* Λ *in a one-to-one way, and possesses an attribute called* electrical charge, *which can be either neutral (0), positive (+) or negative (-);*
- $w_1, \ldots, w_d$ *are strings over* Γ*, describing the* initial multisets *of objects placed in a number of d membranes of* μ*; notice that* w_i *is assigned to membrane i;*
- R *is a finite* set of rules *over* $\Gamma \cup \Delta$*:*
  1. $[a \rightarrow w]_h^\alpha$ object evolution rules
     An object $a \in \Gamma$ *is rewritten into the multiset* w*, if* a *is placed inside a membrane labelled by* h *with charge* α*. An object* a *can be deleted by considering* w *the empty multiset* $\emptyset$*. Notice that these rules allow only to rewrite objects from* Γ*, but not from* Δ*.*
  2. $a[\ ]_h^\alpha \rightarrow [b]_h^\beta$ send-in communication rules
     An object a *is sent into a membrane labelled by* h *and with charge* α*, becoming* b*; also, the charge of* h *is changed to* β*. If* $b \in \Delta$*, then* $a = b$ *must hold.*
  3. $[a]_h^\alpha \rightarrow b[\ ]_h^\beta$ send-out communication rules
     An object a*, placed into a membrane labelled by* h *and having charge* α*, is sent out of membrane* h *and becomes* b*; simultaneously, the charge of* h *is changed to* β*. If* $b \in \Delta$*, then* $a = b$ *must hold.*
  4. $[a]_h^\alpha \rightarrow b$ dissolution rules
     An object a*, placed into a membrane labelled by* h *and having charge* α *dissolves membrane hand becomes* b*. All object contained in membrane* h *are released in the parent membrane of* h*.*

Each configuration $\mathcal{C}_i$ of a P system with active membranes and input objects is described by the current membrane structure, including the electrical charges, together with the multisets of objects located in the corresponding membranes. The initial configuration of such a system is denoted by $\mathcal{C}_0$. An evolution step from the current configuration $\mathcal{C}_i$ to a new configuration $\mathcal{C}_{i+1}$, denoted by $\mathcal{C}_i \Rightarrow \mathcal{C}_{i+1}$, is done according to the principles:

- Each object and membrane is involved in at most one communication rule per step.
- Each membrane could be involved in several object evolution rules that can be applied in parallel inside it.
- The application of rules is maximally parallel: the only objects and membranes that do not evolve are those associated with no rule, or only to rules that are not applicable due to the electrical charges.
- When several conflicting rules could be applied at the same time, a non-deterministic choice is performed; this implies that multiple configurations can be reached as the result of an evolution step.
- In each computation step, all the chosen rules are applied simultaneously.
- Any object sent out from the skin membrane cannot re-enter it.

A *halting evolution* of such a system Π is a finite sequence of configurations $\overrightarrow{\mathcal{C}} = (\mathcal{C}_0, \ldots, \mathcal{C}_k)$, such that $\mathcal{C}_0 \Rightarrow \mathcal{C}_1 \Rightarrow \ldots \Rightarrow \mathcal{C}_k$, and no rules can be applied any more in $\mathcal{C}_k$. A *non-halting* evolution $\overrightarrow{\mathcal{C}} = (\mathcal{C}_i \mid i \in \mathbb{N})$ consists of an infinite evolution $\mathcal{C}_0 \Rightarrow \mathcal{C}_1 \Rightarrow \ldots$, where the applicable rules are never exhausted.

Example 1. Addition is trivial; we consider n objects a and m objects b placed in a membrane 0 with charge $+$. The rule $[b \rightarrow a]_h^+$ says that an object b is transformed in one object a. Such a rule is applied in parallel as many times as possible. Consequently, all objects b are erased. The remaining number of objects a represents the addition $n + m$. More examples can be found in [5].

In order to solve decision problems (i.e., decide languages over an alphabet Σ), we use *families* of recognizer P systems $\mathbf{\Pi} = \{\Pi_x \mid x \in \Sigma^*\}$ that respect the following conditions: (1) all evolutions halt; (2) two additional objects *yes* (successful evolution) and *no* (unsuccessful evolution) are used; (3) one of the objects *yes* and *no* appears in the halting configuration [16]. Each input x is associated with a P system Π_x that decides the membership of x in the language $L \subseteq \Sigma^*$ by accepting or rejecting it. The mapping $x \vdash \Pi_x$ must be efficiently computable for each input length [12].

In this paper we use a logarithmic space uniformity condition [17].

Definition 2. *A family of P systems $\mathbf{\Pi} = \{\Pi_x \mid x \in \Sigma^*\}$ is said to be $(\mathbf{L}, \mathbf{L})$-uniform if the mapping $x \vdash \Pi_x$ can be computed by two deterministic logarithmic space Turing machines F (for "family") and E (for "encoding") as follows:*

- *F computes the mapping $1^n \vdash \Pi_n$, where Π_n represents the membrane structure with some initial multisets and a specific input membrane, while n is the length of the input x.*
- *E computes the mapping $x \vdash w_x$, where w_x is a multiset encoding the specific input x.*
- *Finally, Π_x is Π_n with w_x added to the multiset placed inside its input membrane.*

In the following definition of space complexity adapted from [17], the input objects do not contribute to the size of the configuration of a P system. In this way, only the actual working space of the P system is measured, and P systems working in sublinear space may be analyzed.

Definition 3. *Given a configuration $\mathcal{C}$, the space size $|\mathcal{C}|$ is defined as the sum of the number of membranes in μ and the number of objects in Γ it contains. If $\overrightarrow{\mathcal{C}}$ is a halting evolution of Π, then $|\overrightarrow{\mathcal{C}}| = max\{|\mathcal{C}_0|, \ldots, |\mathcal{C}_k|\}$ or, in the case of a non-halting evolution $\overrightarrow{\mathcal{C}}$, $|\overrightarrow{\mathcal{C}}| = sup\{|\mathcal{C}_i| \mid i \in \mathbb{N}\}$. The space required by Π itself is then $|\Pi| = sup\{|\overrightarrow{\mathcal{C}}| \mid \overrightarrow{\mathcal{C}}$* is an evolution of *$\Pi\}$.*

Notice that $|\Pi| = \infty$ if Π has an evolution requiring infinite space or an infinite number of halting evolutions that can occur such that for each $k \in \mathbb{N}$ there exists at least one evolution requiring most than k steps.

3 Solving the SAT Problem with Active Membranes

At the beginning of 2005, Gh. Păun wrote:

> *"My favourite question (related to complexity aspects in P systems with active membranes and with electrical charges) is that about the number of polarizations. Can the polarizations be completely avoided? The feeling is that this is not possible - and such a result would be rather sound: passing from no polarization to two polarizations amounts to passing from non-efficiency to efficiency."*

This conjecture (problem F in [14]) can be formally described in terms of membrane computing complexity classes as follows:

$$P = PMC_{\mathcal{AM}^0(+d,-n,+e,+c)}$$

where

- $PMC_{\mathcal{R}}$ indicates that the result holds for P systems with input membrane;
- $+d$ indicates that dissolution rules are permitted;
- $-n$ indicates that only division rules for elementary membranes are allowed;
- $+e$ indicates that evolution rules are permitted;
- $+c$ indicates that communication rules are permitted.

The SAT problem checks the satisfiability of a propositional logic formula in conjunctive normal form (CNF). Let $\{x_1, x_2, \ldots, x_n\}$ be a set of propositional variables. A formula in CNF is of the form $\varphi = C_1 \wedge C_2 \wedge \cdots \wedge C_m$ where each C_i, $1 \leq i \leq m$ is a disjunction of the form $C_i = y_1 \vee y_2 \vee \cdots \vee y_r$ $(r \leq n)$, where each y_j is either a variable x_k or its negation $\neg x_k$.

We present some attempts to solve this conjecture by providing algorithms solving the SAT problem using P systems with active membranes with neither polarizations nor division, but using exponential pre-computed initial configurations constructed by additional P systems in polynomial time. As usually done in the membrane computing community, we construct effectively a system of membranes that solves the problem.

3.1 Solving SAT Problem by Using a Pre-computed Alphabet

In this section, we propose a polynomial time solution to the SAT problem using the polarizationless P systems with active membranes, without division, but with a pre-computed alphabet. For any instance of SAT we construct effectively a system of membranes that solves it. Formally, we prove the following result:

Theorem 1. *The SAT problem can be solved by a* **polarizationless** *P system with active membranes and* **without division**, *but with an exponential alphabet pre-computed in linear time with respect to the number of variables and the number of clauses, i.e.,*

$$P = PMC_{\mathcal{AM}^0(+d,+e,+c,pre(\alpha))}.$$

where $pre(\alpha)$ indicates that a pre-computed alphabet is permitted.

Proof. Let us consider a propositional formula

$$\varphi = C_1 \wedge C_2 \wedge \cdots \wedge C_m$$

where each $C_i, 1 \leq i \leq m$ is a disjunction of the form

$$C_i = y_1 \vee y_2 \vee \cdots \vee y_r (r \leq n),$$

where each y_j is either a variable x_k or its negation $\neg x_k$.

We construct a P system with active membranes able to check the satisfiability of φ. The P system is given by $\Pi = (\Gamma, \Lambda, \mu, w_1, \ldots, w_d, R)$, where:

- $\Gamma = \{z_i \mid 0 \leq i \leq max\{m,n\}\} \cup$
  $\cup \{s_i \mid i = t_1 \ldots t_n, t_j \in \{0,1\}$ and $1 \leq j \leq n\} \cup \{yes, no\}$.
  The alphabet $\{s_i \mid i = t_1 \ldots t_n, t_j \in \{0,1\}$ and $1 \leq j \leq n\}$ to be placed inside the input membrane 0 can be generated, starting from an object s, using the rules:
  - $s \rightarrow s_0 s_1$;
  - $s_i \rightarrow s_{i0} s_{i1}$, for $i = t_1 \ldots t_k$ where $t_j \in \{0,1\}$ and $1 \leq j \leq k < n$.

  Thus all the possible assignments for the n variable $\{x_1, x_2, \ldots, x_n\}$ are created. The rules are applied until the length k of i in the second rule equals n. For example, s_{100} over $\{x_1, x_2, x_3\}$ represents the assignment $x_1 = 1$, $x_2 = 0$ and $x_3 = 0$ (1 stands for *true*, while 0 stands for *false*). The input alphabet can be computed in linear (polynomial) time by using an additional device, for instance P systems with replicated rewriting [8].
- $\Lambda = \{0, c_1, \ldots, c_m, h\}$, with $c_i = z_1 \ldots z_n$, $1 \leq i \leq m$ where
  - $z_j = 1$ if x_j appears in C_i;
  - $z_j = 0$ if $\neg x_j$ appears in C_i;
  - $z_j = \star$ if neither x_j nor $\neg x_j$ appear in C_i.

  For example $c_1 = 1 \star 0$ over the set of variables $\{x_1, x_2, x_3\}$ represents the disjunction $c_1 = x_1 \vee \neg x_3$.
- $\mu = [[[\cdots[[[\ ]_0]_{c_1}]_{c_2} \cdots]_{c_{m-1}}]_{c_m}]_h$.
- $w_0 = z_0$.
- $w_i = \lambda$, for all $i \in \Lambda \backslash \{0\}$.
- The set R contains the following rules:
  1. $[z_0]_0 \rightarrow z_0$
     After the input is placed inside membrane 0, membrane 0 is dissolved, and its content is released in the upper membrane labelled with c_1.
  2. $[s_i]_{c_j} \rightarrow s_i[\ ]_{c_j}$
     if i and j have at least one position with the same value (either 0 or 1);
  3. $[s_i]_{c_m} \rightarrow yes$
     if i and m have at least one position with the same value (either 0 or 1). An assignment s_i is sent out of a membrane c_m if there is at least one position in i and j that is equal, namely an assignment to a variable x_k such that it makes C_j true. Once an object yes is generated, another object yes cannot be created because membrane c_m was dissolved and the rule $[s_i]_{c_m} \rightarrow yes$ cannot be applied. For example, if $c_1 = 1 \star 0$ and s_{101}

(as described above), then this means that s_{101} satisfies the clause coded by $c_1 = 1 \star 0$ since both have 1 on their first position, and this is enough to make true a disjunction.

4. $[z_0 \to z_1]_{c_1}$
5. $[z_i]_{c_i} \to [\ ]_{c_i} z_{i+1}$, for $1 \leq i \leq m-1$
6. $[z_m]_{c_m} \to no$
   The object z_0 waits a step after membrane 0 is dissolved in order to allow the other objects s_i to go through the c_j membranes. The object z_i then is communicated through the c_j membranes. Once z_m reached the membrane c_m, if membrane c_m still exists (i.e., the rule $[s_i]_{c_m} \to yes$ was not applied), then the answer *no* is generated. Once an object *yes* or *no* is generated, other objects *yes* or *no* cannot be created because membrane c_m was dissolved, and neither rule $[s_i]_{c_m} \to yes$ nor $[z_m]_{c_m} \to no$ can be applied.
7. $[yes]_h \to yes[\ ]_h$
8. $[no]_h \to no[\ ]_h$
   The answer *yes* or *no* regarding the satisfiability is sent out of the skin.

3.2 Solving SAT Problem Using a Pre-computed Initial Structure

In this section, we propose a polynomial time solution to the SAT problem using the polarizationless P systems with active membranes and without division, but with a pre-computed structure. For any instance of SAT we construct effectively a system of membranes that solves it. The fact that each membrane can be subject to at most one communication rule per step is needed when generating all possible assignments to be verified. Formally, we prove the following result:

Theorem 2. *The SAT problem can be solved by a* **polarizationless** *P system with active membranes and* **without division**, *but with an initial exponential structure pre-computed in linear time with respect to the number of variables and the number of clauses, i.e.,*

$$P = PMC_{\mathcal{AM}^0(+d,+e,+c,pre(\mu))}.$$

where $pre(\mu)$ indicates that a pre-computed structure is permitted.

Proof. Let us consider a propositional formula

$$\varphi = C_1 \wedge C_2 \wedge \cdots \wedge C_m$$

where each $C_i, 1 \leq i \leq m$ is a disjunction of the form

$$C_i = y_1 \vee y_2 \vee \cdots \vee y_r (r \leq n),$$

where each y_j is either a variable x_k or its negation $\neg x_k$.

We construct a P system with active membranes able to check the satisfiability of φ. The P system is given by $\Pi = (\Gamma, \Lambda, \mu, w_1, \ldots, w_d, R)$, where:

- $\Gamma = \{a_i, t_i, t'_i, f_i, f'_i \mid 1 \leq i \leq n\} \cup \{z_i \mid 0 \leq i \leq 4 \times n + 2 \times m\} \cup \{yes, no\}$.

- $\Lambda = \{0, \ldots, n, c_1, \ldots, c_m, h\}$, $1 \leq i \leq m$.
- $\mu = [[[[\ldots]_2[\ldots]_2]_1[[\ldots]_2[\ldots]_2]_1]_0]_h$, where
  - each membrane i contains two membranes $i+1$ for $0 \leq i \leq n-1$;
  - each membrane n contains a membrane structure $[[\ldots[\ ]_{c_m}\cdots]_{c_1}]_{c_0}$;
  - membrane 0 is the input membrane.

  Graphically, the membrane structure μ can be represented as a tree:

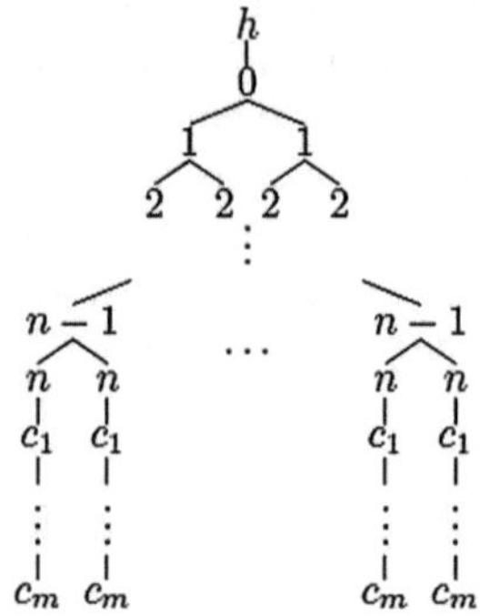

  This membrane structure can be generate in linear (polynomial) time with respect to the number of variables and the number of clauses. This is done by using an additional device that starts from a membrane structure $[[\ ]_0]_h$, with object 0 placed inside membrane 0 and rules of the form:
  - $[i \to (i+1)'\ (i+1)']_i$, for $0 \leq i \leq n-1$
  - $i' \to [i]_i$, for $1 \leq i \leq n$
  - $n \to [c_2]_{c_1}$
  - $c_k \to [c_{k+1}]_{c_k}$, for $2 \leq k \leq m-1$
  - $c_m \to [\ ]_{c_m}$.
- $w_0 = a_1 z_0$.
- $w_i = \lambda$, for all $i \in \Lambda \backslash \{0\}$.
- The set R contains the following rules:
  1. $[z_i \to z_{i+1}]_0$, for all $0 \leq i < 4 \times n + 2 \times m$
     These rules count the time needed for producing the truth assignments for the n variables inside the membranes labelled by n ($3 \times n$ steps), then to dissolve the membranes labelled by c_j, $1 \leq j \leq m$ ($2 \times m$ steps), and for an y object to reach the membrane labelled by 0 (n steps).
  2. $[a_i \to t_i f_i]_{i-1}$, for $1 \leq i \leq n$
  3. $t_i[\ ]_i \to [t_i]_i$, for $1 \leq i \leq n$
  4. $f_i[\ ]_i \to [f_i]_i$, for $1 \leq i \leq n$
  5. $[t_i \to t'_i t'_i a_{i+1}]_i$, for $1 \leq i \leq n-1$
  6. $t'_i[\ ]_k \to [t_i]_k$, for $i+1 \leq k \leq n$
  7. $[t_i \to t'_i t'_i]_k$, for $i+1 \leq k \leq n-1$
  8. $[f_i \to f'_i f'_i a_{i+1}]_i$, for $1 \leq i \leq n-1$
  9. $f'_i[\ ]_k \to [f_i]_k$, for $i+1 \leq k \leq n$
  10. $[f_i \to f'_i f'_i]_k$, for $i+1 \leq k \leq n-1$
     In membranes n we create all possible assignments for the n variable $\{x_1, x_2, \ldots, x_n\}$. It starts from an object a_1 placed initially in membrane

labelled by 0. Each a_i is used to create t_i and f_i that are then send in one of the two membranes labelled by i placed in membrane $i-1$. In fact each membrane i receives either t_i or f_i, and this is possible because a membrane can be involved in only one communication rule of an evolution step. After an object t_i or f_i reaches a membrane i, it generates two new copies of it to be sent inside membranes $i+1$ together with an object a_{i+1} that is used then to construct the assignments over variable x_{i+1}.

11. $t_i[\,]_{c_j} \to [t_i]_{c_j}$, if x_i appears in C_j
12. $[t_i]_{c_j} \to t_i$, for $1 \leq i \leq n$, $1 \leq j < m$
13. $[t_i]_{c_m} \to y$, for $1 \leq i \leq n$
14. $f_i[\,]_{c_j} \to [t_i]_{c_j}$, if $\neg x_i$ appears in C_j
15. $[f_i]_{c_j} \to f_i$, for $1 \leq i \leq n$, $1 \leq j \leq m$
16. $[f_i]_{c_m} \to y$, for $1 \leq i \leq n$.
   An assignment t_i (f_i) is sent into a membrane c_j if there is an assignment to a variable x_k ($\neg x_k$) such that it makes C_j true. Once all membranes labelled by c_i are dissolved inside a membrane labelled by n, an object y is generated.
17. $[y]_k \to [\,]_k y$, for $k \in \Lambda \backslash \{0, h\}$
18. $[y]_0 \to yes$
19. $[z_{4\times n+2\times m}]_0 \to no$.
   The object z_0 waits for $4\times n+2\times m$ steps in order to allow dissolving the membrane labelled by 0 if this still exists (i.e., the rule $[y]_0 \to yes$ was not applied), then the answer *no* is generated. Once an object *yes* or *no* is generated, other objects *yes* or *no* cannot be created because membrane c_m was dissolved, and neither rule $[y]_0 \to yes$ nor $[z_{4\times n+2\times m}]_0 \to no$ can be applied.
20. $[yes]_h \to yes[\,]_h$
21. $[no]_h \to no[\,]_h$.
   The answer *yes* or *no* regarding the satisfiability is sent out of the skin.

Example 2. We illustrate this algorithm and the evolution of a system Π constructed for the propositional formula $\psi = (x_1 \vee x_2) \wedge (\neg x_1 \vee \neg x_2)$.

Thus, m = n = 2. The initial configuration of the systems, constructed by an additional device that starts from a membrane structure $[[\,]_0]_h$, with object 0 placed inside membrane 0 and rules of the form:

- $[0 \to 1'\ 1']_0$ and $[1 \to 2'\ 2']_1$
- $1' \to [1]_1$ and $2' \to [2]_2$
- $2 \to [c_2]_{c_1}$ and $c_2 \to [\,]_{c_2}$.

The obtained structure is

$$[[[[[[\,]_{c_2}]_{c_1}]_2[[[\,]_{c_2}]_{c_1}]_2]_1[[[[\,]_{c_2}]_{c_1}]_2[[[\,]_{c_2}]_{c_1}]_2]_1 a_1 z_0]_0]_h$$

Graphically, the membrane structure μ can be represented as a tree:

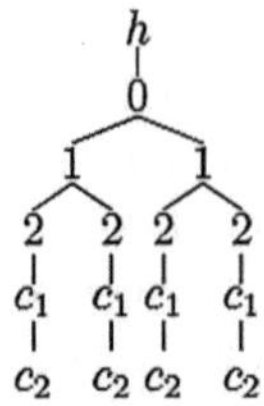

Using the set R of rules $1 \div 21$, the computation proceeds as follows:

$$
\begin{aligned}
& [[[[[\ ]_{c_2}]_{c_1}]_2[[[\ ]_{c_2}]_{c_1}]_2]_1[[[[\ ]_{c_2}]_{c_1}]_2[[[\ ]_{c_2}]_{c_1}]_2]_1 a_1 z_0]_0]_h \\
\Rightarrow & [[[[[\ ]_{c_2}]_{c_1}]_2[[[\ ]_{c_2}]_{c_1}]_2]_1[[[[\ ]_{c_2}]_{c_1}]_2[[[\ ]_{c_2}]_{c_1}]_2]_1 t_1 f_1 z_1]_0]_h \\
\Rightarrow & [[[[[\ ]_{c_2}]_{c_1}]_2[[[\ ]_{c_2}]_{c_1}]_2 t_1]_1[[[[\ ]_{c_2}]_{c_1}]_2[[[\ ]_{c_2}]_{c_1}]_2 f_1]_1 z_2]_0]_h \\
\Rightarrow & [[[[[\ ]_{c_2}]_{c_1}]_2[[[\ ]_{c_2}]_{c_1}]_2 t'_1 t'_1 a_2]_1[[[[\ ]_{c_2}]_{c_1}]_2[[[\ ]_{c_2}]_{c_1}]_2 f'_1 f'_1 a_2]_1 z_3]_0]_h \\
\Rightarrow & [[[[[\ ]_{c_2}]_{c_1} t_1]_2[[[\ ]_{c_2}]_{c_1} t_1]_2 t_2 f_2]_1[[[[\ ]_{c_2}]_{c_1} f_1]_2[[[\ ]_{c_2}]_{c_1} f_1]_2 t_2 f_2]_1 z_4]_0]_h \\
\Rightarrow & [[[[[\ ]_{c_2}]_{c_1} t_1 t_2]_2[[[\ ]_{c_2}]_{c_1} t_1 f_2]_2]_1[[[[\ ]_{c_2}]_{c_1} f_1 t_2]_2[[[\ ]_{c_2}]_{c_1} f_1 f_2]_2]_1 z_5]_0]_h \\
\Rightarrow & [[[[[\ ]_{c_2} t_1]_{c_1} t_2]_2[[[\ ]_{c_2} t_1]_{c_1} f_2]_2]_1[[[[\ ]_{c_2} t_2]_{c_1} f_1]_2[[[\ ]_{c_2}]_{c_1} f_1 f_2]_2]_1 z_6]_0]_h \\
\Rightarrow & [[[[\ ]_{c_2} t_1 t_2]_2[[\ ]_{c_2} t_1 f_2]_2]_1[[[\ ]_{c_2} t_2 f_1]_2[[[\ ]_{c_2}]_{c_1} f_1 f_2]_2]_1 z_7]_0]_h \\
\Rightarrow & [[[[\ ]_{c_2} t_1 t_2]_2[[f_2]_{c_2} t_1]_2]_1[[[f_1]_{c_2} t_2]_2[[[\ ]_{c_2}]_{c_1} f_1 f_2]_2]_1 z_8]_0]_h \\
\Rightarrow & [[[[\ ]_{c_2} t_1 t_2]_2[y t_1]_2]_1[[y t_2]_2[[[\ ]_{c_2}]_{c_1} f_1 f_2]_2]_1 z_9]_0]_h \\
\Rightarrow & [[[[\ ]_{c_2} t_1 t_2]_2[t_1]_2 y]_1[[t_2]_2[[[\ ]_{c_2}]_{c_1} f_1 f_2]_2 y]_1 z_{10}]_0]_h \\
\Rightarrow & [[[[\ ]_{c_2} t_1 t_2]_2[t_1]_2]_1[[t_2]_2[[[\ ]_{c_2}]_{c_1} f_1 f_2]_2]_1 y y z_{11}]_0]_h \\
\Rightarrow & [[[\ ]_{c_2} t_1 t_2]_2[t_1]_2]_1[[t_2]_2[[[\ ]_{c_2}]_{c_1} f_1 f_2]_2]_1 y z_{12} yes]_h \\
\Rightarrow & [[[\ ]_{c_2} t_1 t_2]_2[t_1]_2]_1[[t_2]_2[[[\ ]_{c_2}]_{c_1} f_1 f_2]_2]_1 y z_{12}]_h yes
\end{aligned}
$$

It can be noticed that even the object z has now the subscript $4 \times n + 2 \times m = 4 \times 2 + 2 \times 2 = 12$, it cannot generate a *no* object because membrane labelled by 0 was already dissolved by an y object in the previous step. Also, even another y object reached the membrane labelled by 0, it cannot generate an *yes* object because membrane labelled by 0 was already dissolved by another y object in a previous step.

4 Natural Computing Modelling of the Polynomial Space Turing Machines

The semi-uniform solutions rely on constructing the system and the solution in polynomial time in order to avoid solving the problem during the evolution of the system. In this context, the initial (exponential) configuration is constructed by another (polynomial) system, and the problem is solved by combining these two systems. In this way, we propose a polynomial solution that uses a polynomial P system for constructing the initial configuration (that is exponential). Related to this step, we show that P systems with active membranes provide an interesting simulation of polynomial space Turing machines by using only logarithmic space and a polynomial number of read-only input objects.

4.1 A Membrane Structure for Simulation

Let M be a single-tape deterministic Turing machine working in polynomial space $s(n)$. Let Q be the set of states of M, including the initial state s; we denote by $\Sigma' = \Sigma \cup \{\sqcup\}$ the tape alphabet which includes the blank symbol $\sqcup \notin \Sigma$. A computation step is performed by using $\delta : Q \times \Sigma' \to Q \times \Sigma' \times \{-1, 0, 1\}$, a (partial) transition function of M which we assume to be undefined on (q, σ) if and only if q is a final state. We describe a uniform family of P systems $\mathbf{\Pi} = \{\Pi_x \mid x \in \Sigma^*\}$ simulating M in logarithmic space.

Let $x \in \Sigma^n$ be an input string, and let $m = \lceil log\ s(n) \rceil$ be the minimum number of bits needed in order to write the tape cell indices $0, \ldots, s(n)$-1 in binary notation. The P system Π_n associated with the input length n and computed as $F(1^n)$ has a membrane structure consisting of $|\Sigma'| \cdot (m+1) + 2$ membranes. The membrane structure contains:

- a skin membrane h;
- an inner membrane c (the input membrane) used to identify the symbol needed to compute the δ function;
- for each symbol $\sigma \in \Sigma'$ of M, the following set of membranes, linearly nested inside c and listed inward:
  - a membrane σ for each symbol σ of the tape alphabet Σ' of M;
  - for each $j \in \{0, \ldots, (m-1)\}$, a membrane labelled by j.

This labelling is used in order to simplify the notations. To respect the one-to-one labelling from Definition 1, the membrane j can be labelled j_σ. Thus in all rules using membranes j, the σ symbol is implicitly considered. Furthermore, the object z_0 is located inside the skin membrane h.

The encoding of x, computed as $E(x)$, consists of a set of objects describing the tape of M in its initial configuration on input x. These objects are the symbols of x subscripted by their position $bin(0), \ldots, bin(n-1)$ (where $bin(i)$ is the binary representation of i on m positions) in x, together with the $s(n) - n$ blank objects subscripted by their position $bin(n), \ldots, bin(s(n)-1)$. The binary representation, together with the polarities of the membranes, is essential when the membrane system has to identify the symbol needed to simulate the δ function (e.g., rule (13)). The multiset $E(x)$ is placed inside the input membrane c. Figure 1 depicts an example.

During the first evolution steps of Π_x, each input object σ_i is moved from the input membrane c to the innermost membrane $(m-1)$ of the corresponding membrane σ by means of the following communication rules:

$$\sigma_i[\ ]_\sigma^0 \to [\sigma_i]_\sigma^0 \quad \text{for} \quad \sigma \in \Sigma',\ bin(0) \leq i < bin(s(n)) \tag{1}$$

$$\sigma_i[\ ]_j^0 \to [\sigma_i]_j^0 \quad \text{for} \quad \sigma \in \Sigma',\ bin(0) \leq i < bin(s(n)),\ 0 \leq j < m \tag{2}$$

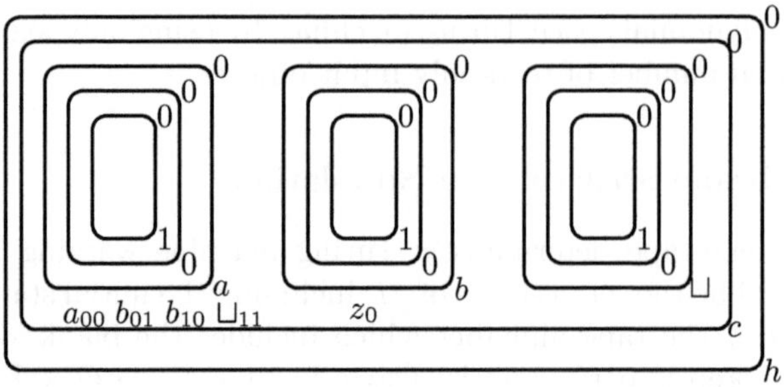

Fig. 1. Initial configuration of the P system Π_3 with tape alphabet $\Sigma' = \{a, b, ⊔\}$, working in space $s(n) = n + 1 = 4$ on the input *abb*.

Since only one communication rule per membrane can be applied during each evolution step of Π_x, all $s(n)$ input objects pass through m membranes, in order to reach the innermost membranes $(m-1)$, in at most $l = s(n) + m$ evolution steps. In the meantime, the subscript of object z_0 is incremented up to $max\{0, l-3\}$ before object z_{l-3} exits and enters membrane c changing the membrane charge from 0 to $+$:

$$[z_t \rightarrow z_{t+1}]_c^0 \qquad \text{for} \quad 0 \leq t < l-3 \tag{3}$$

$$[z_{l-3}]_c^0 \rightarrow z_{l-3}[\ ]_c^0 \tag{4}$$

$$z_{l-3}[\ ]_c^0 \rightarrow [z_{l-3}]_c^+ \tag{5}$$

The object z_{l-3} is rewritten to a multiset of objects containing an object z' (used in rule (10)) and $|\Sigma'|$ objects z_+ (used in rules (7))

$$[z_{l-3} \rightarrow z' \underbrace{z_+ \cdots z_+}_{|\Sigma'|\text{copies}}]_c^+ \tag{6}$$

The objects z_+ are used to change the charges from 0 to $+$ for all membranes $\sigma \in \Sigma'$ using parallel communication rules, and then are deleted:

$$z_+[\ ]_\sigma^0 \rightarrow [\#]_\sigma^+ \quad \text{for} \quad \sigma \in \Sigma' \tag{7}$$

$$[\# \rightarrow \emptyset]_\sigma^+ \qquad \text{for} \quad \sigma \in \Sigma' \tag{8}$$

In the meantime, the object z' is rewritten into z'' (in parallel with rule (7)), and then, in parallel with rule (8), into s_{00} (where s is the initial state of M):

$$[z' \rightarrow z'']_c^+ \tag{9}$$

$$[z'' \rightarrow s_{00}]_c^+ \tag{10}$$

The configuration reached by Π_x encodes the initial configuration of M (Fig. 2):

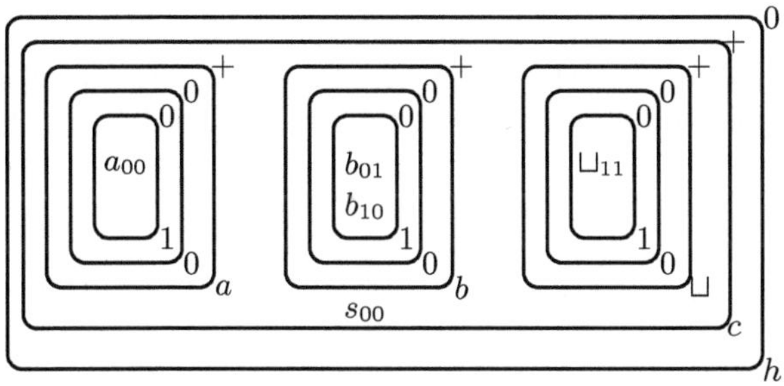

Fig. 2. Configuration of Π_x (from Fig. 1) encoding the initial configuration of M on input $x = abb$ and using $s(|x|) = 4$ tape cells.

An arbitrary configuration of M on input x is encoded by a configuration of Π_x as it is described in Fig. 3:

- membrane c contains the state-object q_i, where q is the current state of M and $i \in \{bin(0), \ldots, bin(s(n) - 1)\}$ is the current position of the tape head;
- membranes $(m - 1)$ contain all input objects;
- all other membranes are empty;
- all membranes are neutrally charged, except those labelled by $\sigma \in \Sigma'$ and by c which all are positively charged.

We employ this encoding because the input objects must be all located in the input membrane in the initial configuration of Π_x (hence they must encode both symbol and position on the tape), and they can never be rewritten.

4.2 Simulating Polynomial Space Turing Machines

Starting from a configuration of the single-tape deterministic Turing machine M, the simulation of a computation step of M by the membrane system Π_x is directed by the state-object q_i. As stated above, q_i encodes the current state

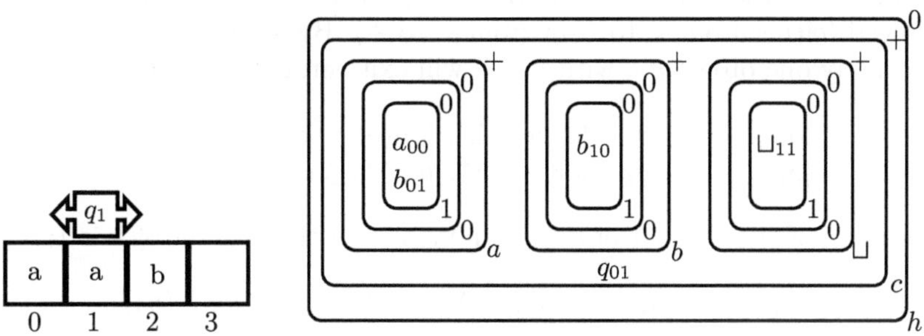

Fig. 3. A configuration of M (from Fig. 1) and the corresponding configuration of Π_x simulating it. The presence of b_{01} inside membrane 1 of a indicates that tape cell 1 of M contains the symbol a.

of M and the position of the head on the tape (in binary format). To simulate the transition function δ of the Turing machine M in state q, it is necessary to identify the actual symbol occurring at tape position i. In order to identify this σ_i object from one of the $(m-1)$ membranes, the object q_i is rewritten into $|\Sigma'|$ copies of q'_i, one for each membrane $\sigma \in \Sigma'$:

$$[q_i \rightarrow \underbrace{q'_i \cdots q'_i}_{|\Sigma'|\text{copies}}\ ]^+_c \quad \text{for } q \in Q,\ bin(0) \leq i < bin(s(n)) \tag{11}$$

The objects q'_i first enter the symbol-membranes in parallel, without changing the charges:

$$q'_i[\ ]^+_\sigma \rightarrow [q'_i]^+_\sigma \quad \text{for } \sigma \in \Sigma',\ q \in Q,\ bin(0) \leq i < bin(s(n)) \tag{12}$$

The object q'_i traverses the membranes $0, \ldots, (m-1)$ while changing their charges such that they represent the bits of i from the least to the most significant one, where a positive charge is interpreted as 1 and a negative charge as 0. For instance, the charges of $[[[\ ]^-_2]^-_1]^+_0$ encode the binary number 001 (that is, decimal 1). By the j-th bit of a binary number is understood the bit from the j-th position when the number is read from right to left (e.g., the 0-th bit of the binary number 001 is 1). The changes of charges are accomplished by the rules:

$$q'_i[\ ]^0_j \rightarrow [q'_i]^\alpha_j \quad \text{for } \sigma \in \Sigma',\ q \in Q,\ bin(0) \leq i < bin(s(n)),\ 0 \leq j < m, \tag{13}$$

where α is $-$ if the j-th bit of i is 0, and α is $+$ if the j-th bit of i is 1.

The membranes j, where $0 \leq j < m$, behave now as "filters" for the input objects σ_k occurring in membrane $(m-1)$: these objects are sent out from each membrane j if and only if the j-th bit of k corresponds to the charge of j.

$$[\sigma_k]^\alpha_j \rightarrow [\ ]^\alpha_j \sigma_k \quad \text{for } \sigma \in \Sigma',\ bin(0) \leq k < bin(s(n)),\ 0 < j < m, \tag{14}$$

where α is $-$ if the j-th bit of k is 0, and α is $+$ if j-th bit of k is 1.

If an object σ_k reaches membrane 0, it is sent outside if the 0-th bit of k corresponds to the charge of membrane 0. In order to signal that it is the symbol occurring at location i of the tape, the charge of the corresponding membrane 0 is changed (either from $+$ to $-$ or from $-$ to $+$). By applying the rules (15) to (17), exactly one object σ_k, with $k = i$, will exit through membrane c:

$$\begin{aligned} &[\sigma_k]^+_0 \rightarrow [\ ]^-_0 \sigma_k \quad \text{for } \sigma \in \Sigma',\ bin(0) \leq k < bin(s(n)) \\ &[\sigma_k]^-_0 \rightarrow [\ ]^+_0 \sigma_k \quad \text{for } \sigma \in \Sigma',\ bin(0) \leq k < bin(s(n)), \end{aligned} \tag{15}$$

where α is $-$ if the j-th bit of k is 0, and α is $+$ if the j-th bit of k is 1;

$$[\sigma_k]^+_\tau \rightarrow \sigma_k[\ ]^-_\tau \quad \text{for } \sigma, \tau \in \Sigma',\ bin(0) \leq k < bin(s(n)). \tag{16}$$

After an σ_i exits from membrane c it gets blocked inside membrane h, by the new charge of membrane c, until it is allowed to move to its new location according to function δ of the Turing machine M. Thus, if another object τ_j reached membrane σ due to the new charge of membrane 0 established by rule (15), τ_j is contained in membrane σ until reintroduced in a membrane (m-1) using rule (2).

$$[\sigma_k]_c^+ \to \sigma_k[\ ]_c^- \quad \text{for } \sigma \in \Sigma', bin(0) \leq k < bin(s(n)) \tag{17}$$

Since there are $s(n)$ input objects, and each of them must traverse at most $(m+1)$ membranes, the object σ_i reaches the skin membrane h after at most $l+1$ steps, where l is as defined in Sect. 4.1 before rule (3). While the input objects are "filtered out", the state-object q_i' "waits" for l steps using the rules:

$$[q_i' \to q_{i,1}'']_{m-1}^{\alpha} \quad \text{for } \sigma \in \Sigma',\ q \in Q,\ bin(0) \leq i < bin(s(n)), \alpha \in \{-,+\} \tag{18}$$

$$[q_{i,t}'' \to q_{i,t+1}'']_{m-1}^{\alpha} \quad \begin{array}{l}\sigma \in \Sigma',\ q \in Q,\ bin(0) \leq i < bin(s(n))\\ \alpha \in \{-,+\},\ 1 \leq t \leq l\end{array} \tag{19}$$

$$[q_{i,l+1}'' \to q_i'']_{m-1}^{\alpha} \quad \text{for } \sigma \in \Sigma',\ q \in Q,\ bin(0) \leq i < bin(s(n)), \alpha \in \{-,+\} \tag{20}$$

In order to reach membrane c, the objects q_i'' are sent out through membranes j ($0 < j \leq m-1$) using rule (21), through membrane 0 by rules (22) and (24), and through membranes $\sigma \in \Sigma'$ by rule (23). While passing through all these membranes, the charges are changed to neutral. This allows the input objects to move back to the innermost membrane $(m-1)$ by using rules of type (2).

$$[q_i'']_j^{\alpha} \to [\ ]_j^0 q_i'' \quad \begin{array}{c}\text{for } \sigma \in \Sigma',\ q \in Q,\ bin(0) \leq i < bin(s(n))\\ 0 < j \leq m-1,\ \alpha \in \{-,+\}\end{array} \tag{21}$$

When q_i'' reaches the membranes 0, only one has the charge different from the 0-th bit of i, thus allowing q_i'' to identify the symbol in tape location i of M:

$$[q_i'']_0^{\alpha} \to [\ ]_0^0 q_i''' \quad \text{for } \sigma \in \Sigma',\ q \in Q,\ bin(0) \leq i < bin(s(n)), \tag{22}$$

where α is $-$ if the 0-th bit of i is 1, and α is $+$ if the 0-th bit of i is 0.

$$[q_i''']_{\sigma}^- \to [\ ]_{\sigma}^0 q_{i,\sigma,1} \quad \text{for } \sigma \in \Sigma',\ q \in Q,\ bin(0) \leq i < bin(s(n)) \tag{23}$$

The other copies of q_i'' are sent out as objects # through membrane 0, and then deleted by rules of type (8):

$$[q_i'']_0^{\alpha} \to [\ ]_0^0 \# \quad \text{for } \sigma \in \Sigma',\ q \in Q,\ bin(0) \leq i < bin(s(n)), \tag{24}$$

where α is $-$ if the 0-th bit of i is 0, and α is $+$ if the 0-th bit of i is 1.

The state-object $q_{i,\sigma,1}$ waits in membrane c for l steps, l representing an upper bound of the number of steps needed for all the input objects to reach the innermost membranes:

$$[q_{i,\sigma,t} \to q_{i,\sigma,t+1}]_c^- \quad \text{for } \sigma \in \Sigma',\ q \in Q,\ bin(0) \leq i < bin(s(n)),\ 1 \leq t < l \tag{25}$$

$$q_{i,\sigma,l}[\ ]_{\sigma}^0 \to [q_{i,\sigma,l}]_{\sigma}^+ \quad \text{for } \sigma \in \Sigma',\ q \in Q,\ bin(0) \leq i < bin(s(n)) \tag{26}$$

$$[q_{i,\sigma,l}]_{\sigma}^+ \to q_{i,\sigma}'[\ ]_{\sigma}^+ \quad \text{for } \sigma \in \Sigma',\ q \in Q,\ bin(0) \leq i < bin(s(n)) \tag{27}$$

The state-object $q'_{i,\sigma}$ now contains all the information needed to compute the transition function δ of the Turing machine M. Suppose $\delta(q,\sigma)=(r,v,d)$ for some $d \in \{-1,0,+1\}$. Then $q'_{i,\sigma}$ sets the charge of membrane v to $-$ and waits for $m+1$ steps, thus allowing σ_i to move to membrane $(m-1)$ of v by using the rules (31), (32) and (2):

$$q'_{i,\sigma}[\ ]_v^+ \rightarrow [q'_{i,\sigma}]_v^+ \quad \text{for } \sigma,v \in \Sigma',\ q \in Q,\ bin(0) \leq i < bin(s(n)) \tag{28}$$
$$[q'_{i,\sigma}]_v^+ \rightarrow q'_{i,\sigma,1}[\ ]_v^- \quad \text{for } \sigma \in \Sigma',\ q \in Q,\ bin(0) \leq i < bin(s(n)) \tag{29}$$
$$[q'_{i,\sigma,1}]_c^- \rightarrow q'_{i,\sigma,1}[\ ]_c^0 \quad \text{for } \sigma \in \Sigma',\ q \in Q,\ bin(0) \leq i < bin(s(n)) \tag{30}$$
$$\sigma_i[\ ]_c^0 \rightarrow [\sigma_i]_c^0 \quad \text{for } \sigma \in \Sigma',\ bin(0) \leq i < bin(s(n)) \tag{31}$$
$$\sigma_i[\ ]_v^- \rightarrow [\sigma_i]_v^- \quad \text{for } \sigma,v \in \Sigma',\ q \in Q,\ bin(0) \leq i < bin(s(n)) \tag{32}$$
$$[q'_{i,\sigma,t} \rightarrow q'_{i,\sigma,t+1}]_h^0 \quad \text{for } \sigma \in \Sigma',\ q \in Q,\ bin(0) \leq i < bin(s(n))1 \leq t \leq m \tag{33}$$

The object $q'_{i,\sigma,m+1}$ is used to change the charges of membranes c and v to $+$, thus preparing the system for the next step of the simulation:

$$q'_{i,\sigma,m+1}[\ ]_c^0 \rightarrow [q'_{i,\sigma,m+1}]_c^+ \quad \text{for } \sigma \in \Sigma',\ q \in Q,\ bin(0) \leq i < bin(s(n)) \tag{34}$$
$$q'_{i,\sigma,m+1}[\ ]_v^- \rightarrow [q'_{i,\sigma,m+1}]_v^- \quad \text{for } \sigma,v \in \Sigma',\ q \in Q,\ bin(0) \leq i < bin(s(n)) \tag{35}$$
$$[q'_{i,\sigma,m+1}]_v^- \rightarrow q''_{i,\sigma}[\ ]_v^+ \quad \text{for } \sigma,v \in \Sigma',\ q \in Q,\ bin(0) \leq i < bin(s(n)) \tag{36}$$

Finally, the state-object $q''_{i,\sigma}$ is rewritten to reflect the change of state and head position, thus producing a configuration of Π_x corresponding to the new configuration of M, as described in Sect. 4.1:

$$[q''_{i,\sigma} \rightarrow r_{i+d}]_c^+ \quad \text{for } bin(0) \leq i < bin(s(n)) \tag{37}$$

The P system Π_x is now ready to simulate the next step of M. If $q \in Q$ is a final state of M, we assume that $\delta(q,\sigma)$ is undefined for all $\sigma \in \Sigma'$; thus we introduce the following rules which halt the P system with the same result (acceptance or rejection) as M:

$$[q_i]_c^+ \rightarrow [\ ]_c^+ yes \quad \text{for } bin(0) \leq i < bin(s(n)),\ \text{if } q \text{ is an accepting state} \tag{38}$$
$$[yes]_h^0 \rightarrow [\ ]_h^0 yes \quad \text{for } bin(0) \leq i < bin(s(n)),\ \text{if } q \text{ is an accepting state} \tag{39}$$
$$[q_i]_c^+ \rightarrow [\ ]_c^+ no \quad \text{for } bin(0) \leq i < bin(s(n)),\ \text{if } q \text{ is a rejecting state} \tag{40}$$
$$[no]_h^0 \rightarrow [\ ]_h^0 no \quad \text{for } bin(0) \leq i < bin(s(n)),\ \text{if } q \text{ is a rejecting state} \tag{41}$$

The simulation directly leads to the following result.

Theorem 3. *Let M be a single-tape deterministic Turing machine working in polynomial space $s(n)$ and time $t(n)$. Then there exists an $(\mathbf{L},\mathbf{L})$-uniform family $\mathbf{\Pi}$ of P systems Π_x with active membranes using object evolution and communication rules that simulates M in space $O(log\ n)$ and time $O(t(n)s(n))$.*

Proof. For each $x \in \Sigma^n$, the P system Π_x can be built from 1^n and x in logarithmic space as it is described in Definition 2; thus, the family $\mathbf{\Pi}$ is $(\mathbf{L},\mathbf{L})$-uniform.

Each P system Π_x uses only a logarithmic number of membranes and a constant number of objects per configuration; thus, Π_x works in space $O(log\ n)$. Simulating one of the $t(n)$ steps of M requires $O(s(n))$ time, an upper bound to the subscripts of objects used to introduce delays during the simulation; thus, the total time is $O(t(n)s(n))$.

5 Conclusion

We proved $P = PMC_{\mathcal{AM}^0(+d,+e,+c,pre(\alpha))}$ and $P = PMC_{\mathcal{AM}^0(+d,+e,+c,pre(\mu))}$ by providing two algorithms for solving the SAT problem using **polarizationless** P system with active membranes and **without division**. For the former equality, the provided algorithm is using an exponential alphabet pre-computed in linear time by a P system with replicated rewriting, while the later one is using an initial exponential structure pre-computed in linear time with respect to the number of variables and clauses by P systems with membrane creation.

In this paper we also provided a simulation of the polynomial space Turing machines by using logarithmic space P systems with active membranes and binary representations for the positions on the tape. A similar approach is presented in [11]. There are important differences in terms of technical details and efficient representation; in comparison to [11], we improve the simulation by reducing the number of membranes (by $|\Sigma'| - 1$) and the number of rules (by $|\Sigma'|\cdot|Q|\cdot s(n)\cdot(5-|\Sigma'|)+|\Sigma'|\cdot|\Sigma'|s(n)\cdot(2\cdot m+1)+|Q|\cdot s(n)-|\Sigma'|\cdot s(n)\cdot(m+3)$). In particular, for the running example, the number of rules is reduced by $14\cdot|Q|+84$. A different approach is presented in [10] where it is claimed that a constant space is sufficient. However, in order to obtain the constant space space, input objects (from Δ) are allowed to create other objects (from Γ) leading to a different and more powerful formalism than the one used by us in this paper.

References

1. Aman, B., Ciobanu, G.: Describing the immune system using enhanced mobile membranes. Electron. Notes Theoret. Comput. Sci. **194**, 5–18 (2008)
2. Aman, B., Ciobanu, G.: Turing completeness using three mobile membranes. In: Calude, C.S., Costa, J.F., Dershowitz, N., Freire, E., Rozenberg, G. (eds.) UC 2009. LNCS, vol. 5715, pp. 42–55. Springer, Heidelberg (2009)
3. Aman, B., Ciobanu, G.: Mobility in Process Calculi and Natural Computing. Natural Computing Series. Springer, New York (2011)
4. Besozzi, D., Ciobanu, G.: A P system description of the Sodium-Potassium pump. In: Mauri, G., Păun, G., Pérez-Jímenez, M., Rozenberg, G., Salomaa, A. (eds.) WMC 2004. LNCS, vol. 3365, pp. 210–223. Springer, Heidelberg (2005)
5. Bonchiş, C., Ciobanu, G., Izbaşa, C.: Encodings and arithmetic operations in membrane computing. In: Cai, J.-Y., Cooper, S.B., Li, A. (eds.) TAMC 2006. LNCS, vol. 3959, pp. 621–630. Springer, Heidelberg (2006)
6. Cavaliere, M.: Evolution-communication P systems. In: Păun, G., Rozenberg, G., Salomaa, A., Zandron, C. (eds.) WMC 2002. LNCS, vol. 2597, pp. 134–145. Springer, Heidelberg (2003)

7. Ciobanu, G., Păun, G., Pérez-Jiménez, M.J. (eds.): Applications of Membrane Computing. Springer, New York (2006)
8. Krishna, S.N., Rama, R.: P systems with replicated rewriting. J. Automata Lang. Comb. **6**(3), 345–350 (2001)
9. Leporati, A., Gutiérrez-Naranjo, M.A.: Solving subset sum by spiking neural P Systems with pre-computed resources. Fundamenta Informaticae **87**(1), 61–77 (2008)
10. Leporati, A., Manzoni, L., Mauri, G., Porreca, A.E., Zandron, C.: Constant-space P systems with active membranes. Fundamenta Informaticae **134**(1–2), 111–128 (2014)
11. Leporati, A., Mauri, G., Porreca, A.E., Zandron, C.: A gap in the space hierarchy of P systems with active membranes. J. Automata Lang. Comb. **19**(1–4), 173–184 (2014)
12. Murphy, N., Woods, D.: The computational power of membrane systems under tight uniformity conditions. Nat. Comput. **10**, 613–632 (2011)
13. Păun, G.: P systems with active membranes: attacking NP-complete problems. J. Automata Lang. Comb. **6**, 75–90 (2001)
14. Păun, G.: Further Twenty Six Open Problems in Membrane Computing. In: Gutiérrez, M.A., et al. (eds.) Third Brainstorming Week on Membrane Computing, pp. 249–262, Fénix Editora, Sevilla (2005)
15. Păun, G., Rozenberg, G., Salomaa, A. (eds.): The Oxford Handbook of Membrane Computing. Oxford University Press, Oxford (2010)
16. Pérez-Jiménez, M.J., Riscos-Núñez, A., Romero-Jiménez, A., Woods, D.: Complexity-membrane division, membrane creation. In: [15], pp. 302–336
17. Porreca, A.E., Leporati, A., Mauri, G., Zandron, C.: Sublinear-space P systems with active membranes. In: Csuhaj-Varjú, E., Gheorghe, M., Rozenberg, G., Salomaa, A., Vaszil, G. (eds.) CMC 2012. LNCS, vol. 7762, pp. 342–357. Springer, Heidelberg (2013)

Abstracting an Operational Semantics to Finite Automata

Nadezhda Baklanova, Wilmer Ricciotti(✉), Jan-Georg Smaus, and Martin Strecker

IRIT (Institut de Recherche en Informatique de Toulouse), Université de Toulouse, Toulouse, France
{wilmer.ricciotti,jan-georg.smaus,martin.strecker}@irit.fr
nbaklanova@gmail.com

Abstract. There is an apparent similarity between the descriptions of small-step operational semantics of imperative programs and the semantics of finite automata, so defining an abstraction mapping from semantics to automata and proving a simulation property seems to be easy. This paper aims at identifying the reasons why simple proofs break, among them artifacts in the semantics that lead to stuttering steps in the simulation. We then present a semantics based on the zipper data structure, with a direct interpretation of evaluation as navigation in the syntax tree. The abstraction function is then defined by an equivalence class construction.

Keywords: Programming language semantics · Abstraction · Finite automata · Formal methods · Verification

1 Introduction

Among the formalisms employed to describe the semantics of transition systems, two particularly popular choices are *abstract machines* and *structural operational semantics* (SOS). Abstract machines (e.g. finite automata, Büchi automata or timed automata [1,4,11]) are widely used for modeling and verifying dynamic systems. An abstract machine can be represented as a directed graph with transition semantics between nodes. The transition semantics is defined by moving a pointer to a current node. Automata are a popular tool for modeling dynamic systems due to the simplicity of the verification of automata systems, which can be carried out in a fully automated way, something that is not generally possible for Turing-complete systems.

This kind of semantics is often extended by adding a background state composed of a set of variables with their values: this is the case of timed automata,

N. Baklanova and M. Strecker were partially supported by the project *Verisync* (ANR-10-BLAN-0310).

W. Ricciotti and J.-G. Smaus are supported by the project AJITPROP (121-AO12-1209) of the Fondation Airbus.

V. Yakovyna et al. (Eds.): ICTERI 2015, CCIS 594, pp. 109–123, 2016.
DOI: 10.1007/978-3-319-30246-1_7

which use background clock variables [2]. The UPPAAL model checker for timed automata extends the notion of background state even further by adding integer and Boolean variables to the state [9] which, however, do not increase the computational power of such timed automata but make them more convenient to use.

Another formalism for modeling transition systems is structural semantics ("small-step", contrary to "big-step" semantics which is much easier to handle but which is inappropriate for a concurrent setting), which uses a set of reduction rules for simplifying a program expression. It has been described in detail in [16] and used, for example, for the Jinja project developing a formal model of the Java language [12]. An appropriate semantic rule for reduction is selected based on the expression pattern and on values of some variables in a state. As a result of reduction the expression and the state are updated. For example, a rule might be:

$$\frac{s' = s(v \longmapsto eval\ expr\ s)}{(Assign\ v\ expr, s) \rightarrow (Unit, s')}\ [\textsc{Assignment}]$$

This kind of rules is intuitive; however, the proofs involving them require induction over the expression structure. A different approach to writing a structural semantics was described in [3,14] for the CMinor language. It uses a notion of continuation which represents an expression as a control stack and deals with separate parts of the control stack consecutively.

$$(Seq\ e1\ e2 \cdot \kappa, s) \rightarrow (e1 \cdot e2 \cdot \kappa, s) \qquad (Empty \cdot \kappa, s) \rightarrow (\kappa, s)$$

Here the "·" operator designates concatenation of control stacks. The semantics of continuations does not need induction over the expression, something which makes proof easier; however it requires more auxiliary steps for maintaining the control stack which do not have direct correspondance in the modeled language.

For modeling non-local transfer of control, Krebbers and Wiedijk [13] present a semantics using (non-recursive) "statement contexts". These are combined with the above-mentioned continuation stacks. The resulting semantics is situated mid-way between [3] and the semantics proposed below.

The present paper describes an approach to translation from structural operational semantics to finite automata extended with background state. All the considered automata are an extension of Büchi automata with background state, i.e. they have a finite number of nodes and edges but can produce an infinite trace. The reason of our interest in abstracting from structural semantics to Büchi automata is our work in progress [5,8]. We are working on a static analysis algorithm for finding possible resource sharing conflicts in multithreaded Java programs. For this purpose we annotate Java programs with timing information and then translate them to a network of timed automata which is later model-checked. The whole translation is formally verified. One of the steps of the translation procedure includes switching from structural operational semantics of a Java-like language to automata semantics. During this step we discovered some problems which we will describe in the next section. The solutions we propose extend well beyond the problem of abstracting a structured language to an automaton. It can also be used for compiler verification, which usually is cluttered up with arithmetic address calculation that can be avoided in our approach.

This article is a revised version of the work we presented at ICTERI [7]. In this new version, we decided to focus on the relationship between zipper-based semantics and big-step operational semantics: this relationship is discussed in Sect. 7.

The contents of the paper has been entirely formalized in the Isabelle proof assistant [15]. We have not insisted on any Isabelle-specific features, therefore this formalization can be rewritten using other proof assistants. The full Isabelle formal development can be found on the web [6].

2 Problem Statement

We have identified the following as the main problems when trying to prove the correctness of the translation between a programming language semantics and its abstraction to automata:

1. Preservation of execution context: an abstract machine always sees all the available nodes while a reduced expression loses the information about previous reductions.
2. Semantic artifacts: some reduction rules are necessary for the functionality of the semantics, but may be missing in the modeled language. Additionally, the rules can produce expressions which do not occur in the original language.

These problems occur independently of variations in the presentation of semantic rules [16] adopted in the literature, such as [12] (recursive evaluation of sub-statements) or [3,14] (continuation-style).

We will describe these two problems in detail, and later our approach to their solution, in the context of a minimalistic programming language which only manipulates Boolean values (a *Null* value is also added to account for errors):

datatype *val* = *Bool bool* | *Null*

The language can be extended in a rather straightforward way to more complex expressions. In this language, expressions are either values or variables:

datatype *expr* = *Val val* | *Var vname*

The statements are those of a small imperative language:

datatype *stmt* =
  Empty — no-op
| *Assign vname val* — assignment: $var := val$
| *Seq stmt stmt* — sequence: $c_1; c_2$
| *Cond expr stmt stmt* — conditional: if e then c_1 else c_2
| *While expr stmt* — loop: while e do c

2.1 Preservation of Execution Context

Problem 1 concerns the loss of an execution context through expression reductions which is a design feature of structural semantics. Let us consider a simple example.

Assume we have a structural semantics for our minimalistic imperative language (some rules of a traditional presentation are shown in Fig. 1): we want to translate a program written in this language into an abstract machine. Assume that the states of variable values have the same representation in the two systems: this means we only need to translate the program expression into a directed graph with different nodes corresponding to different expressions obtained by reductions of the initial program expression.

$$\frac{s' = s(v \longmapsto \mathit{eval}\ \mathit{expr}\ s)}{(\mathit{Assign}\ v\ \mathit{expr}, s) \rightarrow (\mathit{Empty}, s')}\ [\text{ASSIGN}]$$

$$\frac{\mathit{eval}\ \mathit{bexp}\ s = \mathit{True}}{(\mathit{Cond}\ \mathit{bexp}\ \mathrm{e1}\ \mathrm{e2}, s) \rightarrow (\mathrm{e1}, s)}\ [\text{CONDT}] \qquad \frac{\mathit{eval}\ \mathit{bexp}\ s = \mathit{False}}{(\mathit{Cond}\ \mathit{bexp}\ \mathrm{e1}\ \mathrm{e2}, s) \rightarrow (\mathrm{e2}, s)}\ [\text{CONDF}]$$

Fig. 1. Semantic rules for the minimal imperative language

On the abstract machine level an *Assign* statement would be represented as a two-state automaton, and the *Cond* as a node with two outgoing edges directed to the automata for the bodies of its branches.

Consider a small program in this language *Cond bexp* (*Assign a* 5) *Empty* and its execution flow.

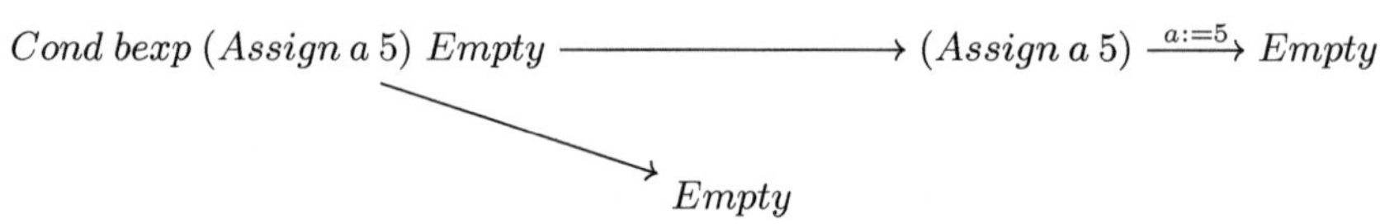

The execution can select any of the two branches depending on the *bexp* value. There are two different *Empty* expressions appearing as results of two different reductions. The corresponding abstract machine would be a natural graph representation for a condition statement with two branches (Fig. 2).

During the simple generation of an abstract machine from a program expression the two *Empty* statements cannot be distinguished although they should be mapped into two different nodes in the graph. We need to add more information about the context into the translation, and it can be done by different ways.

A straightforward solution would be to add some information in order to distinguish between the two *Empty* expressions. If we add unique identifiers to each subexpression of the program, they will allow us to know exactly which subexpression we are translating (Fig. 3). The advantage of this approach is its simplicity, however, it requires additional functions and proofs for identifier management.

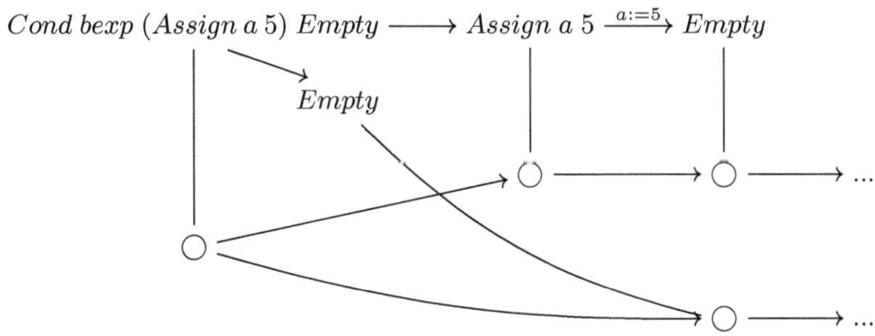

Fig. 2. The execution flow and the corresponding abstract machine for the program *Cond bexp* (*Assign a* 5) *Empty*

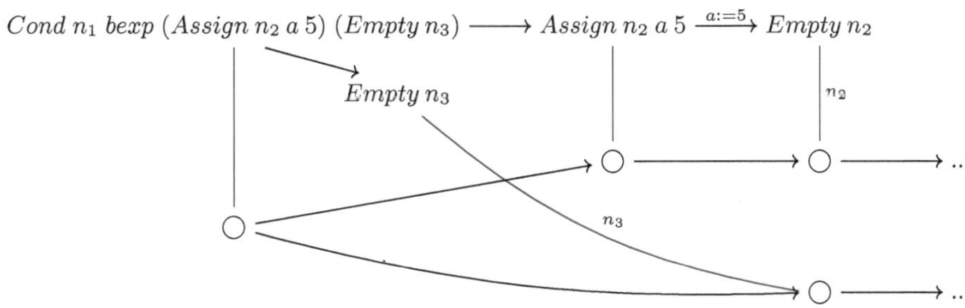

Fig. 3. The execution flow and the corresponding abstract machine for the program with subexpression identifiers *Cond* n_1 *bexp* (*Assign* n_2 *a* 5) (*Empty* n_3)

Another solution for the problem proposed in this paper involves usage of a special data structure to keep the context of the translation. There are known examples of translations from subexpression-based semantics [12] and continuation-based semantics [14] to abstract machines. However, all these translations do not address the problem of context preservation during the translation.

2.2 Semantic Artifacts

The second problem appears because of the double functionality of the *Empty* expression: it is used to define an empty operator which does nothing as well as the final expression for reductions which cannot be further reduced. The typical semantic rules for a sequence of expressions look as shown on Fig. 4.

Here the *Empty* expression means that the first expression in the sequence has been reduced up to the end, and we can start reducing the second expression. However, any imperative language translated to an assembly language would not have an additional operator between the two pieces of code corresponding to the first and the second expressions. The rule SEQ2 must be marked as a silent transition when translated to an automaton, or the semantic rules have to be changed.

$$\frac{(e1, s) \rightarrow (e1', s')}{(Seq\ e1\ e2, s) \rightarrow (Seq\ e1'\ e2, s')}\ [\text{SEQ1}] \qquad \frac{}{(Seq\ Empty\ e2, s) \rightarrow (e2, s)}\ [\text{SEQ2}]$$

Fig. 4. Semantic rules for the sequence of two expressions

3 Zipper-Based Semantics of Imperative Programs

3.1 The Zipper Data Structure

Our plan is to propose an alternative technique to formalize operational semantics that will make it easier to preserve the execution context during the translation to an automata-based formalism. Our technique is built around a zipper data structure, whose purpose is to identify a location in a tree (in our case: a *stmt*) by the subtree below the location and the rest of the tree (in our case: of type *stmt-path*). In order to allow for an easy navigation, the rest of the tree is turned inside-out so that it is possible to reach the root of the tree by following the backwards pointers. The following definition is a straightforward adaptation of the zipper for binary trees discussed in [10] to the *stmt* data type:

datatype *stmt-path* =
  PTop
| *PSeqLeft stmt-path stmt* | *PSeqRight stmt stmt-path*
| *PCondLeft expr stmt-path stmt* | *PCondRight expr stmt stmt-path*
| *PWhile expr stmt-path*

Here, *PTop* represents the root of the original tree, and for each constructor of *stmt* and each of its sub-*stmts*, there is a "hole" of type *stmt-path* where a subtree can be fitted in. A location in a tree is then a combination of a *stmt* and a *stmt-path*:

datatype *stmt-location* = *Loc stmt stmt-path*

Given a location in a tree, the function *reconstruct* reconstructs the original tree *reconstruct* :: *stmt* ⇒ *stmt-path* ⇒ *stmt*, and *reconstruct-loc* (*Loc c sp*) = *reconstruct c sp* does the same for a location.

fun *reconstruct* :: *stmt* ⇒ *stmt-path* ⇒ *stmt* **where**
  reconstruct c PTop = *c*
| *reconstruct c* (*PSeqLeft sp c2*) = *reconstruct* (*Seq c c2*) *sp*
| *reconstruct c* (*PSeqRight c1 sp*) = *reconstruct* (*Seq c1 c*) *sp*
| *reconstruct c* (*PCondLeft e sp c2*) = *reconstruct* (*Cond e c c2*) *sp*
| *reconstruct c* (*PCondRight e c1 sp*) = *reconstruct* (*Cond e c1 c*) *sp*
| *reconstruct c* (*PWhile e sp*) = *reconstruct* (*While e c*) *sp*

fun *reconstruct-loc* :: *stmt-location* ⇒ *stmt* **where**
  reconstruct-loc (*Loc c sp*) = *reconstruct c sp*

3.2 Semantics

Our semantics is a small-step operational semantics describing the effect of the execution of a program on a certain program state. For each variable, the state yields *Some* value associated with the variable, or *None* if the variable is unassigned. More formally, the state is a mapping $vname \Rightarrow val\ option$. Defining the evaluation of an expression in a state is then standard.

Before commenting the rules of our semantics, let us discuss which kind of structure we are manipulating. The semantics essentially consists in moving around a pointer within the syntax tree. As explained in Sect. 3.1, a position in the syntax tree is given by a *stmt-location*. However, during the traversal of the syntax tree, we visit each position at least twice (and possibly several times, for example in a loop): before executing the corresponding statement, and after finishing the execution. We therefore add a Boolean flag, where *True* is a marker for "before" and *False* for "after" execution.

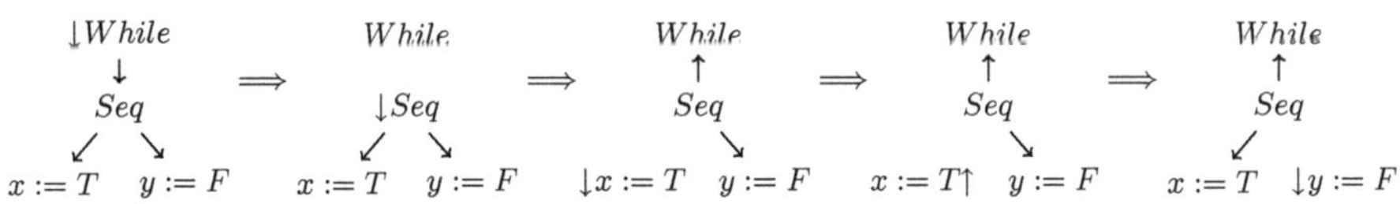

Fig. 5. Example of execution of small-step semantics

As an example, consider the execution sequence depicted in Fig. 5 (with assignments written in a more readable concrete syntax), consisting of the initial steps of the execution of the program $While\ (e,\ Seq(x := T,\ y := F))$. The before (resp. after) marker is indicated by a downward arrow before (resp. an upward arrow behind) the current statement. The condition of the loop is omitted because it is irrelevant here. The middle configuration would be coded as $((Loc\ (x := T)\ (PSeqLeft\ (PWhile\ e\ PTop)\ (y := F))),\ True)$.

Altogether, we obtain a syntactic configuration (*synt-config*) which combines the location and the Boolean flag. The semantic configuration (*sem-config*) manipulated by the semantics adjoins the *state*, as defined previously.

type-synonym *synt-config* = *stmt-location* × *bool*
type-synonym *sem-config* = *synt-config* × *state*

The rules of the small-step semantics of Fig. 7 fall into two categories: before execution of a statement s (of the form $((l,\ True),\ s)$) and after execution (of the form $((l,\ False),\ s)$); there is only one rule of this latter kind: SFALSE.

Let us comment on the rules in detail:

- SEMPTY executes the *Empty* statement just by swapping the Boolean flag.
- SASSIGN is similar, but it also updates the state for the assigned variable.
- SSEQ moves the pointer to the substatement c_1, pushing the substatement c_2 as continuation to the statement path.
- SCONDT and SCONDF move to the *then-* respectively *else-* branch of the conditional, depending on the value of the condition.

$$\begin{array}{l}
\textbf{fun } \textit{next-loc} :: \textit{stmt} \Rightarrow \textit{stmt-path} \Rightarrow (\textit{stmt-location} \times \textit{bool}) \textbf{ where}\\
\quad \textit{next-loc } c \textit{ PTop} = (\textit{Loc } c \textit{ PTop}, \textit{ False})\\
\mid \textit{next-loc } c\ (\textit{PSeqLeft } sp\ c_2) = (\textit{Loc } c_2\ (\textit{PSeqRight } c\ sp),\ \textit{True})\\
\mid \textit{next-loc } c\ (\textit{PSeqRight } c_1\ sp) = (\textit{Loc } (\textit{Seq } c_1\ c)\ sp,\ \textit{False})\\
\mid \textit{next-loc } c\ (\textit{PCondLeft } e\ sp\ c_2) = (\textit{Loc } (\textit{Cond } e\ c\ c_2)\ sp,\ \textit{False})\\
\mid \textit{next-loc } c\ (\textit{PCondRight } e\ c_1\ sp) = (\textit{Loc } (\textit{Cond } e\ c_1\ c)\ sp,\ \textit{False})\\
\mid \textit{next-loc } c\ (\textit{PWhile } e\ sp) = (\textit{Loc } (\textit{While } e\ c)\ sp,\ \textit{True})
\end{array}$$

Fig. 6. Finding the next location

$$\frac{}{((\textit{Loc Empty } sp,\ \textit{True}),\ s) \rightarrow ((\textit{Loc Empty } sp,\ \textit{False}),\ s)}\ [\text{SEmpty}]$$

$$\frac{}{((\textit{Loc } (\textit{Assign } vr\ vl)\ sp,\ \textit{True}),\ s) \rightarrow ((\textit{Loc } (\textit{Assign } vr\ vl)\ sp,\ \textit{False}),\ s(vr \mapsto vl))}\ [\text{SAssign}]$$

$$\frac{}{((\textit{Loc } (\textit{Seq } c_1\ c_2)\ sp,\ \textit{True}),\ s) \rightarrow ((\textit{Loc } c_1\ (\textit{PSeqLeft } sp\ c_2),\ \textit{True}),\ s)}\ [\text{SSeq}]$$

$$\frac{\textit{eval } e\ s = \textit{Bool True}}{((\textit{Loc } (\textit{Cond } e\ c_1\ c_2)\ sp,\ \textit{True}),\ s) \rightarrow ((\textit{Loc } c_1\ (\textit{PCondLeft } e\ sp\ c_2),\ \textit{True}),\ s)}\ [\text{SCondT}]$$

$$\frac{\textit{eval } e\ s = \textit{Bool False}}{((\textit{Loc } (\textit{Cond } e\ c_1\ c_2)\ sp,\ \textit{True}),\ s) \rightarrow ((\textit{Loc } c_2\ (\textit{PCondRight } e\ c_1\ sp),\ \textit{True}),\ s)}\ [\text{SCondF}]$$

$$\frac{\textit{eval } e\ s = \textit{Bool True}}{((\textit{Loc } (\textit{While } e\ c)\ sp,\ \textit{True}),\ s) \rightarrow ((\textit{Loc } c\ (\textit{PWhile } e\ sp),\ \textit{True}),\ s)}\ [\text{SWhileT}]$$

$$\frac{\textit{eval } e\ s = \textit{Bool False}}{((\textit{Loc } (\textit{While } e\ c)\ sp,\ \textit{True}),\ s) \rightarrow ((\textit{Loc } (\textit{While } e\ c)\ sp,\ \textit{False}),\ s)}\ [\text{SWhileF}]$$

$$\frac{sp \neq \textit{PTop}}{((\textit{Loc } c\ sp,\ \textit{False}),\ s) \rightarrow (\textit{next-loc } c\ sp,\ s)}\ [\text{SFalse}]$$

Fig. 7. Small-step operational semantics

- SWhileT moves to the body of the loop.
- SWhileF declares the execution of the loop as terminated, by setting the Boolean flag to *False*.
- SFalse comes into play when execution of the current statement is finished. We then move to the next location, provided we have not already reached the root of the syntax tree and the whole program terminates.

The move to the next relevant location is accomplished by function *next-loc* (Fig. 6) which intuitively works as follows: upon conclusion of the first substatement in a sequence, we move to the second substatement. When finishing the body of a loop, we move back to the beginning of the loop. In all other cases, we move up the syntax tree, waiting for rule SFALSE to relaunch the function.

4 Target Language: Automata

4.1 Syntax

As usual, our automata are a collection of nodes and edges, with a distinguished initial state. In this general definition, we will keep the node type *'n* abstract. It will later be instantiated to *synt-config*. An edge connects two nodes; moving along an edge may trigger an assignment to a variable (*AssAct*), or have no effect at all (*NoAct*).

An automaton *'n ta* is a record consisting of a set of *nodes*, a set of *edges* and an initial node *init-s*. An edge has a *source* node, an *action* and a destination node *dest*. Components of a record are written between ⦇ ... ⦈.

4.2 Semantics

An automaton state is a node, together with a *state* as in Sect. 3.2.

type-synonym *'n ta-state* = *'n* ∗ *state*

Executing a step of an automaton in an automaton state (l, s) consists of selecting an edge starting in node l, moving to the target of the edge and executing its action. Automata are non-deterministic; in this simplified model, we have no guards for selecting edges.

$$\frac{l = \mathit{source}\ e \qquad e \in \mathit{set}\ (\mathit{edges}\ \mathit{aut}) \quad l' = \mathit{dest}\ e \qquad s' = \mathit{action\text{-}effect}\ (\mathit{action}\ e)\ s}{\mathit{aut} \vdash (l,\ s) \rightarrow (l',\ s')}\ [\text{ACTION}]$$

5 Automata Construction

The principle of abstracting a statement to an automaton is simple; the novelty resides in the way the automaton is generated via the zipper structure: as nodes, we choose the locations of the statements (with their Boolean flags), and as edges all possible transitions of the semantics.

To make this precise, we need some auxiliary functions. We first define a function *all-locations* of type *stmt* ⇒ *stmt-path* ⇒ *stmt-location list* which gathers all locations in a statement, and a function *nodes-of-stmt-locations* which adds the Boolean flags.

As for the edges, the function *synt-step-image* yields all possible successor configurations for a given syntactic configuration. This is of course an over-approximation of the behavior of the semantics, since some of the source tree locations may be unreachable during execution.

fun *synt-step-image* :: *synt-config* ⇒ *synt-config list* **where**
synt-step-image (*Loc Empty sp*, *True*) = [(*Loc Empty sp*, *False*)]
| *synt-step-image* (*Loc* (*Assign vr vl*) *sp*, *True*) = [(*Loc* (*Assign vr vl*) *sp*, *False*)]
| *synt-step-image* (*Loc* (*Seq c1 c2*) *sp*, *True*) = [(*Loc c1* (*PSeqLeft sp c2*), *True*)]
| *synt-step-image* (*Loc* (*Cond e c1 c2*) *sp*, *True*) =
[(*Loc c1* (*PCondLeft e sp c2*), *True*), (*Loc c2* (*PCondRight e c1 sp*), *True*)]
| *synt-step-image* (*Loc* (*While e c*) *sp*, *True*) =
[(*Loc c* (*PWhile e sp*), *True*), (*Loc* (*While e c*) *sp*, *False*)]
| *synt-step-image* (*Loc c sp*, *False*) = (*if sp* = *PTop then* [] *else* [*next-loc c sp*])

Together with the following definitions:

fun *action-of-synt-config* :: *synt-config* ⇒ *action* **where**
action-of-synt-config (*Loc* (*Assign vn vl*) *sp*, *True*) = *AssAct vn vl*
| *action-of-synt-config* (*Loc c sp*, *b*) = *NoAct*

definition *edge-of-synt-config* :: *synt-config* ⇒ *synt-config edge list* **where**
edge-of-synt-config s =
map(λ *t*. ⦇*source* = *s*, *action* = *action-of-synt-config s*, *dest* = *t*⦈)(*synt-step-image s*)
definition *edges-of-nodes* :: *synt-config list* ⇒ *synt-config edge list* **where**
edges-of-nodes nds = *concat* (*map edge-of-synt-config nds*)

we can define the translation function from statements to automata:

fun *stmt-to-ta* :: *stmt* ⇒ *synt-config ta* **where**
stmt-to-ta c =
(*let nds* = *nodes-of-stmt-locations* (*all-locations c PTop*) *in*
⦇ *nodes* = *nds*, *edges* = *edges-of-nodes nds*, *init-s* = ((*Loc c PTop*), *True*) ⦈)

6 Simulation Property

We recall that the nodes of the automaton generated by *stmt-to-ta* are labeled by configurations (location, Boolean flag) of the syntax tree. The simulation lemma (Lemma 1) holds for automata with appropriate closure properties: a successor configuration wrt. a transition of the semantics is also a label of the automaton (*nodes-closed*), and analogously for edges (*edges-closed*) or both nodes and edges (*synt-step-image-closed*).

The simulation statement is a typical commuting-diagram property: a step of the program semantics can be simulated by a step of the automaton semantics, for corresponding program and automata states. For this correspondence, we use the notation ≈, even though it is just plain syntactic equality in our case.

Lemma 1 (Simulation property)
Assume that synt-step-image-closed aut and (((*lc*, *b*), *s*) ≈ ((*lca*, *ba*), *sa*)). *If* ((*lc*, *b*), *s*) → ((*lc′*, *b′*), *s′*), *then there exist lca′*, *ba′*, *sa′ such that* (*lca′*, *ba′*) ∈ *set* (*nodes aut*) *and the automaton performs the same transition: aut* ⊢ ((*lca*, *ba*), *sa*) → ((*lca′*, *ba′*), *sa′*) *and* ((*lc′*, *b′*), *s′*) ≈ ((*lca′*, *ba′*), *sa′*).

The proof is a simple induction over the transition relation of the program semantics and is almost fully automatic in the Isabelle proof assistant.

We now want to get rid of the precondition *synt-step-image-closed aut* in Lemma 1. The first subcase (edge closure), is easy to prove. Node closure is more difficult and requires the following key lemma:

Lemma 2
If lc $\in$ *set* (*all-locations c PTop*) *then set* (*map fst* (*synt-step-image* (*lc*, *b*))) $\subseteq$ *set* (*all-locations c PTop*).

With this, we obtain the desired.

Lemma 3 (Closure of automaton). *synt-step-image-closed (stmt-to-ta c).*

For the proofs, see [6].

Let us combine the previous results and write them more succinctly, by using the notation $\rightarrow^*$ for the reflexive-transitive closure for the transition relations of the small-step semantics and the automaton. Whenever a state is reachable by executing a program c in its initial configuration, then a corresponding ($\approx$) state is reachable by running the automaton generated with function *stmt-to-ta*:

Theorem 1
If ((*Loc c PTop*, *True*), *s*) $\rightarrow^*$ (*cf'*, *s'*) *then* $\exists$ *cfa' sa'*. *stmt-to-ta c* $\vdash$ (*init-s* (*stmt-to-ta c*), *s*) $\rightarrow^*$ (*cfa'*, *sa'*) $\wedge$ (*cf'*, *s'*) $\approx$ (*cfa'*, *sa'*).

Obviously, the initial configuration of the semantics and the automaton are in the simulation relation $\approx$, and for the inductive step, we use Lemma 1.

7 Relationship with Big-Step Semantics

The rules of the zipper-based semantics (Fig. 7) share an unusual feature: none of them is recursive. In other words, while in standard small-step semantics a transition is usually defined by a derivation tree built by combining several rules, in our semantics the derivation is a very simple "tree" composed of a single rule. This is a distinguishing characteristic of zipper semantics, which can be understood better when we consider, at least informally, how it relates to other styles, and to natural (big-step) semantics in particular.

For this reason, let us take a look at the evaluation of a simple statement (the sequential composition of three assignments) of our minimalistic language according to both styles. For natural semantics, we use the notation $s, c \Downarrow s'$ to mean that a complete evaluation of the statement c in the state s yields an updated state s'. Moreover, syntactic sugar is used for conciseness to represent assignment, sequential composition, and Boolean values.

$$\dfrac{\dfrac{s, a := T \Downarrow s(a \mapsto T) \qquad s(a \mapsto T), b := F \Downarrow s(a \mapsto T, b \mapsto F)}{s, (a := T; b := F) \Downarrow s(a \mapsto T, b \mapsto F)} \qquad s(a \mapsto T, b \mapsto F), c := a \Downarrow s(a \mapsto T, b \mapsto F, c \mapsto T)}{s, (a := T; b := F; c := a) \Downarrow s(a \mapsto T, b \mapsto F, c \mapsto T)}$$

The corresponding evaluation in zipper-based semantics is a chain of transitions (... is used to omit the parts of the zipper that are not relevant here):

$$
\begin{aligned}
&((\mathit{Loc}\ (a := T; b := F; c := a)\ \mathit{PTop}, \mathit{True}), s)\\
\rightarrow\ &((\mathit{Loc}\ (a := T; b := F)\ \ldots, \mathit{True}), s)\\
\rightarrow\ &((\mathit{Loc}\ (a := T)\ \ldots, \mathit{True}), s)\\
\rightarrow\ &((\mathit{Loc}\ (a := T)\ \ldots, \mathit{False}), s(a \mapsto T))\\
\rightarrow\ &((\mathit{Loc}\ (b := F)\ \ldots, \mathit{True}), s(a \mapsto T))\\
\rightarrow\ &((\mathit{Loc}\ (b := F)\ \ldots, \mathit{False}), s(a \mapsto T, b \mapsto F))\\
\rightarrow\ &((\mathit{Loc}\ (a := T; b := F)\ \ldots, \mathit{False}), s(a \mapsto T, b \mapsto F))\\
\rightarrow\ &((\mathit{Loc}\ (c := a)\ \ldots, \mathit{True}), s(a \mapsto T, b \mapsto F))\\
\rightarrow\ &((\mathit{Loc}\ (c := a)\ \ldots, \mathit{False}), s(a \mapsto T, b \mapsto F, c \mapsto T))\\
\rightarrow\ &((\mathit{Loc}\ (a := T; b := F; c := a)\ \mathit{PTop}, \mathit{False}), s(a \mapsto T, b \mapsto F, c \mapsto T))
\end{aligned}
$$

The reader can directly verify that each transition in the zipper semantics corresponds to a step in the depth first visit of the derivation tree in big-step semantics. In particular, when the zipper is flagged with the Boolean *True*, the visit is proceeding from the root towards the leaves; when the flag is *False*, we are going back from the leaves to the root.

This is true in general: the steps of a complete evaluation of a statement in zipper semantics (i.e. a chain of transitions ending on *PTop* and flagged with *False*) are in one-one correspondence with the steps of the depth-first visit of an equivalent derivation tree in big-step semantics, and vice-versa. The zipper can then be explained as a structure which keeps track of the current position in the visit of the derivation tree: since the derivation tree is coherent with the AST of the statement being evaluated, a zipper on the AST can often be used as a more convenient alternative to a zipper on the derivation tree. We will make this remark more precise, although without pretense of being entirely formal.

The rules of big-step semantics, in the most general form, derive a conclusion $c, s \Downarrow s'$ from a fixed number of recursive premises of the same form, possibly guarded by a side condition. We present a technique to obtain a zipper-based semantics equivalent to a given big-step semantics, under the following simplifying assumptions:

- each evaluation judgment of the big-step semantics distinguishes an input (the statement c and the initial state s) and an output (the final state s');
- in the case of the evaluation of a compound statement, the recursive premises correspond to the evaluation of some of its sub-statements, or to another evaluation of the compound statement (generally, in an updated state);
- the recursive premises of all rules are listed naturally according to the order of evaluation, in such a way that the output of a premise can be employed as part of the input of the following premises;
- a single side condition is evaluated before all other premises (it can, therefore, refer to the input of the conclusion judgment, but to no other input or output).

In symbols, the evaluation of a compound statement $(T\ \overrightarrow{z}\ c_1 \cdots c_n)$ (where the c_i are its sub-statements and $\overrightarrow{z}$ its other sub-expressions) will be enacted by rules in the following form:

$$\frac{\begin{array}{c} d_1, s_0 \Downarrow s_1 \\ d_1, s_1 \Downarrow s_2 \\ \cdots \\ d_k, s_{k-1} \Downarrow s_k \end{array}}{(T\ \overrightarrow{z}\ c_1 \cdots c_n), s_0 \Downarrow f(s_k, (T\ \overrightarrow{z}\ c_1 \cdots c_n))} \quad (\text{if } P((T\ \overrightarrow{z}\ c_1 \cdots c_n), s_0))$$

where:

- each d_i is either a sub-statement c_j (for some j) or the full compound statement $(T\ \overrightarrow{z}\ c_1 \cdots c_n)$
- the function f is used to allow some final manipulation of the state s_k according to the shape of the statement $(T\ \overrightarrow{z}\ c_1 \cdots c_n)$.

The big-step rule is translated to $k+1$ zipper-based rules (where k is the number of recursive premises). In the zipper rules, configurations are composed of a statement location, a Boolean representing whether we are at the beginning or at the end of the execution of the statement, and the state, as in the case of our small imperative language. To state the translation, we assume that the evaluated statement $(T\ \overrightarrow{z}\ c_1 \cdots c_n)$ is located in a generic path *sp*. If we use $PT_1, \ldots, PT_n$ as names for the statement path constructors corresponding to the statement constructor T, we can express the locations l_i associated to each of the statements d_i of the rule premises as follows:

- if $d_i = c_j$, then $l_i = \mathit{Loc}\ c_j\ (PT_j\ sp\ \overrightarrow{z}\ c_1 \cdots c_{j-1}\ c_{j+1} \cdots c_n)$
- if $d_i = (T\ \overrightarrow{z}\ c_1 \cdots c_n)$, then $l_i = \mathit{Loc}\ (T\ \overrightarrow{z}\ c_1 \cdots c_n)\ sp$.

Then, we produce the following zipper-based rules:

- one initial rule:

$$\frac{P((T\ \overrightarrow{z}\ c_1 \cdots c_n), s_0)}{((\mathit{Loc}\ (T\ \overrightarrow{z}\ c_1 \cdots c_n)\ sp, \mathit{True}), s) \rightarrow ((l_1, \mathit{True}), s)}$$

- $k-1$ intermediate rules, one for each $i = 1, \ldots, k-1$:

$$((l_i, \mathit{False}), s) \rightarrow ((l_{i+1}, \mathit{True}), s)$$

- one final rule:

$$((l_k, \mathit{False}), s) \rightarrow ((\mathit{Loc}\ (T\ \overrightarrow{z}\ c_1 \cdots c_n)\ sp, \mathit{False}), f(s, (T\ \overrightarrow{z}\ c_1 \cdots c_n)))$$

In the special case where $k = 0$, i.e. there are no recursive premises, everything collapses to a single translated rule:

$$\frac{P((T\ \overrightarrow{z}\ c_1 \cdots c_n), s_0)}{\begin{array}{l}((\mathit{Loc}\ (T\ \overrightarrow{z}\ c_1 \cdots c_n)\ sp, \mathit{True}), s) \rightarrow \\ \quad ((\mathit{Loc}\ (T\ \overrightarrow{z}\ c_1 \cdots c_n)\ sp, \mathit{False}), f(s, (T\ \overrightarrow{z}\ c_1 \cdots c_n)))\end{array}}$$

In the case of our minimalistic language, the zipper on the statement is a precise approximation of a zipper on the derivation tree of big-step semantics: this allows us to state the two semantics are equivalent:

Fact 2. *For all statement paths sp, we have*

$$c, s \Downarrow s' \Longleftrightarrow ((Loc\ c\ sp, True), s) \rightarrow^* ((Loc\ c\ sp, False), s')$$

In the case of more complex languages, the $\Longleftarrow$ direction might not hold if the zipper on statements does not univocally identify positions in the big-step evaluation tree. In this case, the zipper semantics can be obtained by annotating each node of the statement-path with the name of the last big-step rule traversed, or by replacing the zipper on statements with a zipper on the derivation tree of big-step evaluations.

As a final remark, let us note that the zipper-based semantics for the minimalistic language presented in the previous sections is an easy refinement of the one we have just described, where all the zipper rules whose source has a *False* flag (i.e. those that we have called *intermediate* and *final*) have been replaced by a single SFALSE rule, employing a *next-loc* function to determine the following location.

8 Conclusions

This paper has presented a new kind of small-step semantics for imperative programming languages, based on the zipper data structure. Our primary aim is to show that this semantics has decisive advantages for abstracting programming language semantics to automata. Even if the generated automata have a great number of silent transitions, these can be removed.

We are currently in the process of adopting this semantics in a larger formalization from Java to Timed Automata [5,8]. As most constructs (zipper data structure, mapping to automata) are generic, we think that this kind of semantics could prove useful for similar formalizations with other source languages. The proofs (here carried out with the Isabelle proof assistant) have a pleasingly high degree of automation that are in sharp contrast with the index calculations that are usually required when naming automata states with numbers.

Renaming nodes from source tree locations to numbers is nevertheless easy to carry out, see the code snippet provided on the web page [6] of this paper. For these reasons, we think that the underlying ideas could also be useful in the context of compiler verification, when converting a structured source program to a flow graph with basic blocs, but before committing to numeric values of jump targets.

References

1. Alur, R., Courcoubetis, C., Dill, D.L.: Model-checking for real-time systems. In: LICS, pp. 414–425. IEEE Computer Society (1990)
2. Alur, R., Dill, D.L.: A theory of timed automata. Theor. Comput. Sci. **126**, 183–235 (1994)

3. Appel, A.W., Blazy, S.: Separation logic for small-step CMINOR. In: Schneider, K., Brandt, J. (eds.) TPHOLs 2007. LNCS, vol. 4732, pp. 5–21. Springer, Heidelberg (2007)
4. Baier, C., Katoen, J.-P.: Principles of Model Checking. MIT Press, Cambridge (2008)
5. Baklanova, N.: Semantics and Proof Methods for a Real-Time Modeling Language. PhD thesis, Université de Toulouse (2014)
6. Baklanova, N., Ricciotti, W., Smaus, J.-G., Strecker, M.: Abstracting an operational semantics to finite automata (formalization) (2014). https://bitbucket.org/Martin_Strecker/abstracting_op_sem_to_automata
7. Baklanova, N., Ricciotti, W., Smaus, J.-G., Strecker, M.: Abstracting an operational semantics to finite automata. In: Proceedings of the 11th International Conference on ICT in Education, Research and Industrial Applications: Integration, Harmonization and Knowledge Transfer, Lviv, Ukraine, 14–16 May 2015, pp. 354–365 (2015)
8. Baklanova, N., Strecker, M.: Abstraction and verification of properties of a real-time java. In: Ermolayev, V., Mayr, H.C., Nikitchenko, M., Spivakovsky, A., Zholtkevych, G. (eds.) ICTERI 2012. CCIS, vol. 347, pp. 1–18. Springer, Heidelberg (2013)
9. Bengtsson, J.E., Yi, W.: Timed automata: semantics, algorithms and tools. In: Desel, J., Reisig, W., Rozenberg, G. (eds.) Lectures on Concurrency and Petri Nets. LNCS, vol. 3098, pp. 87–124. Springer, Heidelberg (2004)
10. Huet, G.: Functional pearl: the zipper. J. Funct. Program. **7**(5), 549–554 (1997)
11. Khoussainov, B., Nerode, A.: Automata Theory and Its Applications. Birkhauser, Boston (2001)
12. Klein, G., Nipkow, T.: A machine-checked model for a Java-like language, virtual machine, and compiler. ACM Trans. Program. Lang. Syst. **28**, 619–695 (2006)
13. Krebbers, R., Wiedijk, F.: Separation logic for non-local control flow and block scope variables. In: Pfenning, F. (ed.) FOSSACS 2013 (ETAPS 2013). LNCS, vol. 7794, pp. 257–272. Springer, Heidelberg (2013)
14. Leroy, X.: A formally verified compiler back-end. J. Autom. Reasoning **43**(4), 363–446 (2009)
15. Nipkow, T., Paulson, L., Wenzel, M.: Isabelle/HOL: A Proof Assistant for Higher-Order Logic. Lecture Notes in Computer Science, vol. 2283. Springer, Heidelberg (2002)
16. Winskel, G.: The Formal Semantics of Programming Languages: An Introduction. MIT Press, Cambridge (1993)

Realisation of Synchronous and Asynchronous Black Boxes Using Machines

Grygoriy Zholtkevych(✉)

School of Mathematics and Computer Science, V.N. Karazin Kharkiv National University, 4 Svobody Sqr., Kharkiv 61022, Ukraine
g.zholtkevych@karazin.ua

Abstract. The intensive development of global solutions that are based on the integration of heterogeneous applications and that do not impede re-engineering leads to the dominance of information systems implemented in accordance with an event-driven architecture. This trend attracts attention of researchers to systems based on event stream processing. In the paper it is proposed to distinguish two classes of event stream processing systems, namely, systems specified by black boxes with synchronous and asynchronous dependences between input and output streams; it is given the definitions for nonanticipation property for black boxes from these two classes; it is shown that such black boxes can be implemented with using machines: Moore machines for synchronous black boxes and pre-machines for asynchronous black boxes.

Keywords: Open system · Black box · Event stream processing · Nonanticipation · State machine · Implementation problem

1 Introduction

A black box is a basic concepts of cybernetics [2]. Actually, specifying the black box that is associated with a system we determine the boundary of the system. In this context the design process of any system can be comprehended as a transformation of the black box that specifies the system being designed into the glass box that implements this black box. Thus, the problem of searching an answer on the question "Does there exist an implementation of the given black box?" is an important problem not only for the general theory of systems and cybernetics in whole, but also for the practice of the system engineering.

In the context of mathematical research a black box is completely specified by its transfer relation (or transfer function if the relation is functional) [7]. This relation determines the dependence on the input impacts of the system responses. As a rule, it is suggested that this dependence is synchronous, i.e. each prime impact causes some response. The implementation problem of a black box has been studied and solved under this suggestion [6,9, and other].

Although the suggestion about synchronisation of input and output is quite natural, but the practice of system engineering shows that it does not hold for

V. Yakovyna et al. (Eds.): ICTERI 2015, CCIS 594, pp. 124–139, 2016.
DOI: 10.1007/978-3-319-30246-1_8

all kinds of systems. The use of event-driven architecture [8] leads to software systems that do not satisfy this suggestion. Event-based architecture enables to decouple components of a system that is making this architectural approach adequate for constructing global scalable distributed systems such as Internet-of-Things [1].

Summing up of this reasoning we can claim that studying the implementation problem of a black box, whose output depends on its input asynchronously, is a topical problem.

The main results of this article were first presented at the XI Conference ICTERI 2015 [10] but as one can see the mentioned text has been essentially improved. Particularly, we have added the section devoted to the formal definition of the concept "nonanticipation" for asynchronous black boxes. Therefore this new text can be considered as independent on the mentioned.

This paper has the following structure:

- Section 2 contains a discussion of prerequisites for the implementation problem, the definition of synchronous and asynchronous black boxes, definitions of basic concepts, and the necessary notation;
- Section 3 explains how the non anticipation property can be generalised for the case of asynchronous black boxes;
- Section 4 contains solution of the implementation problem.

2 Motivation and Preliminaries

In this section, the necessity to introduce the concept of an asynchronous black box is motivated. Then we give the notation and necessary formal definitions to specify the mathematical models of the corresponding objects.

2.1 Synchronous and Asynchronous Black Boxes

The traditional approach to the description of a system as a black box suggests that each input impact is accompanied by synchronised with it system response that, in general, depends on the sequence of all previous impacts (see Fig. 1). Most researchers take this approach when the specification problem for the external behaviour of a system is discussed. This approach was adopted also

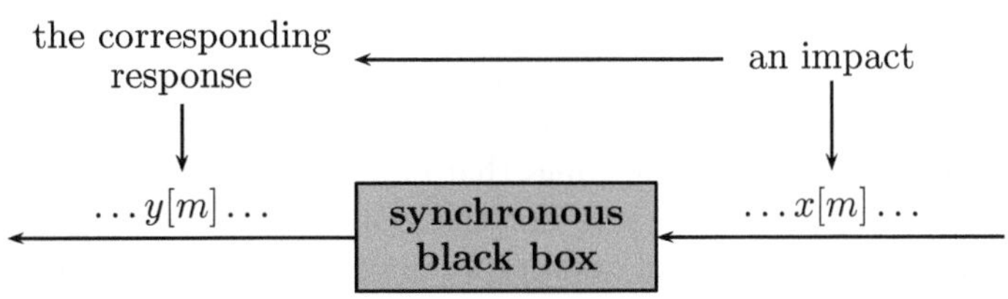

Fig. 1. A synchronous black box

by M.D. Mesarovic and Y. Takahara to build a mathematical model of dynamical systems [7]. In the context of this paper, this approach is studied in detail in [6,9].

However, a synchronous interaction is not typical for distributed systems that are now being built in accordance with the event-driven architecture and its modifications. The paper [5] presents the main examples of applications that require asynchronous approach to modelling the corresponding black boxes. We cite some of these examples.

Example 1. See [5, p. 7, Example 1]. A patient is hooked up to multiple monitors that perform various measurements. The measurements take the form of events, which are then analysed by an event processing system. The system can be configured individually for each patient. Some combinations of events can be identified as threats. This example demonstrates the use of event processing to allow timely response to emergency situations for patients.

Example 2. See [5, p. 7, Example 2]. In an airline luggage handling system a radio-frequency identification (RFID) tag is attached to every piece of luggage. RFID readers are located along the luggage route (the sorting device, the cart going to the aircraft, the aircrafts unloading dock, and more). Events from the RFID readers are analysed to provide exception alerts, such as luggage is on the wrong cart; luggage did not arrive at the aircraft; luggage did not even arrive at the sorting device; as well as a routine alert when luggage is approaching the carousel. This example demonstrates the use of event processing for detecting and eliminating errors within an automated processing system.

Example 3. See [5, p. 8, Example 5]. A financial institution wishes to detect frauds or a financial regulator wishes to catch illegal trading patterns. They collect events from banking or trading systems and analyze them. Certain patterns of activity might suggest that a person is possibly (but not necessarily) in the process of committing a fraud or other illegal activity. This example demonstrates the use of event processing to detect evolving phenomena.

Example 4. See [5, p. 8, Example 6]. An emergency control system informs and directs first responders and people at risk in case of an incident (for example, a fire or the leakage of hazardous materials). In this case the event is a report on an incident, and the main focus of the system is the dissemination of information: who should be informed about what and at what time, given the nature of the incident.

Example 5. See [5, p. 8, Example 8]. A manufacturing plant management system diagnoses mechanical failures based on observable symptoms. In this case the events are symptoms, describing things that do not work properly, and the main purpose of the event processing is to find the root cause of these symptoms. This example demonstrates the use of event processing for problem determination and resolution.

Example 6. See [5, p. 9, Example 10]. A social networking site starts a multi-party chat when five people from a group are online. In this case an event occurs when a person goes online or offline. Event processing is used to analyse these events to decide when to start a chat session. This example demonstrates the use of event processing for real-time collaboration.

These examples demonstrate that synchronous handling of event streams cannot be used to solve the corresponding problems and we need to utilize a solution similar to the one that is shown in Fig. 2.

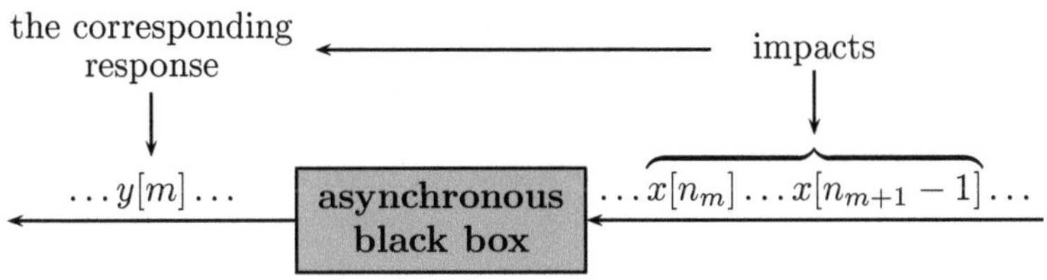

Fig. 2. An asynchronous black box

These examples show also that an asynchronous behaviour is typical for various classes of systems and studying an asynchronous black box has not only theoretical interest.

2.2 Basic Definitions and Notation

Here we give brief survey of some matters and explain the basic notation used below.

At the paper we use the denotation $\mathbb{N}$ for the natural series with 0.

For a set X (it is usually finite) we use the notation:

- X^* denotes the set of all finite sequences (words) whose elements belong to X;
- ε denotes the empty word;
- X^+ denotes the set $X^* \setminus \{\varepsilon\}$;
- X^ω denotes the set of all (infinite) sequences whose elements belong to X;
- X^∞ denotes the union of the sets X^* and X^ω.

Further, we use the denotation $\|\boldsymbol{u}\|$ for the length of the word $\boldsymbol{u} \in X^*$ and assume that $\|\boldsymbol{x}\| = +\infty$ for any infinite sequence $\boldsymbol{x} \in X^\omega$.

To refer to the k-th member of a word $\boldsymbol{u} \in X^*$ (or a sequence $\boldsymbol{x} \in X^\omega$) the denotation $\boldsymbol{u}[k]$ (or $\boldsymbol{x}[k]$ respectively) is used.

For a word $\boldsymbol{u} \in X^*$ whose length is equal or greater than n (or a sequence $\boldsymbol{x} \in X^\omega$) by $\boldsymbol{u}[0:n]$ (or $\boldsymbol{x}[0:n]$ respectively) we denote the word $u[0] \dots u[n-1]$ (or $x[0] \dots x[n-1]$).

Similarly, for a word $\boldsymbol{u} \in X^*$ whose length is greater than or equal to n (or a sequence $\boldsymbol{x} \in X^\omega$) by $\boldsymbol{u}[n:]$ (or $\boldsymbol{x}[n:]$ respectively) we denote the word $u[n] \dots u[\|\boldsymbol{u}\| - 1]$ (or the sequence $x[n]x[n+1] \dots$).

We use also the denotation $\boldsymbol{u} \cdot X^{\omega}$ (or $\boldsymbol{u} \cdot X^{*}$) where $\boldsymbol{u} \in X^{+}$ to refer to the set of all sequences (or words respectively) whose beginnings coincide with $\boldsymbol{u}$.

Taking into account that below we deal with partially defined mappings the following notation is introduced:

$f\colon X \dashrightarrow Y$	denotes the partial mapping f from the set X into the set Y;
$f(x)\uparrow$	denotes that the partial function f is not defined on the element x;
$f(x)\downarrow$	denotes that the partial function f is defined on the element x;
$f(x)\downarrow= y$	denotes that the partial function f is defined on the element x and the corresponding value equals y.

Finally, some class of subsets in X^{*} (or X^{∞}) plays an important role further, namely: a subset $A \subset X^{*}$ (or $A \subset X^{\infty}$) is called prefix-closed if for any $n \in \mathbb{N}$ and $\boldsymbol{x} \in A$ such that $\|\boldsymbol{x}\| > n$ the word $\boldsymbol{x}[0:n]$ belongs A.

3 Nonanticipation Property for Black Boxes

A real open system must meet the requirement: its response can depend only on information received in the past and the present, and the response has no chance to depend on any information from the future. Therefore, correct models describing open systems cannot have ability to predict unerringly future. Such an inability to predict unerringly the future is referred the nonanticipation property.

In this section we remind the definition of the nonanticipation property for a black box, whose output depends on input synchronously. Then we generalise this definition for the case of an asynchronous interdependence between input and output. Finally, we discuss logical correspondences between these definitions.

3.1 Nonanticipation Property: Case of Synchronous Black Box

Thus we begin by recalling the case definition of nonanticipation property for a black box with a functional transfer relation.

Definition 1. *We say that a mapping $T\colon X^{\omega} \to Y^{\infty}$ satisfies the* ***synchronous nonanticipation property*** *(briefly SN-property) if*

$$\begin{aligned}&\textit{for any } \boldsymbol{x} \in X^{\omega},\quad n \in \mathbb{N} \textit{ such that } n \leq \|T\boldsymbol{x}\|, \textit{ and} \\ &\boldsymbol{x}' \in \boldsymbol{x}[0:n] \cdot X^{\omega} \textit{ the following equation is fulfilled:} \\ &(T\boldsymbol{x}')[0:n] = (T\boldsymbol{x})[0:n].\end{aligned} \tag{SN}$$

Example 7 (Main Example for the SN-property). Let a partial mapping $A\colon X^{+} \dashrightarrow Y$ with the prefix-closed domain be given then we can define the mapping $T_A\colon X^{\omega} \to Y^{\infty}$ using Algorithm 1. It is easy to see that the mapping T_A defined by Algorithm 1 satisfies the SN-property.

We sum up the discussion of Example 7 in the following proposition.

Require: $\boldsymbol{x} \in X^{\omega}$ and $A\colon X^{+} \dashrightarrow Y$ with the prefix-closed domain
Ensure: printing the output sequence corresponding to $T_A\boldsymbol{x}$

buff = [ ]
while True **:**
  evnt, $\boldsymbol{x} = \boldsymbol{x}[0], \boldsymbol{x}[1:]$
  buff.*append*(evnt)
  if A(buff)$\uparrow$ **: continue**
  else : *print*(A(buff))

Algorithm 1: The Operational Definition for T_A

Proposition 1. *Let $A\colon X^{+} \dashrightarrow Y$ be a partial mapping with the prefix-closed domain then Algorithm 1 defines uniquely the mapping $T_A\colon X^{\omega} \to Y^{\infty}$, which satisfies the SN-property.*

Note that the converse statement is evidently true too.

Proposition 2. *If a mapping $T\colon X^{\omega} \to Y^{\infty}$ satisfies the SN-property then there exists the unique partial mapping $A\colon X^{+} \dashrightarrow Y$ with the prefix-closed domain such that $T \simeq T_A$.*

Proof. Indeed, one can define the required partial mapping A as follows:

if for $\boldsymbol{u} \in X^{+}$ the exists $\boldsymbol{x} \in \boldsymbol{u} \cdot X^{\omega}$ such that $\|\boldsymbol{u} \leq \|T\boldsymbol{x}\|\|$ then
$$A\boldsymbol{u}\downarrow = (T\boldsymbol{x})[\|\boldsymbol{u}\| - 1]$$
otherwise $A\boldsymbol{u}\uparrow$.

The SN-property ensures the correctness of this definition, prefix-closedness of the domain for A, and the validity of the equality $T \simeq T_A$. □

Thus, we may combine the Propositions 1 and 2 in the following theorem.

Theorem 1. *Let $T\colon X^{\omega} \to Y^{\infty}$ be a mapping then T satisfies the SN-property if and only if there exists the partial mapping $A\colon X^{+} \dashrightarrow Y$ with prefix-closed domain such that $T \simeq T_A$.*

Note 1. Of course, the results of this subsection are known (see, for example, [9]) and we mentioned about them only for completeness of the presentation.

3.2 Nonanticipation Property: Case of Asynchronous Black Box

In this subsection we define the non anticipation property for the case whenever input and output of the black box are in an asynchronous interdependence.

Definition 2. *We say that a mapping $T\colon X^{\omega} \to Y^{\infty}$ satisfies the **asynchronous nonanticipation property** (briefly AN-property) if*

for any $\boldsymbol{x} \in X^{\omega}$ and $n \in \mathbb{N}$ the inequality $n \leq \|T\boldsymbol{x}\|$ implies the existence of $k \geq n$ such that for every $\boldsymbol{x}' \in \boldsymbol{x}[0:k] \cdot X^{\omega}$ the following is true: $(T\boldsymbol{x}')[0:n] = (T\boldsymbol{x})[0:n]$. (AN)

Example 8 (Main Example for the AN-property). Let a partial mapping $A\colon X^+ \dashrightarrow Y$ be given then we can define the mapping $T_A\colon X^\omega \to Y^\infty$ using Algorithm 1.

It is easy to see that the mapping T_A defined by Algorithm 1 satisfies the AN-property. Indeed, for $\boldsymbol{x} \in X^\omega$ and n such that $n \leq \|T_A\boldsymbol{x}\|$ we choose as k the number of iteration that prints n-th output symbol. This choice ensures the fulfilment of the conditions of Definition 2.

We sum up the consideration of Example 8 in the following proposition.

Proposition 3. *Let $A\colon X^+ \dashrightarrow Y$ be a partial mapping then Algorithm 1 defines uniquely the mapping $T_A\colon X^\omega \to Y^\infty$, which satisfies the AN-property.*

We show that this example is the most general, i.e. the following theorem is true.

Theorem 2. *Let $T\colon X^\omega \to Y^\infty$ be a mapping satisfying the AN-property then there exists the unique partial mapping $A\colon X^+ \dashrightarrow Y$ such that $T \simeq T_A$.*

To prove the theorem we need the following auxiliary statement.

Lemma 1. *Let $T\colon X^\omega \to Y^\infty$ be a mapping satisfying the AN-property, $\boldsymbol{x}$ be an element of X^ω, and n be a natural number less than or equal to $\|T\boldsymbol{x}\|$ then for the set*

$$K_n^T(\boldsymbol{x}) = \{k \in \mathbb{N} \mid k \geq n \wedge (\forall \boldsymbol{x}' \in \boldsymbol{x}[0:k])(T\boldsymbol{x}')[0:n] = (T\boldsymbol{x})[0:n]\}$$

there exists the unique natural number $k_n^T(\boldsymbol{x})$ such that

$$K_n^T(\boldsymbol{x}) = \{k \in \mathbb{N} \mid k \geq k_n^T(\boldsymbol{x})\}.$$

Proof. If $k \in K_n^T(\boldsymbol{x})$ and $k' > k$ then it is evident that $k' \in K_n^T(\boldsymbol{x})$. Now the statement of lemma follows from the well-foundedness of the natural series. □

Proof (of Theorem 2). Let us consider the function $k_n^T(\boldsymbol{x}) = \min K_n^T(\boldsymbol{x})$ then define $A\boldsymbol{u} = (T\boldsymbol{x})[k_{\|\boldsymbol{u}\|}^T(\boldsymbol{x}) - 1]$ where $\boldsymbol{x}$ is any member of $\boldsymbol{u} \cdot X^\omega$. The correctness of the definition is ensured by the previous lemma. □

Corollary 1. *A mapping $T\colon X^\omega \to Y^\infty$ satisfies the AN-property if and only if there exists a partial mapping $A\colon X^+ \dashrightarrow Y$ such that $T \simeq T_A$. In this case the partial mapping A is defined uniquely.*

At the end of the section we discuss the case whenever $k_n^T(\boldsymbol{x}) = n$ for all $\boldsymbol{x} \in X^\omega$ and $0 \leq n \leq \|T\boldsymbol{x}\|$.

It is evident that if $T\colon X^\omega \to Y^\infty$ satisfies the SN-property then T satisfies the AN-property and $k_n^T(\boldsymbol{x}) = n$ for all $\boldsymbol{x} \in X^\omega$ and $n \leq \|T\boldsymbol{x}\|$. The converse is true too.

Proposition 4. *Let $T\colon X^\omega \to Y^\infty$ be a mapping satisfying the AN-property and $k_n^T(\boldsymbol{x}) = n$ for any $\boldsymbol{x} \in X^\omega$ and $n \leq \|T\boldsymbol{x}\|$ then this mapping satisfies the SN-property.*

Proof. In this case in Definition 2 k and n are coincident and, hence, AN-property is coincident with SN-property. □

4 Implementation Problem for Black Boxes

In this section we give a solution of the implementation problem for synchronous and asynchronous black boxes. Of course, the solution for synchronous black boxes is well-known and we mention it only for the completeness of our presentation and providing the unification of concepts and notation for both synchronous and asynchronous black boxes.

4.1 Implementation of Synchronous Black Box

Automata. We start our consideration reminding the definition of an automaton.

Definition 3. *A triple $\mathcal{A}(X, Z_{\mathcal{A}}, \delta_{\mathcal{A}})$ is called an automaton if X is a finite alphabet of impacts, $Z_{\mathcal{A}}$ is a set of states of the automaton, $\delta_{\mathcal{A}}\colon Z_{\mathcal{A}} \times X \dashrightarrow Z_{\mathcal{A}}$ is a partial mapping, which is called the transition function of the automaton.*

Note 2. The transition function can always be transformed into the total mapping by including an additional element "$*$" into $Z_{\mathcal{A}}$ and determining $\delta_{\mathcal{A}}(z, x) = *$ if $\delta_{\mathcal{A}}(z, x) \uparrow$ and $\delta_{\mathcal{A}}(*, x) = *$ for any $x \in X$. Taking this into account we suppose that $\delta_{\mathcal{A}}\colon Z_{\mathcal{A}} \times X \to Z_{\mathcal{A}}$ is a total mapping.

An automaton behaviour is determined by a right action of the monoid X^* on the state set $Z_{\mathcal{A}}$ [3].

Proposition 5. *Let $\mathcal{A}(X, Z_{\mathcal{A}}, \delta_{\mathcal{A}})$ be an automaton and its extended transition function be the mapping $\delta^*_{\mathcal{A}}\colon Z_{\mathcal{A}} \times X^* \to Z_{\mathcal{A}}$ defined recursively by formulas* (1)

$$\begin{array}{lll} \delta^*_{\mathcal{A}}(z, \varepsilon) & = z & \textit{for any } \; z \in Z_{\mathcal{A}}; \\ \delta^*_{\mathcal{A}}(z, \boldsymbol{u}x) & = \delta_{\mathcal{A}}(\delta^*_{\mathcal{A}}(z, \boldsymbol{u}), x) & \textit{for } \; z \in Z_{\mathcal{A}}, \; \boldsymbol{u} \in X^*, \; x \in X \end{array} \tag{1}$$

then $\delta^*_{\mathcal{A}}$ is a right action of the monoid X^* on the set $Z_{\mathcal{A}}$.

Proof. To prove the proposition it is sufficient to check the equality

$$\delta^*_{\mathcal{A}}(z, \boldsymbol{u}'\boldsymbol{u}'') = \delta^*_{\mathcal{A}}(\delta^*_{\mathcal{A}}(z, \boldsymbol{u}'), \boldsymbol{u}'')$$

for any $z \in Z_{\mathcal{A}}$, $\boldsymbol{u}', \boldsymbol{u}'' \in X^*$. The corresponding checking is a simple exercise in the application of mathematical induction on the length of $\boldsymbol{u}''$. □

Moore Machine. Usually, automata associate with black boxes in the following manner.

Firstly, the class of Moore machines is defined.

Definition 4. *Let $\mathcal{A}(X, Z_{\mathcal{A}}, \delta_{\mathcal{A}})$ be an automaton then the corresponding (reachable) Moore machine is a quintuple $\mathcal{M}(X, Z_{\mathcal{A}}, \delta_{\mathcal{A}}, z^0_{\mathcal{M}}, \lambda_{\mathcal{M}})$, where $z^0_{\mathcal{M}}$ is some fixed state of $\mathcal{A}$ called the initial state of the machine and $\lambda_{\mathcal{M}}\colon Z_{\mathcal{A}} \to Y$ is a mapping called the output function of the machine, if the condition of reachability*

$$\textit{for any } \; z \in Z_{\mathcal{A}} \; \textit{ there exists } \; \boldsymbol{u} \in X^* \; \textit{ such that } \; z = \delta^*_{\mathcal{A}}(z^0_{\mathcal{M}}, \boldsymbol{u}) \tag{2}$$

holds.

Then for a Moore machine is determined its reaction function.

Definition 5. *Let $\mathcal{M}(X, Z_{\mathcal{A}}, \delta_{\mathcal{A}}, z^0_{\mathcal{M}}, \lambda_{\mathcal{M}})$ be a Moore machine then its reaction function $A_{\mathcal{M}} \colon X^+ \to Y$ is determined by the formula*

$$A_{\mathcal{M}}(\boldsymbol{u}) = \lambda_{\mathcal{M}}(\delta_{\mathcal{A}}(z^0_{\mathcal{M}}, \boldsymbol{u})). \tag{3}$$

Finally, we define the transfer function $T_{\mathcal{M}} \colon X^\omega \to Y^\omega$ for the machine $\mathcal{M}(X, Z_{\mathcal{A}}, \delta_{\mathcal{A}}, z^0_{\mathcal{M}}, \lambda_{\mathcal{M}})$ using its reaction function $A_{\mathcal{M}}$ and Algorithm 1.

Note 3. If the transition function of a Moore machine is partial then a transition of the machine into the state "*" is considered as the prohibition of a response on any impact.

Posing of the Implementation Problem. The preceding arguments show that machines can be considered as glass boxes. Therefore we pose the following problem.

Problem 1 (Implementation Problem for Synchronous Black Boxes). Let we have a mapping $T \colon X^\omega \to Y^\omega$ that holds the SN-property.

Then it is required to describe the properties of the mapping that ensures the existence of a More machine $\mathcal{M}(X, Z_{\mathcal{A}}, \delta_{\mathcal{A}}, z^0_{\mathcal{M}}, \lambda_{\mathcal{M}})$ such that $T_{A_{\mathcal{M}}} \simeq T$.

Existence of a Solution for the Implementation Problem. It is known that Moore machines are glass boxes for all synchronous black boxes [6,9]. I.e. SN-property is necessary and sufficient to implement the corresponding black box with using some Moore machine. Below we present the corresponding reasoning for the completeness of the presentation.

Thus we assume that two alphabets (the input alphabet X and the output alphabet Y) and the transfer function $T \colon X^\omega \to Y^\omega$ are given. If T satisfies the SN-property then we can select the corresponding mapping $A \colon X^+ \to Y$ as it has been established in Theorem 1.

Now let us choose

1. $Z_{\mathcal{F}} = X^*$;
2. $\delta_{\mathcal{F}}(\boldsymbol{u}, x) = \boldsymbol{u}x$ for $x \in X$ and $\boldsymbol{u} \in X^*$

and consider the triple $\mathcal{F}(X, Z_{\mathcal{F}}, \delta_{\mathcal{F}})$.

Lemma 2. *The triple $\mathcal{F}(X, Z_{\mathcal{F}}, \delta_{\mathcal{F}})$ is an automaton such that the right action $\delta^*_{\mathcal{F}} \colon Z_{\mathcal{F}} \times X^* \to Z_{\mathcal{F}}$ associated with it satisfies the equation*

$$\delta^*_{\mathcal{F}}(\boldsymbol{u}, \boldsymbol{v}) = \boldsymbol{u}\boldsymbol{v} \tag{4}$$

for all $\boldsymbol{u}, \boldsymbol{v} \in X^*$.

Proof. Checking is reduced to a simple application of the mathematical induction. □

Now the following theorem is evident.

Theorem 3. *Let us consider the Moore machine $\mathcal{F}^A(X, Z_{\mathcal{F}}, \delta_{\mathcal{F}}, z^0_{\mathcal{F}A}, \lambda_{\mathcal{F}A})$ where $z^0_{\mathcal{F}A} = \varepsilon$ and $\lambda_{\mathcal{F}A}(\boldsymbol{u}) = A\boldsymbol{u}$ then $A \simeq A_{\mathcal{F}A}$.*

Minimal Solution for the Implementation Problem. The solution that is given in the previous subsection for the Implementation Problem is too redundant because the state set of the corresponding Moore machine contains too many indistinguishable states. Below we demonstrate the method to eliminate the lack of the construction.

Let us choose

1. $Z_{\mathcal{S}^A} = \{f\colon X^+ \to Y \mid f(\_) = A(\boldsymbol{u}_f \cdot \_) \text{ for some } \boldsymbol{u}_f \in X^*\}$;
2. $\delta_{\mathcal{S}^A}(f,x)(\_) = f(x \cdot \_)$ for $x \in X$ and $f \in Z_{\mathcal{S}^A}$

and consider the triple $\mathcal{S}^A(X, Z_{\mathcal{S}^A}, \delta_{\mathcal{S}^A})$.

Lemma 3. *The triple $\mathcal{S}^A(X, Z_{\mathcal{S}^A}, \delta_{\mathcal{S}^A})$ is an automaton such that the right action $\delta^*_{\mathcal{S}^A} : Z_{\mathcal{S}^A} \times X^* \to Z_{\mathcal{S}^A}$ associated with it satisfies the equation*

$$\delta^*_{\mathcal{S}^A}(f,\boldsymbol{u})(\_) = f(\boldsymbol{u} \cdot \_) \tag{5}$$

for all $\boldsymbol{u} \in X^*$ and $f \in Z_{\mathcal{S}^A}$.

Proof. Primarily, we should show that $\delta_{\mathcal{S}^A}(f,x) \in Z_{\mathcal{S}^A}$ if $f \in Z_{\mathcal{S}^A}$ and $x \in X$. Indeed, $f \in Z_{\mathcal{S}^A}$ implies that there exists $\boldsymbol{u}_f \in X^*$ such that $f(\boldsymbol{v}) = A(\boldsymbol{u}_f\boldsymbol{v})$ for any $\boldsymbol{v} \in X^+$. Therefore, $\delta_{\mathcal{S}^A}(f,x)(\boldsymbol{v}) = f(x\boldsymbol{v}) = A(\boldsymbol{u}_f(x\boldsymbol{v})) = A((\boldsymbol{u}_f x)\boldsymbol{v})$ and $\boldsymbol{u}_{\delta_{\mathcal{S}^A}(f,x)} = \boldsymbol{u}_f x$.
Now one can prove (5) using mathematical induction by length of $\boldsymbol{u}$. □

Theorem 4. *Let us consider the Moore machine $\mathcal{M}^A(X, Z_{\mathcal{S}^A}, \delta_{\mathcal{S}^A}, z^0_{\mathcal{M}^A}, \lambda_{\mathcal{M}^A})$ where $z_{\mathcal{M}^A} = A$ and $\lambda_{\mathcal{M}^A}(f) = A(\boldsymbol{u}_f)$ then $A \simeq A_{\mathcal{M}^A}$.*

Proof. It is evident that $A \in Z_{\mathcal{S}^A}$ and $\boldsymbol{u}_A = \varepsilon$.
Further, taking into account the previous lemma one can obtain

$$\begin{aligned} A_{\mathcal{M}^A}(\boldsymbol{u}) =& \lambda_{\mathcal{M}^A}(\delta^*_{\mathcal{S}^A}(z_{\mathcal{M}^A}, \boldsymbol{u})) = \\ & A\left(\boldsymbol{u}_{\delta^*_{\mathcal{S}^A}(z_{\mathcal{M}^A},\boldsymbol{u})}\right) = A(\boldsymbol{u}_{z_{\mathcal{M}^A}}\boldsymbol{u}) = A(\varepsilon\boldsymbol{u}) = A(\boldsymbol{u}). \end{aligned}$$

Hence, $A \simeq A_{\mathcal{M}^A}$. □

Thus, we prove that the Moore machine $\mathcal{M}^A(X, Z_{\mathcal{S}^A}, \delta_{\mathcal{S}^A}, z^0_{\mathcal{M}^A}, \lambda_{\mathcal{M}^A})$ implements the synchronous black box with transfer function T. Our goal is to prove that this is the minimal implementation.

Theorem 5. *Let $\mathcal{M}(X, Z_{\mathcal{A}}, \delta_{\mathcal{A}}, z^0_{\mathcal{M}}, \lambda_{\mathcal{M}})$ be a Moore machine that implements a synchronous black box with transfer function T and $A\colon X^+ \to Y$ such that $T \simeq T_A$ then there exists the surjective mapping $\mu\colon Z_{\mathcal{A}} \to Z_{\mathcal{S}^A}$ such that*

1. *$\mu(z^0_{\mathcal{M}}) = z^0_{\mathcal{M}^A}$;*
2. *$\mu(\delta_{\mathcal{A}}(z,x)) = \delta_{\mathcal{S}^A}(\mu(z),x)$ for any $z \in Z_{\mathcal{A}}$ and $x \in X$;*
3. *$\lambda_{\mathcal{M}}(z) = \lambda_{\mathcal{M}^A}(\mu(z))$ for any $z \in Z_{\mathcal{A}}$.*

Proof. First of all, we define the mapping μ.

Let z be an arbitrary element of $Z_{\mathcal{A}}$ then taking into account (2) we can find $\boldsymbol{u}_z \in X^*$ such that $z = \delta^*_{\mathcal{A}}(z^0_{\mathcal{M}}, \boldsymbol{u}_z)$. Suppose that there exists another $\boldsymbol{v}_z \in X^*$ such that $z = \delta^*_{\mathcal{A}}(z^0_{\mathcal{M}}, \boldsymbol{v}_z)$.

Under this supposition we obtain

$$\begin{aligned} A(\boldsymbol{u}_z x) =&\lambda_{\mathcal{M}}(\delta^*_{\mathcal{A}}(z^0_{\mathcal{M}}, \boldsymbol{u}_z x)) = \lambda_{\mathcal{M}}(\delta^*_{\mathcal{A}}(\delta^*_{\mathcal{A}}(z^0_{\mathcal{M}}, \boldsymbol{u}_z), x)) = \\ &\lambda_{\mathcal{M}}(\delta_{\mathcal{A}}(z, x)) = \lambda_{\mathcal{M}}(\delta^*_{\mathcal{A}}(\delta^*_{\mathcal{A}}(z^0_{\mathcal{M}}, \boldsymbol{v}_z), x)) = \\ &\lambda_{\mathcal{M}}(\delta^*_{\mathcal{A}}(z^0_{\mathcal{M}}, \boldsymbol{v}_z x)) = A(\boldsymbol{v}_z x) \end{aligned}$$

for any $x \in X$.

Therefore, the correspondence $z \mapsto A(\boldsymbol{u}_z \cdot \_)$ determines correctly some mapping $\mu \colon Z_{\mathcal{A}} \to Z_{\mathcal{S}^A}$.

Now let us check that the mapping μ is surjective. Indeed, let us take an arbitrary f belonging to $Z_{\mathcal{M}^A}$. Then there exists $\boldsymbol{u}_f \in X^*$ such that $f(\_) = A(\boldsymbol{u}_f \cdot \_)$. Let $z = \delta^*_{\mathcal{A}}(z^0_{\mathcal{M}}, \boldsymbol{u}_f)$ then $\mu(z)(\_) = A(\boldsymbol{u}_f \cdot \_) = f(\_)$.

Now it remains to verify properties 1–3.

Note that property 1 is evident and the property 2 is easily proved using mathematical induction by length of $\boldsymbol{u}$.

To prove property 3 note the following

$$\lambda_{\mathcal{M}}(z) = \lambda_{\mathcal{M}}(\delta^*_{\mathcal{A}}(z^0_{\mathcal{M}}, \boldsymbol{u}_z)) = A(\boldsymbol{u}_z) = \lambda_{\mathcal{M}^A}(\delta^*_{\mathcal{S}^A}(z^0_{\mathcal{M}^A}, \boldsymbol{u}_z)) = \lambda_{\mathcal{M}^A}(\mu(z)).$$

This complete the proof. □

4.2 Implementation of Asynchronous Black Box

Pre-automata. The notion of a pre-automaton had been introduced in [4] by replacing the action with the partial action in the definition.

Definition 6. *A triple $\mathcal{P}(X, Z_{\mathcal{P}}, \delta^*_{\mathcal{P}})$ is called a pre-automaton if X is a finite alphabet of impacts, $Z_{\mathcal{P}}$ is a set of states of the pre-automaton, $\delta^*_{\mathcal{P}}$ is a right partial action of the monoid X^* on the set $Z_{\mathcal{P}}$, i.e. it is a partial mapping $\delta^*_{\mathcal{P}} \colon Z_{\mathcal{P}} \times X^* \dashrightarrow Z_{\mathcal{P}}$ such that*

1. *$\delta^*_{\mathcal{P}}(z, \varepsilon) \downarrow = z$ for all $z \in Z_{\mathcal{P}}$;*
2. *if $\delta^*_{\mathcal{P}}(z, \boldsymbol{u}') \downarrow$ and $\delta^*_{\mathcal{P}}(\delta^*_{\mathcal{P}}(z, \boldsymbol{u}'), \boldsymbol{u}'') \downarrow$ then $\delta^*_{\mathcal{P}}(z, \boldsymbol{u}'\boldsymbol{u}'') \downarrow = \delta^*_{\mathcal{P}}(\delta^*_{\mathcal{P}}(z, \boldsymbol{u}'), \boldsymbol{u}'')$ for all $z \in Z_{\mathcal{P}}$ and $\boldsymbol{u}', \boldsymbol{u}'' \in X^*$;*
3. *if $\delta^*_{\mathcal{P}}(z, \boldsymbol{u}') \downarrow$ and $\delta^*_{\mathcal{P}}(z, \boldsymbol{u}'\boldsymbol{u}'') \downarrow$ then $\delta^*_{\mathcal{P}}(\delta^*_{\mathcal{P}}(z, \boldsymbol{u}'), \boldsymbol{u}'') \downarrow = \delta^*_{\mathcal{P}}(s, \boldsymbol{u}'\boldsymbol{u}'')$ for all $z \in Z_{\mathcal{P}}$ and $\boldsymbol{u}', \boldsymbol{u}'' \in X^*$.*

Now we describe some method that allows us to construct a pre-automaton using an automaton.

Suppose that we have taken some automaton $\mathcal{A}(X, Z_{\mathcal{A}}, \delta_{\mathcal{A}})$. Let us define the pre-automaton $\mathcal{P}(X, Z_{\mathcal{P}}, \delta^*_{\mathcal{P}})$ in the following manner:

1. choose as $Z_{\mathcal{P}}$ an arbitrary subset of $Z_{\mathcal{A}}$;
2. define the partial mapping $\delta^*_{\mathcal{P}}\colon Z_{\mathcal{P}} \times X^* \dashrightarrow Z_{\mathcal{P}}$ as follows for $z \in Z_{\mathcal{P}}$ and $\boldsymbol{u} \in X^*$ let assign that

$$\begin{aligned} &\delta^*_{\mathcal{P}}(z, \boldsymbol{u})\uparrow && \text{if } \delta^*_{\mathcal{A}}(z, \boldsymbol{u}) \notin Z_{\mathcal{P}} && \text{and} \\ &\delta^*_{\mathcal{P}}(z, \boldsymbol{u})\downarrow = \delta^*_{\mathcal{A}}(z, \boldsymbol{u}) && \text{if } \delta^*_{\mathcal{A}}(z, \boldsymbol{u}) \in Z_{\mathcal{P}}. \end{aligned}$$

Proposition 6. *The triple defined by the previous construction is a pre-automaton.*

Proof. Indeed, item (1) of the construction ensures that item (1) of Definition 6 is satisfied. Further, item (2) of the construction and Proposition 5 implies that items (2) and (3) of Definition 6 are satisfied. □

Taking into account this proposition we call the constructed pre-automaton a restriction of the automaton $\mathcal{A}(X, Z_{\mathcal{A}}, \delta_{\mathcal{A}})$ to the subset $Z_{\mathcal{P}}$.

The assertion just proved demonstrates that the method to obtain pre-automata consists in hiding part of the states.

The converse assertion proved in [4] as Globalisation Theorem ensures that the method considered above is the most general method to obtain pre-automata.

Moore Pre-machine. Pre-automata are associated with black boxes similarly to automata.

Firstly, the class of Moore pre-machines is defined.

Definition 7. *Let $\mathcal{P}(X, Z_{\mathcal{P}}, \delta^*_{\mathcal{P}})$ be a pre-automaton then the corresponding Moore pre-machine is a quintuple $\mathcal{M}(X, Z_{\mathcal{P}}, \delta^*_{\mathcal{P}}, z^0_{\mathcal{M}}, \lambda_{\mathcal{M}})$, where $z^0_{\mathcal{M}}$ is some fixed element of $Z_{\mathcal{P}}$ called the initial state of the pre-machine and $\lambda_{\mathcal{M}}\colon Z_{\mathcal{P}} \to Y$ is a mapping called the output function of the pre-machine, if the condition of reachability*

$$\textit{for any } \; z \in Z_{\mathcal{P}} \; \textit{ there exists } \; \boldsymbol{u} \in X^* \; \textit{ such that } \; \delta^*_{\mathcal{P}}(z^0_{\mathcal{M}}, \boldsymbol{u})\downarrow = z \tag{6}$$

holds.

Then for a Moore pre-machine is determined its reaction function.

Definition 8. *Let $\mathcal{M}(X, Z_{\mathcal{P}}, \delta^*_{\mathcal{P}}, z^0_{\mathcal{M}}, \lambda_{\mathcal{M}})$ be a Moore pre-machine then its reaction function $A_{\mathcal{M}}\colon X^+ \dashrightarrow Y$ is determined in the following manner*

$$\begin{aligned} &A_{\mathcal{M}}(\boldsymbol{u})\uparrow && \textit{if } \; \delta^*_{\mathcal{M}}(z^0_{\mathcal{M}}, \boldsymbol{u})\uparrow && \textit{and} \\ &A_{\mathcal{M}}(\boldsymbol{u})\downarrow = \lambda_{\mathcal{M}}(\delta^*_{\mathcal{P}}(z^0_{\mathcal{M}}, \boldsymbol{u})) && \textit{if } \; \delta^*_{\mathcal{M}}(z^0_{\mathcal{M}}, \boldsymbol{u})\downarrow . \end{aligned}$$

Finally, we define the transfer function $T_{\mathcal{M}}\colon X^\omega \to Y^\infty$ for the pre-machine $\mathcal{M}_{\mathcal{P}}$ using its reaction function $A_{\mathcal{M}}$ and Algorithm 1.

Posing of the Implementation Problem. Now we pose the following problem.

Problem 2 (Implementation Problem for Asynchronous Black Boxes). Let we have a mapping $T\colon X^\omega \to Y^\infty$ that holds the AN-property.

Then it is required to describe the properties of the mapping that ensures the existence of a More pre-machine $\mathcal{M}(X, Z_\mathcal{P}, \delta_\mathcal{P}, z^0_\mathcal{M}, \lambda_\mathcal{M})$ such that $T_{A_\mathcal{M}} \simeq T$.

Existence of Solution of the Implementation Problem. Thus we assume that two alphabets (the input alphabet X and the output alphabet Y) and the transfer function $T\colon X^\omega \to Y^\infty$ are given that satisfies the AN-property. In this case Corollary 1 ensures the possibility to select the partial mapping $A\colon X^+ \dashrightarrow Y$ such that $T \simeq T_A$.

Let us choose

1. $Z_\mathcal{F} = X^*$;
2. $\delta_\mathcal{F}(\boldsymbol{u}, x) = \boldsymbol{u}x$ for $x \in X$ and $\boldsymbol{u} \in X^*$

and consider the triple $\mathcal{F}(X, Z_\mathcal{F}, \delta_\mathcal{F})$. In Proposition 5 has been established that this triple is an automaton.

Now let us choose $Z_{\mathcal{F}^A} \subset Z_\mathcal{F}$ in the following manner:

$$Z_{\mathcal{F}^A} = \{\boldsymbol{u} \in X^* \mid A\boldsymbol{u}\downarrow\} \bigcup \{\varepsilon\}.$$

Selecting restriction of the automaton $\mathcal{F}$ on the set $Z_{\mathcal{F}^A}$ we obtain the pre-automaton $\mathcal{F}^A(X, Z_{\mathcal{F}^A}, \delta^*_{\mathcal{F}^A})$.

Theorem 6 (Existence of Solutions for the Synthesis Problem). *Let us consider the Moore pre-machine $\mathcal{M}(X, Z_{\mathcal{F}^A}, \delta^*_{\mathcal{F}^A}, z^0_\mathcal{M}, \lambda_\mathcal{M})$, where*

$$\begin{aligned} &z^0_\mathcal{M} = \varepsilon;\\ &\lambda_\mathcal{M}(\boldsymbol{u}) = A\boldsymbol{u} \quad \textit{if} \quad A\boldsymbol{u}\downarrow;\\ &\lambda_\mathcal{M}(\varepsilon) \quad \textit{is defined arbitrary,} \end{aligned}$$

then $A_\mathcal{M} \simeq A$.

Proof. Really, $\mathcal{M}$ is a Moore pre-machine (see Proposition 6).
Hence we need to prove that $A_\mathcal{M}\boldsymbol{u}\downarrow$ if and only if $A\boldsymbol{u}\downarrow$ and the equality $A_\mathcal{M}\boldsymbol{u} = A\boldsymbol{u}$ holds on the common domain. But this follows immediately from Lemma 2 and the specification of the pre-machine $\mathcal{M}$. □

Minimal Solution for the Implementation Problem. Now we need to eliminate the redundancy of the proposed problem solution. We do similarly it as we have done it for the SN-case studied above.

Let us choose

1. $Z_{\mathcal{S}^A} = \{f\colon X^+ \dashrightarrow Y \mid f(\_) \simeq A(\boldsymbol{u}_f \cdot \_) \text{ for some } \boldsymbol{u}_f \in X^* \text{ such that } A\boldsymbol{u}_f\downarrow\}$;
2. $\delta^*_{\mathcal{S}^A}(f, \boldsymbol{u})\uparrow$ if $f(\boldsymbol{u} \cdot \_) \notin Z_{\mathcal{S}^A}$; $\delta^*_{\mathcal{S}^A}(f, \boldsymbol{u})(\_) \simeq f(\boldsymbol{u} \cdot \_)$ if $f(\boldsymbol{u} \cdot \_) \in Z_{\mathcal{S}^A}$

and consider the triple $\mathcal{S}^A(X, Z_{\mathcal{S}^A}, \delta^*_{\mathcal{S}^A})$.

Lemma 4. *The triple $\mathcal{S}^A(X, Z_{\mathcal{S}^A}, \delta^*_{\mathcal{S}^A})$ is a pre-automaton.*

Proof. Note that $\delta^*_{\mathcal{S}^A}(f,\varepsilon)(\_) \simeq f(\varepsilon\,\_) \simeq f(\_)$ therefore property (1) of Definition 6 is true.

Suppose that $\delta^*_{\mathcal{S}^A}(f,\boldsymbol{u}')\downarrow$ and $\delta^*_{\mathcal{S}^A}(\delta^*_{\mathcal{S}^A}(f,\boldsymbol{u}'),\boldsymbol{u}'')\downarrow$ then

firstly, $\delta^*_{\mathcal{S}^A}(f,\boldsymbol{u}')(\_) \simeq f(\boldsymbol{u}'\cdot\_) \simeq A((\boldsymbol{u}_f\boldsymbol{u}')\cdot\_)$ and $A(\boldsymbol{u}_f\boldsymbol{u}')\downarrow$ and
secondly, $\delta^*_{\mathcal{S}^A}(\delta^*_{\mathcal{S}^A}(f,\boldsymbol{u}'),\boldsymbol{u}'')(\_) \simeq f((\boldsymbol{u}'\boldsymbol{u}'')\cdot\_) \simeq A((\boldsymbol{u}_f\boldsymbol{u}'\boldsymbol{u}'')\cdot\_)$ and $A(\boldsymbol{u}_f\boldsymbol{u}'\boldsymbol{u}'')\downarrow$.

Further,

$$\delta^*_{\mathcal{S}^A}(f,\boldsymbol{u}'\boldsymbol{u}'')(\_) \simeq f((\boldsymbol{u}'\boldsymbol{u}'')\cdot\_) \simeq A((\boldsymbol{u}_f\boldsymbol{u}'\boldsymbol{u}'')\cdot\_)$$

and taking into account the previously statements we obtain that $\delta^*_{\mathcal{S}^A}(f,\boldsymbol{u}') \simeq \delta^*_{\mathcal{S}^A}(\delta^*_{\mathcal{S}^A}(f,\boldsymbol{u}'),\boldsymbol{u}'')$ and property (2) of Definition 6 is true.
The validity of property (3) of Definition 6 is established by the similar way. □

Theorem 7. *Let $\mathcal{M}^A(X, Z_{\mathcal{S}^A}, \delta^*_{\mathcal{S}^A}, z^0_{\mathcal{M}^A}, \lambda_{\mathcal{M}^A})$ be the Moore pre-machine where $z_{\mathcal{M}^A} \simeq A$ and $\lambda_{\mathcal{M}^A}(f) = A(\boldsymbol{u}_f)$ then $A \simeq A_{\mathcal{M}^A}$.*

Proof. Taking into account the previous lemma we need to check that $A(\_) \simeq \lambda_{\mathcal{M}^A}(\delta^*_{\mathcal{S}^A}(z^0_{\mathcal{M}^A},\_))$. Indeed, $A\boldsymbol{u}\downarrow$ if and only if $\delta^*_{\mathcal{S}^A}(z^0_{\mathcal{M}^A},\boldsymbol{u})\downarrow$ by definition and in this case

$$\lambda_{\mathcal{M}^A}(\delta^*_{\mathcal{S}^A}(z^0_{\mathcal{M}^A},\boldsymbol{u})) = \lambda_{\mathcal{M}^A}(A(\boldsymbol{u}\cdot\_)) = A(\boldsymbol{u}).$$

This complete the proof. □

Thus, we prove that the Moore pre-machine $\mathcal{M}^A(X, Z_{\mathcal{S}^A}, \delta^*_{\mathcal{S}^A}, z^0_{\mathcal{M}^A}, \lambda_{\mathcal{M}^A})$ implements the asynchronous black box with transfer function T. Our goal is to prove that this is the minimal implementation.

Theorem 8. *Let $\mathcal{M}(X, Z_{\mathcal{P}}, \delta^*_{\mathcal{P}}, z^0_{\mathcal{M}}, \lambda_{\mathcal{M}})$ be a Moore pre-machine that implements an asynchronous black box with transfer function T and $A\colon X^+ \dashrightarrow Y$ such that $T \simeq T_A$ then there exists the surjective mapping $\mu\colon Z_{\mathcal{P}} \to Z_{\mathcal{S}^A}$ such that*

1. $\mu(z^0_{\mathcal{M}}) = z^0_{\mathcal{M}^A}$;
2. $\delta^*_{\mathcal{A}}(z,\boldsymbol{u})\downarrow$ *implies* $\delta^*_{\mathcal{S}^A}(\mu(z),\boldsymbol{u})\downarrow = \mu(\delta^*_{\mathcal{A}}(z,\boldsymbol{u}))$ *for any* $z \in Z_{\mathcal{A}}$ *and* $\boldsymbol{u} \in X^*$;
3. $\lambda_{\mathcal{M}}(z) = \lambda_{\mathcal{M}^A}(\mu(z))$ *for any* $z \in Z_{\mathcal{A}}$.

We obtain the proof of the corresponding theorem modifying the proof of Theorem 5.

Proof (of Theorem 8). First of all, we define the mapping μ.
Let z be an arbitrary element of $Z_{\mathcal{P}}$ then taking into account (6) we can find $\boldsymbol{u}_z \in X^*$ such that $\delta^*_{\mathcal{P}}(z^0_{\mathcal{M}},\boldsymbol{u}_z)\downarrow = z$. Suppose that there exists another $\boldsymbol{v}_z \in X^*$ such that $\delta^*_{\mathcal{P}}(z^0_{\mathcal{M}},\boldsymbol{v}_z)\downarrow = z$.

Under this supposition we obtain

$$A(\boldsymbol{u}_z\boldsymbol{u})\downarrow = \lambda_{\mathcal{M}}(\delta^*_{\mathcal{P}}(z^0_{\mathcal{M}},\boldsymbol{u}_z\boldsymbol{u})\downarrow = \lambda_{\mathcal{M}}(\delta^*_{\mathcal{P}}(\delta^*_{\mathcal{P}}(z^0_{\mathcal{M}},\boldsymbol{u}_z),\boldsymbol{u}))\downarrow = \lambda_{\mathcal{M}}(\delta^*_{\mathcal{P}}(z,\boldsymbol{u}))$$

and

$$A(\boldsymbol{v}_z\boldsymbol{u}) \downarrow = \lambda_{\mathcal{M}}(\delta^*_{\mathcal{P}}(z^0_{\mathcal{M}}, \boldsymbol{v}_z\boldsymbol{u})) \downarrow = \lambda_{\mathcal{M}}(\delta^*_{\mathcal{P}}(\delta^*_{\mathcal{P}}(z^0_{\mathcal{M}}, \boldsymbol{v}_z), \boldsymbol{u})) \downarrow = \lambda_{\mathcal{M}}(\delta^*_{\mathcal{P}}(z, \boldsymbol{u}))$$

for any $\boldsymbol{u} \in X^*$ such that $A(\boldsymbol{u}_z\boldsymbol{u})$ (and respectively $A(\boldsymbol{v}_z\boldsymbol{u})$) is defined.

Therefore, the correspondence $z \mapsto A(\boldsymbol{u}_z \cdot)$ determines correctly some mapping $\mu \colon Z_{\mathcal{A}} \to Z_{\mathcal{S}^A}$.

Now let us check that the mapping μ is surjective. Indeed, let us take an arbitrary f belonging to $Z_{\mathcal{M}^A}$. Then there exists $\boldsymbol{u}_f \in X^*$ such that $f(\_) = A(\boldsymbol{u}_f \cdot \_)$ and $A(\boldsymbol{u}_f)\downarrow$.

Let $z = \delta^*_{\mathcal{A}}(z^0_{\mathcal{M}}, \boldsymbol{u}_f)$ then $\mu(z)(\_) = A(\boldsymbol{u}_f \cdot \_) = f(\_)$.

Now it remains to verify properties 1–3.

Note that property 1 is evident and the property 2 is easily proved using mathematical induction by length of $\boldsymbol{u}$.

To prove property 3 note the following

$$\lambda_{\mathcal{M}}(z) = \lambda_{\mathcal{M}}(\delta^*_{\mathcal{P}}(z^0_{\mathcal{M}}, \boldsymbol{u}_z)) \downarrow = A(\boldsymbol{u}_z)$$

and

$$\lambda_{\mathcal{M}^A}(\mu(z)) = \lambda_{\mathcal{M}^A}(\delta^*_{\mathcal{S}^A}(z^0_{\mathcal{M}^A}, \boldsymbol{u}_z)) \downarrow = A(\boldsymbol{u}_z).$$

Therefore, $\lambda_{\mathcal{M}}(z) = \lambda_{\mathcal{M}^A}(\mu(z))$. This complete the proof. □

5 Conclusion

Thus, we can summarize that the paper gives the algebraic analysis for the problem of implementation black boxes by machines. The main results of the analysis are the following

- the concepts of synchronous and asynchronous black boxes have been introduced. This allows us to study not only systems with the immediate response to each prime impact, but also systems, whose response depends on a sequence of prime impacts;
- the nonanticipation property has been formulated for asynchronous black boxes. It has been shown that this formulation generalises the corresponding property for synchronous black boxes;
- the complete solution of the implementation problem has been given for both synchronous and asynchronous black boxes. The machines that realise the corresponding transfer functions are based on pre-automata, which had been introduced by author jointly with Prof. M. Dokuchaev and Prof. B. Novikov in earlier papers (see, for example, [4]).

It should be emphasised that issues dealing with computational properties of pre-machines has not been considered in the paper. The coverage of these issues requires a separate study.

References

1. Atzori, L., Iera, A., Morabito, G.: The internet of things: a survey. Comput. Netw. **54**(15), 2787–2805 (2010)
2. Ashby, W.R.: An Introduction to Cybernetics. Chapman & Hall, London (1956)
3. Clifford, A.H., Preston, G.B.: The Algebraic Theory of Semigroups, vol. 1. AMS, Providence (1961)
4. Dokuchaev, M., Novikov, B., Zholtkevych, G.: Partial actions and automata. Algebra Discrete Math. **11**(2), 51–63 (2011)
5. Etzion, O., Niblett, P.: Event Processing in Action. Manning Publications Co., Greenwich (2011)
6. Glushkov, V.M.: Some problems in the synthesis of digital automata. USSR Comput. Math. Math. Phys. **1**(3), 399–446 (1962)
7. Mesarovic, M.D., Takahara, Y.: General Systems Theory: Mathematical Foundation. Academic Press, New York (1975)
8. Michelson, B.M.: Event-driven architecture overview. Patricia Seybold Group (2006)
9. Trakhtenbrot, B.A., Barzdin, J.M.: Finite Automata: Behaviour and Synthesis. North-Holland Publishing Company, Amsterdam (1973)
10. Zholtkevych, G.: Realisation of "Black Boxes" using machines. In: Ermolayev, V., et al. (eds.) ICT in Education, Research, and Industrial Applications. CEUR–WS, pp. 326–337 (2015). http://ceur-ws.org/Vol-1356/paper_32.pdf

Analysis of Boundary States of Multi-state System by Direct Partial Logic Derivatives

Elena Zaitseva(✉), Vitaly Levashenko, Jozef Kostolny, and Miroslav Kvassay

Department of Infromatics,
University of Zilina, Univerzitna 8215/1, 010 26 Zilina, Slovakia
{elena.zaitseva, vitaly.levashenko, jozef.kostolny, miroslav.kvassay}@fri.uniza.sk

Abstract. Multi-State System (MSS) is mathematical model that is used in reliability engineering for the representation of initial investigated object (system). In a MSS, both the system and its components may experience more than two states (performance levels). One of possible description of MSS is a structure function that is defined correlation between a system components states and system performance level. The investigation of a structure function allows obtaining different properties, measures and indices for MSS reliability. For example, boundary system's states, probabilities of a system performance levels and other measures are calculated based a structure function. In this paper mathematical approach of Direct Partial Logical Derivatives is proposed for calculation of boundary states of MSS.

Keywords: Multi-state system · Multiple-valued logic · Direct partial logic derivatives · Boundary state

1 Introduction

Reliability is considered as an important characteristic of any modern system. How-ever, modern systems are very complex and, therefore, their reliability analysis is a challenging task. The complexity of these systems results from the fact that they consist of a huge amount of elements with various behaviour. Examples of such systems include electrical transmission systems, gas grids [1, 2] or healthcare systems [3]. Distribution grids are typical examples of network systems. They represent large systems consisting of many (not necessarily) hardware elements with different properties, e.g. generating units, different types of transmission lines, and demand centres in the case of electrical grids. Similarly, a healthcare system is a typical instance of socio-technical systems composing of a lot of highly variable elements (components) that can be classified as hardware, software, organizational, and human [1]. This variety of components of complex systems causes that such systems can operate at many different levels of performance and, therefore, their analysis is more difficult than the analysis of other systems.

One of the principal tasks of reliability engineering is investigation of influence of individual system components on system activity. Results of such analysis are useful in

V. Yakovyna et al. (Eds.): ICTERI 2015, CCIS 594, pp. 140–155, 2016.
DOI: 10.1007/978-3-319-30246-1_9

optimization of system availability or in planning system maintenance. This investigation requires creation of a model of the considered system. Several types of mathematical models are used in reliability analysis. The first ones are known as *Binary-State Systems* (BSSs) because they permit defining only two states in system/components performance – functioning and failure. BSSs have been widely used in classical approaches of reliability engineering [4]. However, they are not very suitable for the analysis of complex systems because their use requires drawing the line between situations in which the system is functioning and when it is considered to be failure. Very often, this is impossible and, therefore, other types of mathematical models are used. According to [1], *Multi-State Systems* (MSSs) are one of the most prospective approaches.

MSSs have been introduced in reliability engineering since 1975 [5–7]. Their main advantage lies in the fact that they allow introducing more than two states in system/components performance [1, 8], i.e. from perfectly functioning, through functioning with restrictions, etc. to completely failed. This indicates that they are very suitable for modelling of complex systems. On the other hand, growing number of states of system components results in dramatic increase of model size, what causes increase of time complexity of the analysis. Therefore, use of MSSs requires development of new and effective methods that could be used to analyse them.

There are several approaches that are used in proposing methods and algorithms for the investigation of MSSs. As a rule, these approaches are based on one of the following four mathematical backgrounds [8]: extensions of Boolean methods, stochastic processes, universal generating function, and Monte Carlo simulation. Each of these approaches is used for some specific tasks relating to evaluation of MSSs. For example, stochastic processes (such as Markov processes) are used to analyse system state transition process [9], universal generating function is useful in optimization problems [10], while Monte Carlo simulation represents a universal tool for reliability assessment of systems consisting of a huge amount of components [11]. If we want to investigate influence of individual system components on the system activity, then the approach based on extensions of Boolean methods can be viewed as one of the most suitable.

The idea of extensions of Boolean methods for the analysis of MSSs lies in the fact that the tools of Boolean algebra have been widely used in reliability analysis of BSSs. This has resulted from the fact that the system structure function, which defines dependency between system state and states of system components, can be viewed as a Boolean function in the case of BSSs [4, 8]. However, this is not true for MSSs. Therefore, some works, e.g. [12, 13], have tried to transform the structure function of a MSS into a Boolean function using Boolean algebra with restrictions [12]. Such transformation allows us to use methods of Boolean algebra in reliability analysis of MSSs. However, this transformation can result in increase of model complexity. To avoid these complications, other authors have proposed using *Multiple-Valued Logic* (MVL) in reliability analysis of MSSs since there are some correlations between the structure function of a MSS and a MVL function [14, 15]. One of the tools of MVL that can be used in the analysis of MSSs is logical differential calculus [16, 17].

Logical differential calculus has been developed for the analysis of dynamic behaviour of Boolean and MVL functions. The central concept of this tool is a logic derivative. There are several types of logic derivatives from which the most interesting are *Direct Partial Logic Derivatives* (DPLDs). Use of DPLDs in reliability analysis of MSSs has been considered in several works, e.g. [15–18]. In those works, it has been shown that DPLDs are useful in calculation of special reliability indices that are named as importance measures. In this paper we propose the application of DPLD for the calculation of exact boundary states that indicate the system state for which the change of one or some of fixed components cause the system performance level decrease or increase. Therefore, they can be used to identify situations in which a degradation of a given component results in a decrease of system performance. Identification of such situations is very important for estimation of component influence on system activity. New indices as probabilities of exact boundary states are introduced in the paper. These indices allow estimating the stability of system in point of view of its availability.

The paper has next structure. Section 2 recalls some basics about structure function and introduce a concept of boundary states of a MSS. Section 3 provides short description of DPLDs computed with respect to one variable and with respect to a vector of several variables (variable vector). Finally, new indices for estimation of MSS boundary states are proposed in Sect. 4, the calculation of these indices are provided based on DPLD.

2 MSS Structure Function

2.1 Structure Function of MSS

A MSS is mathematical model that is used for the description of the system of n components. The i-th system component state is denoted as x_i ($i = 1, \ldots, n$). Consider simple variant of a MSS where the system components and system have equal number of states and performance levels. Each component in such mathematical representation has m states that are indicated as 0 for the complete failure and as m-1 for perfect functioning. Suppose, that the system has m performance level too: from the complete failure (it is 0) to the perfect functioning (it is m-1). The system performance levels depend on components states and this dependency is defined by the structure function $\phi(\boldsymbol{x})$ identically:

$$\phi(x_1, x_2, \ldots, x_n) = \phi(x) : \{0, 1, \ldots, m-1\}^n \to \{0, 1, \ldots, m-1\}. \quad (1)$$

In the mathematical point of view the structure function (1) corresponds with the definition of a MVL function [19]. Therefore the mathematical approaches of MVL can be used in qualification and quantification analysis of MSS. But the structure function (1) allows representing the very small class of real system for which the number of system performance levels and number of every component states are equal. As a rule, the real-world system has different numbers of states for different components and these numbers are not equal to number of performance levels and the structure function of such system is defined as:

$$\phi(x) : \{0, 1, \ldots, m_1 - 1\} \times \ldots \times \{0, 1, \ldots, m_n - 1\} \rightarrow \{0, 1, \ldots, M - 1\}, \quad (2)$$

where m_i is number of states for i-th system component ($i = 1, \ldots, n$) and M is number of a system performance levels.

The Eq. (2) is not a MVL function. The interpretation of the Eq. (2) as a MVL function needs additional transformation. Some formal changes in the interpretation of the structure function (2) allow to consider this function as an *incompletely specified MVL function*. The first of them it is definition of value of incompletely specified MVL function. In this case the maximal value of numbers of components states and number of system performance level is interpreted as an value of incompletely specified MVL function $m_{\max} = \mathrm{MAX}\{m_1, \ldots, m_n, M\}$. The second changes in formal interpretation of the structure function is addition of real values of m_i ($i = 1,.., n$) and M to value of incompletely specified MVL function $m_{\max}$. And the structure function (2) as an incompletely specified MVL function can be defined as:

$$\phi'(x) : \{0, 1, \ldots, m_{\max} - 1\}^n \rightarrow \{0, 1, \ldots, m_{\max} - 1\}. \quad (3)$$

The interpretation of the structure function (2) as an incompletely specified MVL function (3) permits to use mathematical approaches of MVL without principal restriction for analysis of properties of the structure function (2). Therefore components states (x_i, $i = 1, \ldots, n$) are interpreted as values of variables of MVL function and system performance levels are considered as values of the MVL function (Fig. 1). And changes of the i-th system component state agrees with changes of the i-th variable value at that the changes of a MSS performance level can be considered as changes of a MVL function. The introduction of these correlations is important for consideration of a MSS boundary states that will be investigated below.

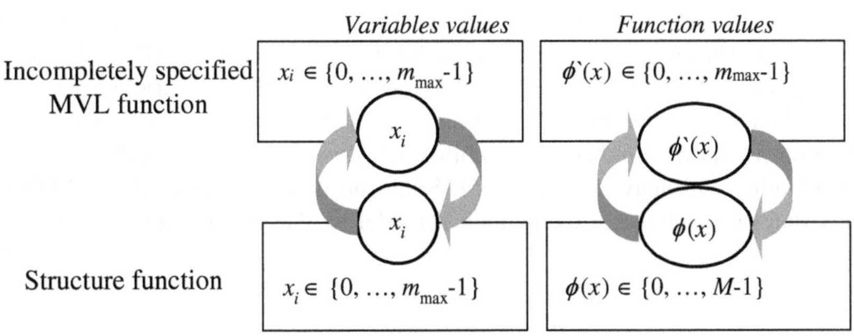

Fig. 1. The correlation of MVL function and structure function.

For example, consider the simple service system (Fig. 2) in a region from paper [18]. This system consists of three components ($n = 3$) – service point 1 (x_1), service point 2 (x_2) and infrastructure (x_3). This system has four performance levels: 0 – non-operational (no customer is satisfied), 1 – partially non-operational (some customers are not satisfied), 2 – partially operational (some customers are satisfied),

3 – fully operational (all customers are satisfied). Next, we assume that the service points are only functional (state 1) or dysfunctional (state 0). The infrastructure can be modelled by 4 quality levels, i.e. from 0 (the quality of the infrastructure is poor) to 3 (the quality is perfect). The structure function of this system according to (2) is defined in Table in Fig. 2 (where $m_1 = m_2 = 2$, $m_3 = 4$ and $M = 4$). Interpret this structure function as incompletely specified MVL function. The value of this function is defined as maximal value of m_1, m_2, m_3, and M and it is $m_{max} = 4$. Therefore two variables x_1 and x_2 must be added by two values: 2 and 3. But values of the structure function are not known and are indicated by "–". The structure function of this system as incompletely specified MVL function is in Table 1.

The system

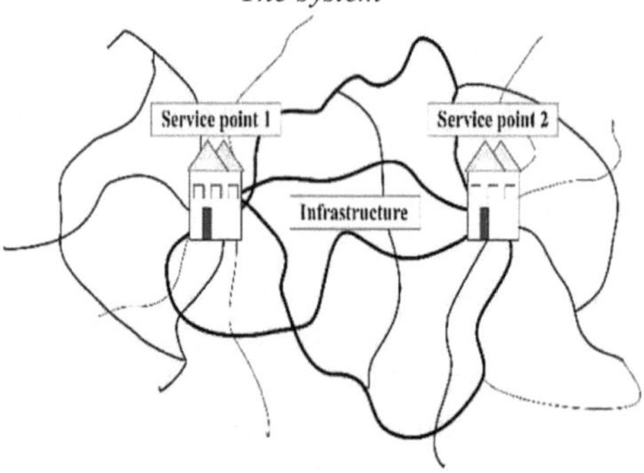

The system structure function

Components states					
x_1	x_2	x_3			
		0	1	2	3
0	0	**0**	**0**	**0**	**0**
0	1	**0**	**1**	**1**	**2**
1	0	**0**	**1**	**1**	**2**
1	1	**0**	**2**	**3**	**3**

Fig. 2. A simple service system and its structure function

Application of the mathematical approach of MVL in reliability engineering has one assumption. This mathematical approach can be used for the analysis of MSS reliability in stationary state or availability only because MVL function is time-independent function [14, 19]. But this assumption is not restriction for the definition of boundary states of a MSS and other reliability indices. Consider the calculation of most important indices in reliability analysis as availability and unavailability. The availability and unavailability of MSS depend on components states. MSS components states are defined in mathematical model by the probabilities of states:

$$p_{i,s} = \Pr\{x_i = s\},\ s = 0, \ldots, m_i - 1. \tag{4}$$

A MSS availability and unavailability based on the conception of the structure function (2) and taking into account the components states probabilities (4) are defined as follows [8]:

$$A(j) = \Pr\{\phi(x) \geq j\},\ j = 1, \ldots, M - 1, \tag{5}$$

$$U = \Pr\{\phi(x) = 0\}. \tag{6}$$

Table 1. The structure function of the simple service system represented as an incompletely specified MVL function

Components states					
x_1	x_2	x_3			
		0	1	2	3
0	0	**0**	**0**	**0**	**0**
0	1	**0**	**1**	**1**	**2**
0	2	–	–	–	–
0	3	–	–	–	–
1	0	**0**	**1**	**1**	**2**
1	1	**0**	**2**	**3**	**3**
1	2	–	–	–	–
1	3	–	–	–	–
2	0	–	–	–	–
2	1	–	–	–	–
2	2	–	–	–	–
2	3	–	–	–	–
3	0	–	–	–	–
3	1	–	–	–	–
3	2	–	–	–	–
3	3	–	–	–	–

But there is the special case of the definition of the system availability for MSS as [8, 15]:

$$A_j = \Pr\{\phi(x) = j\}, j = 1, \ldots, M - 1 \tag{7}$$

In this paper Definitions (7) and (6) for a MSS availability and unavailability will be used. Consider a coherent MSS. There are next assumptions for structure function of a coherent MSS [8]: (*a*) the structure function (2) is monotone and $\phi(\boldsymbol{s}) = s$ ($s \in \{0, \ldots, m\text{-}1\}$), and (*b*) all components are *s*-independent and are relevant to the system.

In papers [6, 7] authors shown that any system state j ($j = 1,\ldots, M$ -1) of a coherent MSS according to the assumption (*b*) can be calculated as the product of probabilities of components states (4) and the system availability for performance level j is sum of probabilities of all possible states for the performance level j. In terms of structure function it means that the system availability (7) can be calculate as the sum of probabilities of all values j of the structure function $\phi(\boldsymbol{x})$ that are computed as product of probabilities of components states.

Illustrate the calculation of the availability (7) by example. Consider the simple service system (Fig. 2) and calculate the availability of this system for the performance level 3. The structure function of this system has two values 3 for the state vectors (x_1 x_2 x_3) = (1, 1, 2) and (x_1 x_2 x_3) = (1, 1, 3). Therefore the availability of the simple service system for the performance level 3 is:

Table 2. The components states probabilities of the simple service system

Components states								
	x_1		x_2		x_3			
	0	1	0	1	0	1	2	3
$p_{i,s}$	0.3	0.7	0.2	0.8	0.2	0.6	0.1	0.1

$$A_3 = \Pr\{\phi(x) = 3\} = \Pr\{\phi(1,1,2) + \Pr\{\phi(1,1,3) = p_{1,1} \cdot p_{2,1} \cdot (p_{3,2} + p_{3,3})$$

Taking into account the components states probabilities for this system shown in Table 2 the availability of this system for the performance level 3 is $A_3 = 0.112$.

The system availability for the performance levels 2 and 1, and unavailability are calculated similar:

$$A_2 = \Pr\{\phi(x) = 2\} = p_{1,1} \cdot p_{2,1} \cdot p_{3,1} + (p_{1,0} \cdot p_{2,1} + p_{1,1} \cdot p_{2,0}) \cdot p_{3,3} = 0.374,$$

$$A_1 = \Pr\{\phi(x) = 1\} = (p_{1,0} \cdot p_{2,1} + p_{1,1} \cdot p_{2,0}) \cdot (p_{3,1} + p_{3,2}) = 0.266$$

$$U = \Pr\{\phi(x) = 0\} = p_{3,0} + p_{1,0} \cdot p_{2,0} \cdot (p_{3,1} + p_{3,2} + p_{3,3}) = 0.248$$

Note, the structure function in Table 1 has one more performance level that is indicated as incompletely specified and marked by "–". These states are depended on the 1-th and 2-nd components states 2 and 3 for which the component state probabilities are equal zero, because these states are not possible: $p_{1,2} = p_{1,3} = p_{2,2} = p_{2,3} = 0$. Therefore the probability of this performance level is zero too.

The system availability for the performance level 2 has maximal value of probability, therefore the service system functioning is more possible as partially operational (some customers are satisfied). The system fault or non-operational (where no customer is satisfied) is characterized by unavailability $U = 0.248$. In comparison with other available performance level this probability is not large.

The system availability and unavailability indicate the probability of the system performance level been, but don't represent the critical states/situation for which a modification of one of components states causes the change of the system performance level, first of all the system degradations. The definition such states are possible by the boundary states of MSS.

2.2 Boundary States of MSS

The conception of boundary states has been proposed for Binary-State System firstly. The boundary state of BSS is defined as system state for which the failure of one system components causes of a system failure [23]. There are different types of boundary states as minimal cut/path sets [14, 23]; exact boundary states [21]. In paper [8] boundary states have been generalized for MSS. The boundary state of MSS must be defined for every system performance level. In papers [24] the boundary states of MSS are interpreted as minimal cut/path sets. Authors of [22] introduced conception of Lower (Upper) Boundary Points of MSS for system performance level j ($j = 0, \ldots, M$-1). The boundary states for system performance level j and component i ($i = 1, \ldots, n$) (named as exact boundary states) has been proposed and considered in papers [20, 21]. In paper [18] and [25] the correlations of these boundary states with minimal cut/path sets and Lower (Upper) Boundary Points are shown accordingly.

The exact boundary states have been considered in paper [15]. These states are system states for which the change of the i-th component state from s to $\tilde{s}$ causes the system performance level change from j to $\tilde{j}$ (s, $\tilde{s} \in \{0, \ldots, m_i$ -1}, $s \neq \tilde{s}$ and j, $\tilde{j} \in \{0, \ldots, M$ -1}, $j \neq \tilde{j}$). The exact boundary state is defined by the exact boundary vector unambiguously. Therefore the exact boundary vectors must be calculated for the definition of exact boundary states. Illustrate the correlation of a system exact boundary state and an exact boundary vector by the example for the service system in Fig. 2.

Determine the exact boundary states of this service system for which the failure of the first component causes the system failure as the change of the system performance level from state 1 to 0. According to Table 1, there are two situations that correspond to this condition. They are possible for the failure of the second component and the third component state 1 or 2. These exact boundary states can be presented as vector states: $\boldsymbol{x} = (x_1, x_2, x_3) = (1 \rightarrow 0{,}0{,}1)$ and $\boldsymbol{x} = (x_1, x_2, x_3) = (1 \rightarrow 0{,}0{,}2)$. Note that the boundary state $\boldsymbol{x} = (x_1, x_2, x_3) = (1 \rightarrow 0{,}0{,}3)$ does not satisfy the condition because the system performance level in this case changes from 1 to 2 depending on the failure of the first component.

One of possible mathematical approaches for the definition of the exact boundary states in MVL is Logical Differential Calculus, in particular the DPLDs [19]. Consider the application of this mathematical approach for analysis of structure function of MSS.

3 Direct Partial Logical Derivatives

3.1 Direct Partial Logical Derivative with Respect to One Variable

The mathematical tool of DPLDs has been proposed in [15] for calculation of an exact boundary states of a MSS. In this paper the definition of DPLDs for MVL function has been adapted for a structure function (1). This definition has been generalized for the structure function (2) in paper [16]. According to [16] DPLD with respect to variable x_i for the structure function (2) permits analyse the system performance level change from j to $\tilde{j}$ when the i-th component state changes from s to $\tilde{s}$:

$$\partial\phi(j \rightarrow \tilde{j})/\partial x_i(s \rightarrow \tilde{s}) = \begin{cases} 1, & \text{if } \phi(s_i, \boldsymbol{x}) = j \text{ and } \phi(\tilde{s}_i, \boldsymbol{x}) = \tilde{j} \\ 0, & \text{other} \end{cases} \tag{8}$$

where $\phi(s_i, \boldsymbol{x}) = \phi(x_1, \ldots, x_{i-1}, s, x_{i+1}, \ldots, x_n)$; $\phi(\tilde{s}, \boldsymbol{x}) = \phi(x_1, \ldots, x_{i-1}, \tilde{s}, x_{i+1}, \ldots, x_n)$; s, $\tilde{s} \in$ {0,…, m_i -1}, $s \neq \tilde{s}$ and j, $\tilde{j} \in$ {0,…, M -1}, $j \neq \tilde{j}$.

There is correlation between exact boundary states and DPLD. Therefore these derivatives can be used for the calculation of exact boundary states and the investigation of influence of the i-th system component changes from s to $\tilde{s}$ to performance level j.

For example, investigate the influence of the first component failure to the fault of the simple service system in Fig. 2. DPLD $\partial\phi(1 \to 0)/\partial x_1(1 \to 0)$ allows to calculate the system state for which this failure causes the system break down. The calculation of this derivative is shown in Fig. 3 in form of flow graph. The derivative $\partial\phi(1 \to 0)/\partial x_1(1 \to 0)$ has two non-zero values that agrees with state vectors: $\boldsymbol{x} = (x_1, x_2, x_3) = (1 \to 0,0,1)$ and $\boldsymbol{x} = (x_1, x_2, x_3) = (1 \to 0,0,2)$. According to the definition of DPLD (8) for these system states the failure of the first system component causes the system failure too. Therefore the service system fails after the failure of the first service point if the second service point isn't functioning and the functioning of the infrastructure conforms state 1 or state 2. The system states $\boldsymbol{x} = (x_1, x_2, x_3) = (1 \to 0,0,1)$ and $\boldsymbol{x} = (x_1, x_2, x_3) = (1 \to 0,0,2)$ are exact boundary states for the first system component failure and the system performance level 1.

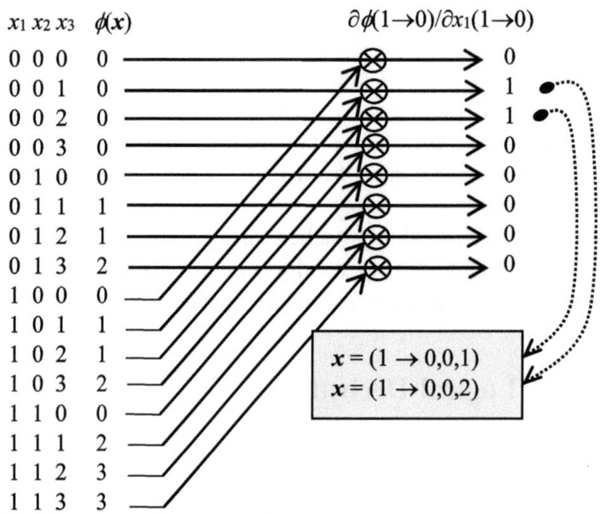

Fig. 3. Calculation of the direct partial logic derivative $\partial\phi(1 \to 0)/\partial x_1(1 \to 0)$.

DPLD (8) allows investigating boundary states of a MSS for which component state x_i change from s to $\tilde{s}$ causes the system performance level change from j to $\tilde{j}$. Therefore, this derivative allows calculating exact boundary states of the i-th system component for MSS performance level j that agree to state vectors $\boldsymbol{x} = (x_1, x_2, \ldots, x_n)$. All possible changes of the i-th system component and their influence to MSS performance level can be investigated based on DPLD (8). But this derivative permits to investigate the influence of one component only. DPLD with respect of variable vector investigates the system state changes depending on changes of states of some system components.

3.2 Direct Partial Logical Derivative with Respect to Variable Vector

DPLD of a structure function $\phi(\boldsymbol{x})$ of n variables with respect to variables vector $x^{(p)} = \left(x_{i_1}, x_{i_2}, \ldots, x_{i_p}\right)$ reflects the fact of changing of function from j to $\tilde{j}$ when the value of every variable of vector $\boldsymbol{x}^{(p)}$ is changing from s to $\ddot{s}$ [16]:

$$\partial\phi(j \to \tilde{j})\Big/\partial x_i(\boldsymbol{s}^{(p)} \to \tilde{\boldsymbol{s}}^{(p)}) = \begin{cases} 1, \text{ if } \phi(s_{i_1}, \ldots, s_{i_p}, \boldsymbol{x}) = j \text{ and } \phi(\tilde{s}_{i_1}, \ldots, \tilde{s}_{i_p}, \boldsymbol{x}) = \tilde{j} \\ 0, \text{ other} \end{cases} \tag{9}$$

In (9) a change of value of i_q-th variable x_{i_q} form s_{i_q} to $\tilde{s}_{i_q}$ agrees with a change of i_q-th MSS component state form s_{i_q} to $\tilde{s}_{i_q}$ ($q = 1, \ldots, p$ and $p < n$). Changes of some components states correspond with change of a variables vector $x^{(p)} = \left(x_{i_1}, \ldots, x_{i_p}\right)$. Every variable values of this vector changes form s_{i_q} to $\tilde{s}_{i_q}$. So, vector $\boldsymbol{x}^{(p)}$ can be interpreted as components states vector or components efficiencies vector.

For example, consider the simple service system (Fig. 2) failure depending on fault of the first service point and reduction of functioning of infrastructure from state 2 to state 1. This system behavior can be presented by the Direct Partial Logic Derivative $\partial\phi(1 \to 0)/\partial x_1(1 \to 0)\, \partial x_3(2 \to 1)$. The calculation of this derivative is shown in Fig. 4.

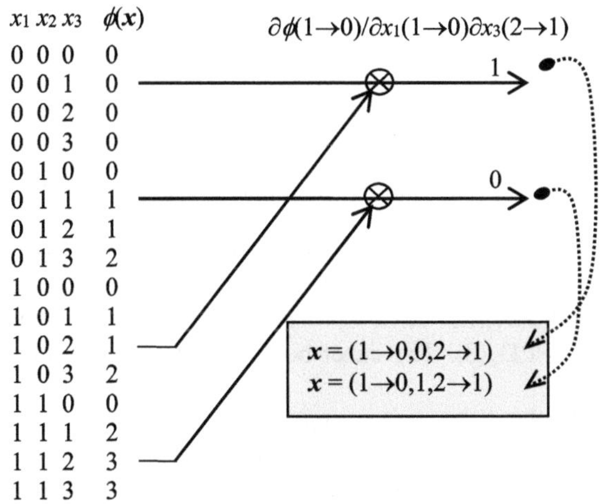

Fig. 4. Calculation of the direct partial logic derivative $\partial\phi(1 \to 0)/\partial x_1(1 \to 0)\, \partial x_3(2 \to 1)$.

The derivative $\partial\phi(1 \to 0)/\partial x_1(1 \to 0)\, \partial x_3(2 \to 1)$ has two values and one of them is non-zero value that agrees with state vector: $\boldsymbol{x} = (x_1, x_2, x_3) = (1 \to 0, 0, 2 \to 1)$. This state vector define of the service system failure depending on the failure of the first service point and deterioration of the infrastructure functioning from state 2 to state 1. Therefore the system state $\boldsymbol{x} = (x_1, x_2, x_3) = (1 \to 0, 0, 2 \to 1)$ can be interpreted as exact boundary state for the first and the third system components of the system performance level 1.

The Direct Partial Logic Derivative with respect to variable vector (15) allows investigating boundary states of a MSS for which simultaneous changes of p components states from s_{i_q} to $\tilde{s}_{i_q}$(q = 1, …, p and $p < n$) causes the system performance level change from j to $\tilde{j}$. Therefore, the Direct Partial Logic Derivative with respect to variable vector allows calculating exact boundary states for MSS performance level j of the i-th system component.

4 The Calculation and Estimation of Exact Boundary States of MSS Based on Direct Partial Logic Derivatives

The exact boundary state of MSS are defined based on the condition that fixed system performance level change depending on the appointed change of one system component state or specified changes of some components states. DPLD with respect to one variable (8) and DPLD with respect to variable vector (9) can be used to investigate change of the system performance level from j to $\tilde{j}$ that are caused by specified changes of one or some system components states. These derivatives have non-zero values of the structure function for system states that satisfy for specified condition: the system performance level change from j to $\tilde{j}$ depending on specified changes of one or some system components states. *Therefor the exact boundary states can be defined as system states that conform to non-zero values of derivatives* (8) *and* (9). In paper [26] new probabilistic indices for exact boundary state that allow estimating the probability of the system boundary/critical states. In this paper this investigation is continued and some new indices are introduced.

Use the symbol $\begin{pmatrix} j\to\tilde{j} \\ x_i \\ s\to\tilde{s} \end{pmatrix}$ for the exact boundary state of MSS performance level j depending on the i-th system component has been introduced in paper [26]. This state is indicated by vector state $\boldsymbol{x} = (x_1,\ldots, x_i,\ldots, x_n) = (a_1,\ldots, s_i,\ldots, a_n)$ for which $\phi(a_1, \ldots, s_i,\ldots, a_n) = j$ and $\phi(a_1,\ldots, \tilde{s}_i,\ldots, a_n) = \tilde{j}$. Therefore this state can be calculated as non-zero value of DPLD (8). The exact boundary state for MSS performance level j depends on p components $x_{i1}, x_{i2}, \ldots, x_{ip}$ $\begin{pmatrix} j\to\tilde{j} \\ x_{i_1}\ldots x_{i_p} \\ s_{i_1}\to\tilde{s}_{i_1}\; s_{ip}\to\tilde{s}_{ip} \end{pmatrix}$ is indicated by vector state $\boldsymbol{x} = (x_1,\ldots, x_{i1},\ldots, x_{ip},\ldots, x_n) = (a_1,\ldots, s_{i1},\ldots, s_{ip},\ldots, a_n)$. This state is calculated as non-zero value of DPLD (9).

In paper [26] some probabilistic indices of the exact boundary states for the coherent MSS have been introduced (Table 3).

The probability of every boundary state $(a_1, \ldots, s_i, \ldots, a_n)$ for MSS performance level j depending on the i-th system component change from s to $\tilde{s}$ is calculated based on the probabilities of components states [26]:

$$P_{(a_1\ldots a_n)}\begin{pmatrix} j\to\tilde{j} \\ x_i \\ s\to\tilde{s} \end{pmatrix} = p_{1,a_1}\cdot\ldots\cdot p_{i-1,a_{i-1}}\cdot p_{i,s_i}\cdot p_{i+1,a_{i+1}}\cdot\ldots\cdot p_{n,a_n} \tag{10}$$

Table 3. Probabilities for the estimation of exact boundary states of MSS defined in paper [26]

The index description	Equation for calculation
The probability of exact boundary state of the i-th component change from s to $\tilde{s}$ and for performance level change from j to $\tilde{j}$	$p\begin{pmatrix} j\to\tilde{j} \\ x_i \\ s\to\tilde{s} \end{pmatrix} = \sum_{\phi(a_1,\ldots,s_i,\ldots,a_n)-j} P_{(a_1\ldots a_n)}\begin{pmatrix} j\to\tilde{j} \\ x_i \\ s\to\tilde{s} \end{pmatrix}$
The probability of exact boundary states of the i-th component for all changes and for performance level change from j to $\tilde{j}$	$p\begin{pmatrix} j\to\tilde{j} \\ x_i \end{pmatrix} = \sum_{s,\tilde{s}} p\begin{pmatrix} j\to\tilde{j} \\ x_i \\ s\to\tilde{s} \end{pmatrix}$
The probability of exact boundary states of the i-th component change from s to $\tilde{s}$ and for all performance level j changes	$p\begin{pmatrix} x_i \\ s\to\tilde{s} \end{pmatrix} = \sum_{j,\tilde{j}} p\begin{pmatrix} j\to\tilde{j} \\ x_i \\ s\to\tilde{s} \end{pmatrix}$
The probability of exact boundary states of the i-th component all changes	$p\begin{pmatrix} x_i \end{pmatrix} = \sum_{s,\tilde{s}} p\begin{pmatrix} x_i \\ s\to\tilde{s} \end{pmatrix}$

The practical application of estimation of a MSS boundary states supposes the calculation of other probabilities, for example, as probability of MSS performance level change depending on all possible changes of the i-th system component. These probabilities are calculated based on the probability of the system boundary state (10) and are presented in Table 3.

In the Table 3 new indices for the analysis of MSS availability are proposed. These indices are probabilities of exact boundary states that allow estimate the critical state/situation of investigated system/object. In particular, these indices allow investigating the influence of different changes the i-th component state s to the fixed performance level.

The similar indices for probabilistic estimation of exact boundary states (Table 3 and 4) can be defined for estimation of exact boundary state for MSS performance level j of p components $x_{i_1}, x_{i_2}, \ldots, x_{i_p}$ $\begin{pmatrix} j\to\tilde{j} \\ x_{i_1}\ldots x_{i_p} \\ s_{i_1}\to\tilde{s}_{i_1}\, s_{i_p}\to\tilde{s}_{i_p} \end{pmatrix}$.

Table 4. New probabilities for the estimation of exact boundary states of MSS

The index description	Equation for calculation
Probability of exact boundary state of i-th component for all decreases from state s and for performance level change from j to $\tilde{j}$	$p\begin{pmatrix} j\to\tilde{j} \\ x_i \\ s\downarrow \end{pmatrix} = \sum_{r=s-1}^{0} p\begin{pmatrix} j\to\tilde{j} \\ x_i \\ s\to r \end{pmatrix}$
Probability of exact boundary state of i-th component for all increases from state s and for performance level change from j to $\tilde{j}$	$p\begin{pmatrix} j\to\tilde{j} \\ x_i \\ s\uparrow \end{pmatrix} = \sum_{r=s+1}^{m-1} p\begin{pmatrix} j\to\tilde{j} \\ x_i \\ s\to r \end{pmatrix}$
Probability of exact board state of i-th component for all changes of state s and for performance level change from j to $\tilde{j}$	$p\begin{pmatrix} j\to\tilde{j} \\ x_i \\ s \end{pmatrix} = p\begin{pmatrix} j\to\tilde{j} \\ x_i \\ s\downarrow \end{pmatrix} + p\begin{pmatrix} j\to\tilde{j} \\ x_i \\ s\uparrow \end{pmatrix}$
Probability of exact board state of i-th component for all decreases from state s and for performance level change from j to $\tilde{j}$	$p\begin{pmatrix} j\to\tilde{j} \\ x_i \end{pmatrix} = \sum_{r=0}^{m-1} p\begin{pmatrix} j\to\tilde{j} \\ x_i \\ r \end{pmatrix}$

Consider the examples of the estimation of exact boundary states for the simple service system (Fig. 2). The components states probabilities for this system are defined in Table 2. Investigate this system failure depending on the first components. DPLD $\partial\phi(1 \to 0)/\partial x_1(1 \to 0)$ represents this system behavior (Fig. 3). This derivative has two non-zero values that conform to two boundary states $\begin{pmatrix} 1\to0 \\ x_1 \\ 1\to0 \end{pmatrix}$: $\boldsymbol{x} = (1, 0, 1)$ and $\boldsymbol{x} = (1, 0, 2)$.

The probabilities of boundary states for the system failure depending on the first component break down $\begin{pmatrix} 1\to0 \\ x_1 \\ 1\to0 \end{pmatrix}$ are calculate according to (16) and are:

$$p\begin{pmatrix} 1\to0 \\ x_1 \\ 1\to0 \end{pmatrix} = p_{(101)}\begin{pmatrix} 1\to0 \\ x_1 \\ 1\to0 \end{pmatrix} + p_{(102)}\begin{pmatrix} 1\to0 \\ x_1 \\ 1\to0 \end{pmatrix} = p_{1,1} \cdot p_{2,0} \cdot p_{3,1} + p_{1,1} \cdot p_{2,0} \cdot p_{3,2} = 0.098 \quad (11)$$

By the similar way the probability of this system failure depending on the breakdown of the second service point is calculated and this probability is $p\begin{pmatrix} 1\to0 \\ x_2 \\ 1\to0 \end{pmatrix} = 0.168$ too. The influence of the infrastructure failure to the fault of the system by the critical state is estimated as $p\begin{pmatrix} 1\to0 \\ x_3 \\ 1\to0 \end{pmatrix} = 0.228$. Therefore the infrastructure failure has maximal influence to the stop of the service system.

Investigate other critical states of this system failure. The critical states can be indicated as exact boundary states of the system. These states correlate to non-zero values of DPLDs $\partial\phi(j \to 0)/\partial x_i(s \to s-1)$ for $j, s \in \{1, 2, 3\}$ (Table 5).

Table 5. The exact boundary states of simple service system calculated based on DPLD

DPLDs	Boundary states for the components		
	x_1	x_2	x_2
$\partial\phi(1 \to 0)/\partial x_i(3 \to 2)$			–
$\partial\phi(1 \to 0)/\partial x_i(3 \to 1)$			–
$\partial\phi(1 \to 0)/\partial x_i(3 \to 0)$			–
$\partial\phi(1 \to 0)/\partial x_i(2 \to 1)$			–
$\partial\phi(1 \to 0)/\partial x_i(2 \to 0)$			(0, 1, 2), (1, 0, 2)
$\partial\phi(1 \to 0)/\partial x_i(1 \to 0)$	(1, 0, 1), (1, 0, 2)	(0, 1, 1), (0, 1, 2)	(0, 1, 1), (1, 0, 1)
$\partial\phi(2 \to 0)/\partial x_i(3 \to 2)$			–
$\partial\phi(2 \to 0)/\partial x_i(3 \to 1)$			–
$\partial\phi(2 \to 0)/\partial x_i(3 \to 0)$			(0, 1, 3), (1, 0, 3)
$\partial\phi(2 \to 0)/\partial x_i(2 \to 1)$			–
$\partial\phi(2 \to 0)/\partial x_i(2 \to 0)$			–
$\partial\phi(2 \to 0)/\partial x_i(1 \to 0)$	(1, 0, 3)	(0, 1, 3)	(1, 1, 1)
$\partial\phi(3 \to 0)/\partial x_i(3 \to 2)$			–
$\partial\phi(3 \to 0)/\partial x_i(3 \to 1)$			–
$\partial\phi(3 \to 0)/\partial x_i(3 \to 0)$			(1, 1, 3)
$\partial\varphi(3 \to 0)/\partial x_i(2 \to 1)$			–
$\partial\varphi(3 \to 0)/\partial x_i(2 \to 0)$			(1, 1, 2)
$\partial\varphi(3 \to 0)/\partial x_i(1 \to 0)$	–	–	–

All critical state for every of components of the service system failure are shown in Table 5. The symbol "–" is in cell, if the critical states are absent for fixed component change. The grey cells agree with the situations where the indicated changes are not possible. The analysis of the exact boundary states in Table 5 shows conditions of the system failure. The system failure can be caused by break down of any system component (one of the service points or the infrastructure), but the degradation the system infrastructure has not influence for the system fault (changes the third component state x_3 from 3 to 2 and from 2 to 1). The probabilistic estimations of the critical states are shown in Table 6. According to these indices the system failure (performance level change from 3 to 0) depending on the third component fault is most possible. The probabilities of other failures of the system (performance level change from 2 to 0 and from 1 to 0) have large values in comparison with probabilities of other critical states. Therefore the third component (the system infrastructure) is most important for the functioning of the system in whole and the support of this component working state must be principal goal of this system maintenance. The index of the system failure depending of all possible changes of one of system components $p(x_i)$ has maximal value for the third component that indicates principal influence of this component to the system failure too.

Therefore the proposed indices for the estimation of the exact boundary states are useful for the analysis of the system availability and its functioning. These indices permit to indicate the system component with maximal influence to the fixed changes of the performance levels. These components will have priority in the maintenance plan.

Table 6. Probabilities for the estimation of critical states of the simple service system

	$p\left(\overset{1\to0}{\underset{1\to0}{x_i}}\right)$	$p\left(\overset{1\to0}{\underset{2\to0}{x_i}}\right)$	$p\left(\overset{2\to0}{\underset{3\to0}{x_i}}\right)$	$p\left(\overset{2\to0}{\underset{1\to0}{x_i}}\right)$	$p\left(\overset{3\to0}{\underset{2\to0}{x_i}}\right)$	$p\left(\overset{3\to0}{\underset{3\to0}{x_i}}\right)$	$p\left(\overset{1\to0}{x_i}\right)$	$p\left(\overset{2\to0}{x_i}\right)$	$p\left(\overset{3\to0}{x_i}\right)$	$p\left(\underset{1\to0}{x_i}\right)$	$p\left(\underset{2\to0}{x_i}\right)$	$p\left(\underset{3\to0}{x_i}\right)$	$p\left(x_i\right)$
x_1	0.098			0.014			0.098	0.014	0	0.112			0.112
x_2	0.168			0.024			0.168	0.024	0	0.192			0.192
x_3	0.228	0.038	–	0.336	–	0.056	0.266	0.336	0.056	0.564	0.038	0.056	0.658

5 Conclusion

The mathematical methods of MVL are used in reliability estimation of MSS. The mathematical background for application of mathematical methods of MVL for reliability analysis of MSS is considered in this paper. The correlation of the structure function (2) and MVL function are shown and proved by means of the conception of incompletely specified MVL function. This background allows using DPLD for analysis of MSS structure function.

In this paper the investigation of boundary values of the structure function of MSS and definition of MSS exact boundary states based on these valued are considered. Conception of exact boundary states is important for the examination of critical states/situation of the system functioning and availability. The analysis of probabilistic indices of exact boundary states allows indicating the system components with most influence and taking into account such components in the maintenance plan.

The analysis of MSS based on the exact boundary states has not limits for the numbers of components (n) and states for every component (m_i), and system performance levels (M) according to the theoretical background. But in real-world applications these numbers have important influence to the structure function dimension (number of structure function elements) that is calculated as:

$$N_{\text{structure function dimension}} = m_1 \times m_1 \times \ldots \times m_n$$

As a rule the number of system performance levels (M) and number of component states (m_i) are defined between two and seven. According to the investigation in papers [16–18] the Direct Partial Logical Derivatives is applicable for systems which have dimension less than ten millions elements. Therefore the proposed method can be useful for the MSS analysis with number of components under ten.

Acknowledgments. This work was partially supported by grant of Scientific Grant Agency of the Ministry of Education of Slovak Republic (Vega 1/0498/14).

References

1. Zio, E.: Reliability engineering: old problems and new challenges. Reliab. Eng. Syst. Saf. **94**, 125–141 (2009)
2. Praks, P., Kopustinskas, V.: Monte-carlo based reliability modelling of a gas network using graph theory approach. In: 2014 Ninth International Conference on Availability, Reliability and Security, pp. 380–386. IEEE (2014)
3. Zaitseva, E., Levashenko, V., Rusin, M.: Reliability analysis of healthcare system. In: FedCSIS 2011 Federated Conference on Computer Science and Information Systems, pp. 169–175. IEEE (2011)
4. Rausand, M., Høyland, A.: System Reliability Theory. John Wiley and Sons Inc., Haboken (2004)
5. Murchland, J.D.: Fundamental concepts and relations for reliability analysis of multistate system. In: Reliability and Fault Tree Analysis, Theoretical and Applied Aspects of System Reliability, SIAM, pp. 581–618 (1975)
6. Barlow, R.E., Wu, A.S.: Coherent systems with multi-state components. Math. Oper. Res. **3**, 275–281 (1978)
7. Hudson, J.C., Kapur, K.C.: Modules in coherent multistate systems. IEEE Trans. Reliab. **32**, 183–185 (1983)
8. Lisnianski, A., Levitin, G.: Multi-state System Reliability: Assessment, Optimization and Applications. World Scientific, Singapore (2003)
9. Xie, M., Dai, Y.-S., Poh, K.-L.: Multi-state system reliability. In: Computing System Reliability Models and Analysis, pp. 207–237. Kluwer Academic Publishers, New York (2004)
10. Levitin, G., Lisniansi, A.: Optimization of imperfect preventive maintenance for multi-state system. Reliab. Eng. Syst. Saf. **67**, 193–203 (2000)

11. Zio, E., Marella, M., Podofillini, L.: A monte carlo simulation approach to the availability assessment of multi-state systems with operational dependencies. Reliab. Eng. Syst. Saf. **92**, 871–882 (2007)
12. Caldarola, L.: Coherent system with multi-state components. Nucl. Eng. Des. **58**, 127–139 (1980)
13. Veeraraghavan, M., Trivedi, K.S.: A combinatorial algorithm for performance and reliability analysis using multistate models. IEEE Trans. Comput. **43**, 229–234 (1994)
14. Reinske, K., Ushakov, I.: Application of graph theory for reliability analysis. Radio i Sviaz, Moscow, USSR (1988) (in Russian)
15. Zaitseva, E.: Reliability analysis of Multi-State System. Dyn. Syst. Geom. Theor. **1**, 213–222 (2003)
16. Zaitseva, E.: Importance analysis of a multi-state system based on multiple-valued logic methods. In: Lisnianski, A., Frenkel, I. (eds.) Recent Advances in System Reliability: Signatures, Multi-state Systems and Statistical Inference, pp. 113–134. Springer, London (2012)
17. Zaitseva, E., Levashenko, V.: Multiple-valued logic mathematical approaches for multi-state system reliability analysis. J. Appl. Logic **11**, 350–362 (2013)
18. Kvassay, M., Zaitseva, E., Levashenko, V.: Minimal cut sets and direct partial logic derivatives in reliability analysis. In: Proceedings of the European Safety and Reliability Conference on Safety and Reliability: Methodology and Applications, pp. 241–248. CRC Press (2014)
19. Miller, M.D., Thornton, M.A.: Multiple Valued Logic: Concepts and Representations. Synthesis Lectures on Digital Circuits and systems. Morgan and Claypool Publishers, San Rafael (2008)
20. Zaitseva, E., Kovalik, S., Levashenko, V., Matiaško, K.: Algorithm for dynamic analysis of multi-state system by structure function. In: IEEE International Conference on Computer as a Tool, pp.1224–1227. IEEE Press (2005)
21. Zaitseva, E.: Dynamic reliability indices for multi-state system. In: The 33th IEEE International Symposium on Multiple-Valued Logic, pp. 287–292. IEEE Press (2003)
22. Boedigheimer, R.A., Kapur, K.C.: Customer-driven reliability models for multistate coherent systems. IEEE Trans. Reliab. **43**, 46–50 (1994)
23. Vachtsevanos, G., Lewis, F.L., Roemer, M., Hess, A., Wu, B.: Intelligent Fault Diagnosis and Prognosis for Engineering Systems. John Wiley and Sons, Hoboken (2006)
24. Yeh, W.C.: A fast algorithm for searching all multi-state minimal cuts. IEEE Trans. Reliab. **57**, 581–588 (2008)
25. Kapur, K.C., Zaitseva, E., Kovalik, S., Matiasko, K.: Customer-driven reliability models and logical differential calculus for reliability analysis of multi state system. J. KONBIN **1**, 39–47 (2006)
26. Zaitseva, E., Levashenko, V., Kostolny, J., Kvassay, M.: Direct partial logic derivatives in analysis of boundary states of multi-state system. In: 11th International Conference on ICT in Education, Research and Industrial Applications: Integration, Harmonization and Knowledge Transfer, pp. 535–549. CEUR-WS (2015)

Author Index

MIX
Papier aus verantwortungsvollen Quellen
Paper from responsible sources
FSC® C105338

If you have any concerns about our products,
you can contact us on
ProductSafety@springernature.com

In case Publisher is established outside the EU,
the EU authorized representative is:
Springer Nature Customer Service Center GmbH
Europaplatz 3, 69115 Heidelberg, Germany

Printed by Libri Plureos GmbH
in Hamburg, Germany